Here We Are

Aarti Namdev Shahani

Here We Are

American Dreams,
American Nightmares

CELADON BOOKS
NEW YORK

www.celadonbooks.com

Designed by Jonathan Bennett

All photographs courtesy of the author.

ISBN 978-1-250-20475-2 (hardcover)
ISBN 978-1-250-20473-8 (ebook)

Our books may be purchased in bulk for promotional, educational, or business use. Please contact your local bookseller or the Macmillan Corporate and Premium Sales Department at 1-800-221-7945, extension 5442, or by email at MacmillanSpecialMarkets@macmillan.com.

First Edition: October 2019

10 9 8 7 6 5 4 3 2 1

To my family, and the many others
who will join us here

Contents

Here
We Are

Prologue

THROUGH A STRANGE COINCIDENCE, I met the man who ran the jail where Dad was locked up.

"How'd a girl like you start visiting Rikers anyway?" he asked me.

"My dad was an inmate there," I said. Not the answer he was expecting.

We were hunched over a tiny oak table in one of those quaint cafés on the Upper East Side. I kept stepping on his toes, not on purpose.

The jailer, Martin Horn, happened to be friends with a genius mentor of mine. Now retired, Martin liked having meandering conversations with journalists. I'm a journalist. Only, I wasn't on my A game. He was the one asking all the good questions, digging deeper.

"Who was the judge in your dad's case?" he asked.

"Why?"

"Maybe I know 'im."

Sure he does. Just like because I'm from Queens, I know everyone there. "Blumenfeld." I humored him. "The judge was Joel Blumenfeld."

"Is that right!" The jailer's eyes lit up. "He's one of my best friends. We go way back, to the Vietnam War days. Really nice guy."

Really nice guy. Quite a tone-deaf way to describe the man who presided over the case that ruined my family, incrementally, over the course of fourteen years.

"I think you'd like Joel. Ya wanna meet 'im?" The jailer loved connecting people. "Lemme know if you're interested." He made it sound as casual as a Tinder date.

"Thanks. I'll let you know."

I said it with disinterest, but that's only because I felt such an intense surge of emotion that my game face kicked in.

These last few years, I'd been trying not to think about the past. By anyone's measure, I took aggressive steps to forget it. But, wherever I turned, there it was. I could never stop feeling like that teenage girl sitting in court, holding her mom's hand, seeing her dad in handcuffs, his once-alert eyes crumbled into an empty stare. No matter how hard I tried to be someone else, that's the girl I always was. Am.

It didn't take longer than a week for me to accept the jailer's offer.

Judge Joel Blumenfeld replied almost instantly. "I hear you on the radio," he wrote in his email. "Why don't you come by next time you're in town?"

When I'm not chasing the skeletons in my family's closet, I'm a correspondent for NPR. I live in California and cover the largest companies on earth, three of which are a short drive from me in Silicon Valley. I was supposed to be scheduling my interview with a billionaire who'd invested early in Facebook and Twitter—not with this judge, who was clearly off my beat. But being a journalist has its perks (namely, access). I get VIP treatment from all kinds of people who otherwise would never give me the time of day.

The judge invited me into his private chambers. That's a place no defendant's kid gets to go—the place behind the courtroom, where he writes his decisions about how long someone is sent to prison or whether the convicted can reopen a case.

I didn't expect that. And, it turns out, I was not ready for it.

I went during one of my business trips to New York. I took the E train into Queens, just like I used to when I'd visit Dad in jail. That was a lifetime ago. Not much had changed: a McDonald's wrapper tossed on the orange subway seat, the train cars rattling on the tracks like there was an earthquake. *Will they ever fix these tracks?*

Exiting the turnstile at Union Turnpike, I was about to make a left for the Rikers bus stop. Muscle memory. Then I remembered that's not where I was going.

I walked down Queens Boulevard and passed the bodega run by Indians (I used to buy Doritos there, back when I was young enough to metabolize Doritos). I spotted the dusty glass storefront with the words

ABOGADO/LAWYER stenciled in huge black letters on a tacky yellow awning and cringed thinking about the crap promises they'd make inside: "We'll beat the charge. I know the judge." As if it were that easy to buy justice in America.

When I got to the Queens Criminal Courthouse, it was smaller than I remembered. Maybe that's because the last time I saw it, I had child eyes.

I put my purse through the scanner and spread my arms like a bird for security. Flashback to teenage me, standing in this exact same spot with Mom, my big brother, Deepak, and my big sister, Angelly. We usually talked a mile a minute. That morning, we were mute. Dad had just been arrested.

"Miss, what's this supposed to be?" The guard pointed to the X-ray, at a black blob inside my bag. "That a baton?"

"No. That's just my shotgun mic." I should have left out the word shotgun. "I use it to record."

"No recording allowed in here."

"I won't record anything," I promised.

That was mostly true. Whatever might get etched into my memory, I hadn't planned to turn on the equipment. It was with me at all times because, my editor told me, you just don't know when a plane might crash. Always be ready for breaking news.

Up in the courtroom, I spotted the pews where the public sits. Flashback to my first time sitting here, in the second row. A defense lawyer walked up to a prosecutor, right after their hearing. I overheard them joking about each other's golf game. *They were golf buddies?* I thought opposing counsel would be at war in all facets of life. Their sliver of an exchange opened my eyes to a basic fact: for most lawyers, justice is just a day job.

I walked toward the swinging doors that separate the bench from the audience. A girlfriend had recently taught me about Stuart Weitzmans, and I'd grabbed a pair off the clearance rack. Today, I'd break them in—a mistake that announced itself in each step. With my pinky toes dying a slow death, I sounded like a bowlegged tap dancer. *I never wear heels. Why the hell did I wear these?*

"Hi, I have an appointment with Judge Blumenfeld." I handed the bailiff my card.

He eyed it and nodded. "Gimme a sec."

A few feet away, there was the witness stand. Flashback to when Dad sat there. He wanted to explain what happened—to lay out the facts of his life, not just the case—and be heard for a moment. He was such a quiet man; it wasn't like him.

"Your honor, may I please—"
The judge cut him off before he finished his sentence.
"Mr. Shahani, I suggest you speak with your lawyer."
Long pause. Lump in Dad's throat. Lump in mine.

In this room, he could not be heard—unless it was to say "I'm guilty."

The bailiff came back and held open the swinging doors. "This way, please."

Three men—probably co-defendants waiting for their hearing—looked at me like, *Where does she think she's going?* I wondered that, too.

I turned a corner and knocked on Judge Blumenfeld's door.

"Young lady, I told you to send me the case number." Those were the first words out of his mouth. A scolding, which he didn't bother to give standing still. He walked right past me over to his desk. No handshake or *Hey, nice to see you after all these years*. Straight to business. Though I wasn't sure what that business was. I didn't have an agenda. I just showed up because I couldn't help myself.

I hadn't seen him so up close before. In my mind's eye, he'd been a granite-faced figure in billowing black robes. Now he was an adorable old man from the nice part of Queens: round, with pink, saggy old-man cheeks—and shorter than me, with or without my heels.

He'd told me in his email to remind him of Dad's indictment number. I guess he'd assumed, reasonably, that I was coming for a legal opinion. I guess I wasn't, because I didn't bother to respond.

Still, he was prepared. Without my asking, before I could sit down, he blurted out a sentence that felt like a punch in the stomach. He said, more or less: "Your dad should never have taken that guilty plea. What a mistake. A jury of his peers in Queens—with all these immigrant business owners—no jury would have convicted him here."

You have to stop and imagine what this felt like.

4

My father was arrested in 1996, along with his little brother. They were running our family business, a wholesale electronics store on Broadway between 27th and 28th Streets in Manhattan. It turns out that we were selling Casio watches and Sharp calculators to the wrong guys—to members of the Cali cartel of Colombia. Dad and Uncle Ratan were charged with money laundering, helping the most notorious drug traffickers in New York City clean their cocaine proceeds.

We hired lawyers. They told us we should not attempt to fight the charges. We agonized over it and followed their advice. And now, when the damage was long done, the man who hit the gavel was telling me what we thought was true all along but couldn't prove: the Shahani family had a hand to play, if only we knew how to play it.

The back of my throat burned, acrid. I wanted to vomit.

The judge seemed oblivious that this could somehow be emotional for me. He talked as if we were teacher and student, dissecting a piece of case law during office hours.

"Here, have a seat." He sat on one end of his sofa and patted the cushion beside him. "You ever ask yourself: Why was the case filed in Queens?"

Socratic method. I felt dizzy. I didn't have an answer. He did.

The fact that it was filed in Queens, he explained, was a sign of its weakness. If it were some high-profile big win for prosecutors, they would have filed it in Manhattan, "with all the media," he said. "They sent it out to me because they didn't have much. They were hoping for big-time drug dealers. Instead, they got your dad and uncle." Two middle-aged men who wore polyester pants and Velcro sneakers from Payless.

The case destroyed Dad's career, his reputation, his will to live. It didn't end when the sentence was over. It spiraled into more punishments than my family or the court ever expected. And now—the truth comes out—it all turned on the most basic miscalculation.

What exactly happened next, I can't remember. Maybe I asked the judge if he was working any interesting cases. Maybe we switched topics entirely and talked about sunny California, my new home. In reality, I wasn't listening. It was a mistake to come. I could literally feel the life I was so meticulously building break at the seams. I needed to get the hell out of his office.

5

It would be rude to dart for the door. I had to chitchat, politely reach for my purse to signal it was getting late. Only, when I did that, the judge reached for an overstuffed folder and pulled out an envelope in mint condition—except for the green certified-mail sticker on the front, which had faded. It was addressed from teenage me to him.

"Do you remember, I called you my pen pal?" he asked, this time with tenderness in his voice.

"That's right." My eyes dropped. I didn't want to look at him anymore. "I wrote you too much."

"Not too much," he said. "It's just that you cared."

Flashback to the first time he called on me in court. I stood up in the back and the adults up front looked puzzled, like, *Why does the judge know this kid?* So many things had gone wrong in the case, I'd decided to write to him directly. I wanted the straightest line to justice, and I knew it wasn't through the lawyers.

Now I glanced at the date. It was postmarked OCT 12, 1999.

"Huh. That was the day before my twentieth birthday. I guess that's how I was celebrating."

"You were such an articulate, passionate kid." He said it like a proud schoolteacher. That's when it hit me: I'm not meeting this judge because he hears me on the radio. I'm meeting him because he remembers me as a teenager.

"You know how many letters I got and never answered," he continued. "But you—I always responded to you."

It's true. He did. Without fail. I'd forgotten about that. I tried to put the envelope back in his hands but he shoved it in mine.

"Keep it. It's for you."

I didn't know it was legal to remove documents from court records. And I didn't want it. But I could tell I wasn't allowed to leave without accepting his gift. "Thank you." I slipped the envelope into my purse and stood up. "I think you've got some defendants waiting."

"I always do!" he said, chipper again.

As I headed for the door, I turned back to ask just one question—not something I expected to ask, but apparently the only question I had about the case. "Do you remember my dad—Namdev Shahani?"

"No. No, I don't," he said.

I wished he did. I knew he wouldn't. Dad's letter to him—my father wrote one, too—landed on the big, fat ignore pile. While the judge could see me, the Good Immigrant who was living the American dream, he could not see the nightmare I came from, which he played a role in creating. My father was invisible to him. To this day. The judge didn't ask, *Whatever came of Mr. Shahani?* I didn't expect any different. Still, it hurt.

Speed-walking from the chambers through the courtroom—the three co-defendants sitting just as they had been—tears streamed down my face. *Why are you doing this, Aarti? This is self-sabotage.*

I was almost thirty when Dad's legal problems ended—nearly half my life spent watching him decay. I had finally left home and was five years into fixing my credit score, which was a far cry from "good." I needed to know I had a future before I could stroll down memory lane.

Let it go, Aarti. Let it go.

Only, I couldn't.

ACT 1
Backstory

I'M GOING TO LET you in on a little secret—the real reason so many people from far away risk everything to come to the United States. It's the backstory you've never heard. But it's so obvious, it'll make you stop and wonder: how does the truth always get so buried? It's the reason my parents came here.

Mom and Dad met over a game of poker in Casablanca. In the crowded salon, people kept coming up to him.

"*Namu-bhai*, when will you bring *Teesri Manzil* already?" someone asked about the latest hit from back home. "I've been waiting forever, *yaar*."

Dad was the *filmwalla*—a film distributor. Not for Hollywood. For Bollywood, which is the world's largest film industry. The B stands for Bombay, where it's based. It was Dad's job to take reels of film and get them to theaters across Morocco, Algeria, and Tunisia. This was the 1960s, when movies were still literally printed on a thin black strip of glossy paper called film.

It was taxing work. He rode around on his bicycle, just like the boy in *Cinema Paradiso*, only with an Arab-world twist. Dad was also the censor. He'd take scissors and cut out each and every scene where a man and woman got too close. And mind you, too close did not mean kissing on the lips. Indians wouldn't go as far as those Americans did. But there was the occasional suggestive shot—cheeks brushing or a long embrace. For the Arabs of North Africa, that was going too far.

"Don't cut too much, *Namu-bhai*," the Hindus at the poker table chided him. "Leave something juicy for those of us who are not Muslim."

Mom and Dad didn't convert to Islam. That fact defined their lives early on. Dad was born in Karachi, which used to be part of India, back when it was still under British rule. While the Brits spent more than three centuries colonizing the subcontinent, they were in a big hurry to leave. They decided four months before departure to divide the land into two parts: Pakistan for Muslims, India for Hindus and Sikhs. The Partition—as it's called—was set for August 15, 1947.

The Brits didn't consult a single astrologer, which was ludicrous. While religions were at war, everyone agreed: consult the star experts before any major decision—be it a wedding, the naming of a child, the divorce of a country. Astrologers jumped up and down, warning the date was ominous. It would result in untold misery.

They were right—though to what extent is unknown, a data point lost in history. The widely cited estimate of 15 million displaced and 1 million killed is a gross understatement, leading scholars say; and there was no serious effort to do a body count.

Dad was six years old at Partition. A gang of men with burning torches and sticks came banging on his family's front door. His mom grabbed the kids and pushed them out the back. "Hide on the terrace," she ordered them. The next day, they were all on a boat sailing from Muslim-held Karachi down to Hindu-held Bombay, with just the clothes on their backs.

Mom was from the same region as Dad—it's called Sindh—but from a different city. She was born in Hyderabad, about a year before Partition. Her real birthday is a mystery. It may have been in August or September. No one can tell for sure. In the middle of a freedom struggle or civil war, it's hard to remember what day a mother goes into labor.

The man in charge of drawing the line through the homelands of 88 million human beings was a lawyer who'd never set foot on the subcontinent. He did, however, go to the same prep school as Britain's prime minister. The Brits believed that with his "objectivity"—modernity's religion, the Western cult of judgment without empathy—the First World would bless our Third World. He used a low-resolution map as his guide.

His final Partition map was not revealed to the leaders of newly independent India and Pakistan until the celebration parties were over. It was a tough morning-after pill to swallow. No side was happy. As politicians squabbled, so too did the masses. Cities that were once cosmopolitan melting pots erupted in tribalism. Muslim babies were put on skewers and roasted. A trainful of Hindus and Sikhs were butchered, arriving into a station as corpses. There were so many dead bodies, dogs turned their noses up at second-grade meat.

Everyone at the poker party in Casablanca had Partition in common—the blood that soaked the streets, their clothes, and, for some, even their own hands. Call them Pakistani or Indian, refugee or expat, they were defined by that day and eager to forget. It was time to live in happier times.

And they were happier. Even if Mom and Dad didn't have a homeland like their ancestors, they did have electricity, flushing toilets, and a chance to flirt with the most intoxicating question the world has ever asked: what is love? Mom and Dad wouldn't be dragged to the altar, made to stand in front of a complete stranger and utter "I do" before ever making eye contact. They'd get to meet and talk first.

From across the room, Mom noticed married women flirting with Dad, manufactured smiles on their heavily painted faces. And, she noticed, Dad did not flirt back. He didn't try to cop a feel like the many handsy men who liked to grab more than their playing cards. Dad kept his hands to himself. *A shy guy,* she thought. She felt something for him.

Dad tried not to stare at Mom, but he couldn't help it. She wore clothes she'd made herself—taking Indian saris and stitching the yards of fabric into Arabian kaftans with belts. (She learned sewing in Barcelona, where her family eventually settled after Partition.) The lustrous black hive on her head was so thick, it looked like a wig. *Is that her real hair?* he wondered, desperately wanting to pull it. He felt something for her.

Their first date was, fittingly, a movie. Mom's little sister sat in between, relaying messages back and forth, the fulcrum in the balancing act between old-fashioned propriety and modern romance.

Dad grew up poor. Mom came from money. So when it was her side that asked him for his hand in marriage, he felt lucky. Acceptance into a world he was not born into was a sign of good karma.

The elders called it an arranged marriage, the union of two good

11

families. The youngsters called it a love marriage, the union of two attractive people. Fashionista weds *filmwalla*. The wedding was picture-perfect. Except for the moment when Mom had a question.

"Mama, Papa, why do you have to clean my husband's feet?" she asked during the ceremony, as her parents hunched over a bowl of water. She thought youngsters were supposed to show respect to their elders, not vice versa.

Her mom slapped her. "Don't talk too much."

The ceremony was in our native language, Sindhi. When the priest wasn't listening, Mom and Dad whispered to each other in French. Between the two, they also spoke Arabic, Spanish, English, Hindi, and Urdu—not from studying, just from living. They had a knack for languages.

Dad encouraged Mom to keep sewing even after marriage. He liked that she had passions outside the home. Mom made him a three-piece suit, which everyone praised—including Dad's mom, my grandmother, Dadi.

Dadi didn't live in Casablanca yet. She was in India, in the same city that happened to be home to the men who'd assassinated Mahatma Gandhi. When Mom visited, she brought Dadi presents—including the gold coins people had given as wedding gifts.

Dadi had seen a lot in her lifetime. Soon after she'd begun menstruating, she was married off to her husband, who was in his thirties or forties. (His first wife had died.) Dadi gave him eleven children: seven boys (future breadwinners), four girls (burdens on the family, who'd need to pay a dowry to marry them off).

For a brief period of time, they were all under one roof. Dadi would line up her army of hungry mouths and rub butter on their faces. Just because they were poor didn't mean they couldn't have bright, shiny skin.

"You're so different from my other daughters-in-law," Dadi praised Mom. "They're not smart like you" and "they don't know how to dress and talk to people like you."

Mom relished the praise. She did feel she was different: not a simple villager but a driven woman with skills. She'd started her own business in Casablanca, as a designer, and got paid to sew wedding trousseaus.

That didn't mean she was a career woman. That concept didn't exist yet. A woman's primary responsibility was her family. And that's why Mom obliged when, one day, Dadi asked her for help.

"My sweet girl," Dadi said. "You and I are great friends. Please tell your husband to bring me to Casablanca. Let's all live together, as a family."

Mom and Dad were renting a flat with marble floors on the rue Chénier. It was the cosmopolitan part of town, a stone's throw from United Nations Square and the Moulin Rouge—a replica of the Paris nightclub. While the flat was only one bedroom, Mom thought they'd figure it out. A lifetime of war and migration had separated her husband's family. Now, with minor inconvenience, she could bring them back together.

When Mom went to Dad, to ask if he'd like Dadi to come live with them, he choked up (which wasn't like him). "I'm so grateful to you that you think of my mother," he said. "I promised my father I would take care of her."

It was a heartwarming idea, in theory. Reality was a different story. If Mom had done her homework, talked to the neighbors while visiting India or the girls in the Shahani family, she would have learned: Dadi was a control freak. No daughter was allowed to set foot outside without interrogation and express permission (extreme even in those days). One of her daughters was so scarred, she refused to visit Dadi after marriage—even though she lived nearby. Mom came to learn the hard way.

Dadi did not come to Casablanca alone. She landed with a younger son who was married and unemployed and an elder son who was married, unemployed, and a belligerent drunk. The fancy apartment started to feel like a slum, sheets and blankets spread across the floor and people tiptoeing around each other, trying to avoid faces and feet on the way to the bathroom. Because Dadi was too old to rough it out, Mom offered the bedroom (which had the only mattress). She didn't mean forever, but that's what it soon became.

While sleeping hours were uncomfortable, waking hours were downright hostile.

"Where are you going?" Dadi began to ask Mom her whereabouts.

"I'm getting fabrics for a trousseau." Mom would try to explain her business.

"Sure you are, you slut! You're seeing other men. I know it."

Then the food became a problem. Mom, who'd learned cooking in Spain and Morocco, made lobster paella and lamb tagine, not chicken tikka masala. Dadi blew a fuse. "What garbage have you brought me?" She and the drunkard son would toss the plates at the wall and, if Mom happened to be in the way, she would duck. The wall looked like a Picasso.

The word "abuse" was not in circulation in those days. Mom did not have a language to describe what was going wrong at home. And neither did Dad.

At the beginning, he pleaded with Dadi. "She didn't grow up in India," he'd say about his wife, hoping it was a small misunderstanding. "Please see, she's trying her best."

His mom fired back: "Look how you talk to me! You promised your father you'd take care of me and now you're forgetting your promise. You have no *akkal*."

Akkal is the word for "sense." But it means much more than that. It means the way God intended the world to be, the natural order of things. Children obey their parents; wives obey their husbands—even in the most extreme tests. Maybe the best analogy for Westerners is that chilling passage in the Old Testament when God commands Abraham to kill his son Isaac. While it's hard to accept—we debate it; we reject it—the point stands: within the logic of that story, if Abraham did not obey God, he would have no *akkal*.

While on the surface both Mom and Dad cowered to Dadi, what was happening beneath—inside each of them—was different. And it's not just because the attacks were aimed at Mom while Dad carried the guilt of wanting to give more to his family than he could afford. It's because, to their core, my parents had different gut instincts about tradition. Dad felt that tradition, with all its imperfections, still provided the stability you needed to survive in a world full of suffering. Mom distrusted tradition. She couldn't pinpoint why, but she sensed it held people back from liberation.

She was disappointed in her husband. Before they married, when Dad was an abstraction to her, she imagined he would be like the great Lord Shiva, doing meditation and power yoga in the face of adversity.

But Dad turned to drinking and smoking instead. He sipped scotch quietly by himself in a corner. And cigarettes—a habit he picked up as a teenager—became an extension of his fingers.

My big brother, Deepak, was born a year into their marriage. When Mom asked Dad to stop smoking, Dadi would jump in. "Don't ever let a woman tell you what to do," she'd scold him, and light two cigarettes. "Come join me, my son."

It took eight years for their next child, Angelly, to be born. Mom had two miscarriages in between. A few months after my sister's birth, something terrible happened. No dishes were shattered. It was something else. Something unspeakable. Mom swallowed a bottle of white pills and tried to make herself sleep forever. When she woke up, a day or two later, she was in a hospital bed. Dad was sitting beside her, his body trembling.

"How can you be so selfish to not think of the children?" His steady voice quavered. "You didn't think of them. You didn't think of me. How can you not think of me?"

"I'm sorry," she whispered.

I was born nine months later, an accident. When Mom and Dad brought me home from the hospital, they assumed Dadi would bring the tray with a few grains of rice and a candle, and put white *tilak* on my newborn forehead. That's what any grandma would do, to give me the protection of my ancestors. That's *akkal*.

But Dadi didn't do that. "What have you brought me?" she shouted. "Another girl!"

"*Hah*, Mama." Mom said yes. She wanted to step inside. It hurt to stand because of the stitches. Doctors had to cut her wider so I would come out.

"You're not a godly person." Dadi began her diatribe. "That's why God gave you another wretched daughter. Now my son will have to work hard for two dowries. He'll kill himself slaving away for you. You don't care about him."

As Dad stood between his wife and mother, immobilized, tears streamed down his face. Mom's too. They loved me. Yet my own grandmother wouldn't so much as hold me, because I was the wrong gender.

"Get her out of my sight." Dadi turned and walked away. "This bitch is bad luck."

15

Was she talking about me or the woman who gave birth to me? It wasn't clear.

My parents didn't know what to do next, in no small part because of their unconventional sleeping arrangements. Dadi had not only taken over the bedroom. She'd ordered Dad to stay with her.

For most people—including my parents—having a grown, married man live in his mother's room is odd. For Dadi, it wasn't. Maybe she had a screw loose because of what she saw during Partition. Maybe she came from a class of elders who felt they had the right to control their children until death. It was a well-known fact that Gandhi, father of the nation, had his grandniece (who was like a daughter) sleep beside him at night.

Like many people in dysfunctional families, Mom just rolled with it. And on special occasions, Dadi let Mom take the master bedroom. Mom assumed tonight, with a newborn, would be one of those nights. Until, that is, Dadi screamed down the hallway: "I don't want her here. Get her out! OUT."

My first night home would not be at home. Dad's best friend, a Moroccan man who'd driven Mom to the hospital when she went into labor, now drove the both of us to another relative's flat. The next day, Dad came and finally agreed to do what Mom had been asking since the incident with the white pills: let's please take our children and go.

So that's our coming to America story. This country became for my parents—and for so many who can't live with their blood—an honorable way out. It's easier to move thousands of miles away than to move across the street. It's easier to say, "We want a better life for the kids" than to say, "I despise you."

My family landed in New York City in 1981. A bit more than half a million foreigners were admitted into the United States that year, joining the ranks of 14 million already here. Like so many of our immigrant brothers and sisters, we ended up in a neighborhood close to the airport.

Flushing, Queens, was one of the most diverse tracts of land on the planet. My childhood was a window into America's multiethnic soul. We were on the coast, but not "coastal elites" by any means. We didn't cling to an ideology about what the world should look like. We simply lived it—and in relative peace.

It is an underappreciated fact of this country that so many poor people from so many other countries can converge, live alongside neighbors who speak different languages and pray to different gods, and yet tribal warfare does not break out. This was the lesson of zip code 11355, where our most aggressive war was with vermin.

The first vacant apartment Mom and Dad saw in America was at the last stop of the 7 train. The super hadn't bothered to clean. It looked like a scene from *Animal House:* pizza boxes strewn on the floor, garbage bags overflowing, roaches crawling over the boxes and bags, and one bag moving on its own because something inside it was pushing.

"¿Eso qué es?" What's jumping in the bag? Mom asked the super in Spanish.

"Acostúmbrate hija." Get used to it, he said. *"Eso es normal aquí."* If the tenants are dirty, that wasn't his problem. Did Mom expect him to clean up other people's mess? *"¿Qué quieres que haga? ¿Limpiarte la casa?"*

Well, yes, she did want him to clean up a vacant unit before showing it. But she sensed she couldn't say that. He seemed like a man who didn't take feedback well.

We needed to find an apartment fast. Mom's baby sister—the same one who crashed my parents' first date in Casablanca—ended up marrying a U.S. citizen and moving to Queens. While she and her husband very generously invited us to stay with them, their small apartment got a little cramped for seven people.

Mom told the super that there were five of us. He said that was too many and couldn't rent the place.

"Tres bebés," Mom clarified. Only two adults. The other three were small children, easy to fit in any corner.

It was a one-bedroom apartment. Though the super put a door on the kitchen pantry and marketed it as a two-bedroom. He wanted about $350 a month. *For this dump!* In Morocco, that would get a palace. Mom and Dad were reeling from sticker shock, in French, when the super interrupted.

"Si quiere, lo coge." Take it or leave it, he said. Otherwise, don't waste his time. *"No quieres, vete."*

Mom, who loved the art of haggling—she'd do it over produce, clothes, cab fares—nudged Dad toward the door. Make it look like they're going to walk. That'll get the super.

He called their bluff. He didn't budge. Not even a penny.

We were not in Casablanca anymore. My parents stopped in their tracks and paid him right there—one month of rent, for which they received a receipt, and another couple hundred, for which there was no receipt. That was his cut.

And so 401—the roach den in the west wing of a 154-unit apartment building—became our first home in America. Mom and Dad could sleep in the same room again.

Though it hardly felt like they had a place to themselves. That's because of the neighbors. Shrieking parents, howling kids, slamming doors, some jerk inevitably kicking the elevator (which was just outside our door), as if that would make it come faster. These were the songs of the building soundtrack.

For Dad, who was an introvert—he craved time to himself—it was noise. What mesmerized him was the local news, with its steady stream of headlines about the Italian mobster John Gotti, the bad-boy millionaire Donald Trump, the vigilantes in red berets who called themselves the Guardian Angels. Dad couldn't believe so many enormous personalities fit into one city. But the neighbors were of no interest.

To Mom, the extrovert, the voices she heard in passing were like trailers to movies she wanted to see. She started a dirt-cheap babysitting service that brought in quick cash and stories. Mom charged one dollar an hour per child. She could take up to four children. That's in addition to my big sister Ang and me. Usually, it was some combination of Kevin, Ahnel, Neha and Nitin, Elijah, Jelani, and Latoya. Elijah took a little extra work because he was still in diapers—the cloth type, not disposable. Mom had to hand wash and iron dry.

Mom wasn't into politics. She cared about people. And that's how she got her crash course in modern history. Countries she hadn't heard of—Guinea, Guyana, Haiti, Dominican Republic—were, like her own homeland, colonized, pillaged, war-ravaged.

All adults were "uncle" or "auntie." Kevin's mom, Auntie Ione, had a job at a hospital and sometimes worked late. One day when she came to pick up Kevin, she found him on Dad's lap. When she reached over, Kevin held on to Dad's collar and said "dada."

She felt horribly self-conscious. Kevin, who was learning to talk, recently used that word with another man. That man responded with a temper tantrum. "I'm not his father. Why the hell is he calling me that?"

Dad didn't mind in the least. He liked it. It was a sign of respect. He smiled and held Kevin a moment longer.

"Thank you," Auntie Ione said.

"What is there to thank?" Dad said. "He's a boy. I'm a father. He can call me Papa."

From then on, that's what Kevin called Dad. It didn't faze him that Kevin was black—the son of a hardworking Jamaican mom and a biological father, a professor from West Africa, who was absent. When adults look at children, it's easier to forget all the biases learned over a lifetime.

With other adults, Dad's walls went straight up. One day he and Mom were in the lobby, waiting for the elevator. A Puerto Rican man wearing rings on all his fingers, with a Mohawk like Mr. T, was waiting, too. He had holes in his acid-washed jeans, in places one should keep covered. My parents didn't know if it was the fashion or if he was too poor to afford a decent pair.

"Let that *bewakoof* go," Dad told Mom in one of their languages. He didn't want his wife in the same elevator as a man who looked like a fool.

"Everyone is God's child," Mom replied.

"God's child? This one is born from the devil."

We arrived with about four thousand dollars. Mom and Dad hid it under a corner of the blue carpet in the Big Bedroom. They assumed we wouldn't need to touch it, that Dad would make so much in America, we'd be able to save and even send cash to Dadi.

They were wrong, devastatingly so. And they were wrong about where the bulk of our money would come from.

Dad set out to find work first. He woke up at 6 A.M. and sat against the wall, sipping his *chai,* the steam from the cup and the smoke of his cigarette rising together. Mom made his *loli* in the kitchen. They didn't speak. Dad needed an hour of quiet before the building soundtrack took over.

Dad put on his suit, a shirt Mom ironed for him, and a favorite tie. He did not understand why American men dressed like little boys—wearing shorts instead of slacks, sneakers instead of dress shoes. At the door, he'd dig out his black leather loafers and *chundhai,* shaking them to toss out the cockroach that might be hiding inside.

Dad was headed to Broadway—the wholesale district—where, he'd heard, a man like him would be snatched up in a heartbeat. With all the languages he spoke, he could cater to just about any of the international clientele. And as if that wasn't enough, he was a numbers guy. Dad had an uncanny ability to memorize large numbers and multiply them in his head. Sometimes, he performed his magic for us.

"What's 13 times 19?" we'd ask.

"247," he'd say.

"What's 187 times 23?"

"4,301."

"What's 346 times 125?"

"43,250."

Had Dad been born in another place and time, he'd be interviewing at a hedge fund or for the foreign service. But that wasn't his destiny. He wasn't in the market for a dream job—something that helped him actualize his self-worth. He just needed cash.

The subway car was already packed at Flushing Main Street, which is where Dad boarded. He didn't understand how more bodies could keep piling in, elbows shoved as new passengers were convinced there must be room for them, if they just pushed hard enough. While elevators in New York had signs that said the maximum capacity, subway cars did not.

Also, men and women mixed together. Back home—if he could call India "home"—that didn't happen. A few too many men thought a woman in public was fair game, to be molested at will. Women needed their own cars.

At Queensboro Plaza, Dad would transfer to a Manhattan-bound N or R train. People clutched their handbags and briefcases like they were about to be mugged. Dad copied, tightening one fist around his briefcase and the other around the plastic strap above his head. The strap was useless. It swayed every time the train swerved. Really, the only thing keeping him upright was the other bodies.

The commute took fifty-five minutes. At Dad's stop, 28th Street, he was carried out in a stampede. *Do all these people already have jobs on Broad-way?* he wondered. Like him and the neighbors in our new building, these commuters came from everywhere. Little hints gave them away: the orange henna in a man's beard, the red slip-ons a woman wore, and many, many smells. Incense, garam masala, coconut oil, shea butter, black soap, fish, vinegar, apple-scented tobacco, Old Spice. It's as if God sprinted the earth with an open bottle and released a globe-trotter's eau de toilette in this one subway station.

Broadway and 28th Street is a short walk from the Empire State Building. Dad had seen this world wonder when he was a young refugee. It was in the movies. Now he was only six blocks away, but it felt too far to visit. When you're on a job hunt, any detour may as well be the distance to Mars.

Dad started on Broadway itself, going to the big shops—the ones that were two stories high, with windows on the ground floor to showcase their radios, videocassette players, watches, handbags, costume jewelry, rayon dresses, Superman and Wonder Woman lunch boxes. They were the original everything stores.

Door knocking did not come naturally to Dad. He was not outgoing like Mom. She'd chat up the whole world. He'd speak only when spoken to. Though when he did open his mouth, it was remarkably easy to like him. He had no rough edges. His voice was calm and precise. He was clearly a smart man.

No. We don't need you.

That's the message he got on his first, second, third try. Too many people from too many countries had already applied for jobs. No help wanted. Dad's pedigree—his languages and math skills and life experience—didn't cross over from the Old World to the New. It—he—was irrelevant.

He gave up on the main road and turned the corner onto the side streets: 27th, 28th, 29th. There, he'd find the smaller businesses without the big windows, hidden from view on the fourth and fifth floors of crumbling buildings, where boxes of merchandise formed columns, creating mazes for rats the size of kittens to play hide-and-seek.

Dad's heart must have sunk when it began sinking in: whatever job he'd land, it would be a step down, not a step up. He wasn't a young man just getting his start in life. He was forty-one years old. There was so much he'd wanted to accomplish. And in New York City, he'd have to begin over again, at the bottom.

The owners of the small stores must have looked at Dad in his suit and had a field day. *Does this FOB really believe the streets are paved with gold?* They'd put him in his place fast.

When Dad came home, he didn't feel like telling Mom about his day. He sat quietly in the corner, smoked his Marlboros, and sipped his scotch. It was exactly what he did in the face of Dadi's wrath. Only now, he couldn't afford to drink Johnnie Walker Red Label neat. He had to add water, to make it last longer.

"How was your day, dahling?" Mom prodded for details. "Dahling" is how Mom and Dad said "darling." They'd picked it up from the movies.

He didn't answer.

"Dahling?" she asked again.

"*Hah*," he said. Yes. He'd visited some stores and would keep going back to Broadway to do whatever work he could find—sweep the streets, shovel the snow, push merchandise up and down the block on a hand truck.

"Oh." Mom was surprised. Given his big brain, she assumed he'd get brain work, not manual labor.

She worried in that moment that Dadi was right, that Mom was bad luck, cursed, bringing misery to her husband. But then she reminded herself that there are small shops in cities all around the world that cater to tourists and the rising middle class, and they're desperate for a man just like Dad. She knew he was overqualified and it would be a brief matter of time before the right door opened.

"It's a very good start," she told him. "From here we'll just keep going further and further."

Her optimism was utterly grating. It was the last thing he needed to hear.

Mom says the first clear sign from God that we were meant to be here came to her on Kissena Boulevard. She was heading to the supermarket. Ang and I were with her, ages three and two. She folded a blanket into her shopping cart and piled us in.

That's when she walked by a bridal shop with two words written in neon orange letters: HELP WANTED. She stopped right then and there to ask for the boss. A man wearing a yarmulke on his head greeted her.

"Do you have papers?" he asked her point-blank.

"No," she said, a little startled at how the truth leapt out. She knew she wasn't supposed to tell anyone we'd overstayed our visas.

"What kind of stitching work can you do?" he asked.

"Anything you need." Even though she'd never made Western bridal gowns, she figured it would be easy enough.

"I have a customer coming in soon. She's not happy with the fitting of the dress we made her. Can you stay and see her?"

Mom glanced at me and Ang. "Yes," she said, knowing that was the only right answer.

The showroom was full of ready-made dresses. One had a bustier top embroidered in translucent sequins; others, lace and satin. A handful were real silk. She found them comely—except for their color. Every single dress was white. That's the color Hindus wear to funerals, to mourn the loss of life. Maybe Christians knew something we didn't about the truth of marriage.

The boss led us down a staircase in the back, helping Mom lift the cart-cum-stroller as we entered a basement with a dozen sewing machines lined up against two walls. Women were hunched over, hard at work, the ornate showroom giving way to a dingy sweatshop.

That was Flushing in a nutshell: the American dream machine, where one person's dreams came true because it was fed, nourished, fattened by the dreams of the others, where the rising middle class stood tall on the hard work of the newest arrivals, who themselves believed they, too, could be the boss one day. Mom had this thought— something she wouldn't even consider in Casablanca. Maybe that's because on Main Street, she'd passed more than one store with a woman in charge.

But first she had to deal with Bridezilla. Mom was thirty-six. The bride who needed alterations was at least ten years younger. Yet she reminded Mom of Dadi.

"What are you doing?" Bridezilla barked from her perch, a small platform in front of a full-length mirror. "Don't you see this?! It's all wrong."

Mom hunched over, pins between her lips, gathering the loose fabric under an armpit. *She shouldn't be so angry,* Mom thought to herself. *I didn't make this mess. I'm trying to fix it.*

"S'il vous plaît." Mom began speaking in French. She was still so new to Queens, she kept mixing up her languages.

"What?" Bridezilla scowled.

The boss gave Ang and me cookies, and he didn't mind us crawling around. The other seamstresses seemed happy to have children in the sweatshop. When Mom finished pinning and remeasuring, the boss asked if she could come back the next day to finish her alterations. Again, no was not an option. Mom said yes.

Childcare was the only problem. Deepak was enrolled in junior high school, where the teacher made it clear he was not allowed to miss class. Dad was making his rounds on Broadway. So Mom did what any parent would do for emergency childcare: she turned to the neighbor she lovingly referred to as "the drug addict."

Now, it's not clear this neighbor was really taking drugs. She may have been, because she didn't seem all there. Either way, she didn't appear to be violent.

Mom sprinted over to the bridal shop and altered the dress without a fuss. Bridezilla tipped her ten dollars. The generosity from such an unlikely source had to be a sign. And when she got back to us girls, we were unscathed.

The boss hired Mom immediately. He paid her per dress, and she sewed so quickly, she made twenty dollars an hour. It wasn't full-time work. It was a few hours here and there. The emergency money under the blue carpet was gone soon enough. But the fact that Mom could make so much and at such a crucial moment for her family's survival—it gave her the sense that she was worth something, and we would survive.

Dad was relieved and proud of Mom. "Very good, dahling." He smiled and kissed her forehead. Though there was, of course, that smidgeon of angst any hardworking man would feel: he was underperforming while his wife was punching above her weight. Maybe this was a feature of America—the strange land where women not only give birth but also pay the bills. What other laws of nature might be broken here?

Migration is not just the intensely personal decision of a couple—on par with marriage or having children. It is a highly impersonal, predictable event—the by-product of networks that have nothing to do with what the heart wants.

Take, for instance, Nari Keplani, who lived two blocks away. Never mind his comb-over—thin strands of hair grown out several inches, flipped over his scalp to cover a shiny bald crown. The man was a godsend—Dad's first friend in America. Though they were long-lost friends, neighbors "back home" in a small town in India, where both landed after Partition.

When we got to Queens, Dad rediscovered Keplani, through a web of people from our ethnic group who used letters and calling cards to stay in touch over the decades. When no landlord would return our call, Keplani was the one who helped us find apartment 401. He also pointed Dad to Broadway.

We began having dinner together; usually we went to the Keplani home. It was a little bigger than ours, in a building where the elevators broke down less often. Like Dad, Keplani couldn't afford to drink his Johnnie Walker neat. But he didn't have to put in as much water—an objective metric that he was doing better in life.

As with the poker nights in Casablanca, it was at these dinners that Mom learned about her husband's life. (Dad came out of his shell, talking with men more readily than with her.) His family of thirteen had had no running water or electricity, she overheard. They used lanterns, not lightbulbs. *My God,* she thought to herself. *I knew he grew up poor—not that poor.* Keplani's family would come by to give food to Dad's family.

Mom also learned that the bosses on Broadway shouted at Dad: *You good-for-nothing! Move faster or I'll get someone younger!* And it turned out Dad's elder brother—the belligerent drunkard who'd made Mom's life miserable in Casablanca—had since cleaned up his act. He had moved to Dubai, then a little-known desert city with a thriving gold market. Another brother of Dad's was in the Middle East too, also in jewels.

"*Namu-bhai,* tell your brothers to send us a few items. We can sell it on Broadway," Keplani said to Dad. "Why work for assholes when we can work for ourselves?"

Dad jumped at it. And, Mom came to learn, he and Keplani got a small office in one of the dingy buildings with the big rats. Dad didn't ask Mom's opinion. What a husband does for money is not his wife's business. She knew that and accepted it.

Though Mom did worry that by bragging about his family abroad, Dad would attract the evil eye. Bragging is what Indians did when we got together. Dreams of grandeur make life a little less humiliating. If we couldn't show off about ourselves, we'd tell tales of our blood relations thriving elsewhere, or of how well the kids are doing. It seemed practically every Indian son in Queens was so exceptional, he was skipping a grade and getting a "double promotion" at school.

Dad became playful again. He'd call Mom *minji vadi gui*, my big butt, because her butt was round and popped out, unlike his concave backside. She liked the teasing. They were laughing again.

In Flushing—Mom didn't notice she was doing this—she actively avoided Indians. She gravitated to people from other countries, who didn't pigeonhole her. With them, she was a blank slate. She could be whoever she wanted to be—which is the spiritual essence of the American dream. The greatest gift of this country is not material wealth so much as the power to re-create oneself. Mom wanted to be more than a wife, and for the first time in her world travels, she did not have to hide it.

Indians scrutinized her. Most had lived on the subcontinent longer than Mom had. They noticed her broken Hindi and that lilting accent that was impossible to place.

"Nina, look how you've worn this sari!" Mrs. Keplani corrected Mom at one dinner. "Why don't you learn to wear it properly! Practice at home before you come out! You look like a *vayari*."

Mom had wrapped the sari around her hips one too many times, cutting short the last ream of fabric that was meant to drape over her shoulder and cover her head. She'd also tied the petticoat too high, so her bare ankles showed.

Mom got defensive: "I have little kids I have to manage with both my hands. Will I take the *chunari* or my children?"

"What nonsense you talk?" Mrs. Keplani said. "You think you're the only one raising kids! I've lived in this country longer than you, and I did it."

Checkmate. Mom lost that battle.

Mrs. Keplani put Mom in her place in more than one way. "They took a neighbor of mine, *yaar*," Mrs. Keplani said one day. The neighbor supposedly went to the grocery store, and when her daughter opened a bag of potato chips without permission, the store employee called the police. "They gave her to immigration." Mrs. Keplani leaned in. "She didn't have papers, like you."

That last line echoed down the long halls of Mom's fears. She didn't stop to question if the story was true—an example of what "law and order" meant in her new home or a tale one newcomer spun to terrify another. She was rattled. She found herself acting differently. When police walked down the street, she'd tense up, walk slower, or turn in a direction she didn't need to go, just to get away from NYPD.

While Mom and Dad didn't talk much, they communicated well about what they earned. Neither of them tried to hide money. At the end of a day, each would put the cash they'd made in the other's hand.

"For you, dahling."

"Thank you, dahling."

This ritual had become such a standard part of life that Mom wanted to crack Dad's skull open after she rummaged through his desk.

Dad got the desk after he started working with Keplani. He kept it in the Big Bedroom, which doubled as his home office. Inside a drawer, Mom found a cashed check—paid to the order of Mrs. Keplani. *Why the hell is my husband writing checks to that woman?* Mom thought to herself. It was for four figures, a mind-blowing amount. *The kids have nothing to wear. We can't eat meat. How can my husband give that woman a thousand when he can't give me a hundred? It must be an affair.*

Mom waited all day for Dad to get home. And when he did, she ripped into him right in front of us: "Why did you write such a big check to Keplani's wife?"

Dad's jaw dropped. Yes, America was different from anywhere else. But whatever corner of earth they landed on, wives have no business talking to their husbands that way. Mom was "eating his head," becoming Americanized. What Dadi had warned of years ago was coming to pass.

Dad widened his eyes, puckered his lips—a warning that used to be enough.

Mom would not back down. "Why did you give her our money?"

"Because they're blackmailing me," he said. The word leapt from his mouth. Blackmail.

"Blackmail?!"

"Hah."

Things were not going as planned. First, Keplani told Dad they'd have to give protection money to the Mafia. Dad hadn't met these men. They didn't walk into the store or leave threatening messages. But, Keplani insisted, they were dangerous and had to be paid off.

Next, jewels were stolen from the safe.

"There were jewels? In a safe?" Mom asked.

One of Dad's brothers had sent him precious stones, to try to sell on Broadway. Whether they came by mail or a friend visiting, Mom didn't know. And before she could pry, there was more.

"I took the phone to call the police," Dad said. But Keplani put his finger on the receiver. "He told me not to report the robbery."

That's when it sunk in. The business was not, as Dad had thought, selling imported items to customers in the wholesale district. The business was milking a dumb illegal for all he was worth.

He didn't cut Keplani off. Dad didn't want to rock the boat. He started telling stories: his rich and generous brothers were having a hard time; the oil sheiks who bought from them were buying less; he couldn't call in more favors. He started making excuses to avoid going into the small office. *"Pait mai dard hai."* He complained of stomachaches and fevers.

Dad started spending sick days in 401, a chair pulled up inches away from the TV, we girls sitting on the floor beside him. We loved having him there, all to ourselves while Mom and Deepak were out. Dad made us chutney sandwiches and *bhindi bhaji*. We watched *The Price Is Right*.

While Dad didn't like how loud Americans can be, their screaming didn't bother him one bit on this game show. When the host came on stage—with his perfectly fitted silver suit and well-coiffed hair—and he asked the retail value of that Palmolive dish soap or Plymouth Voyager, Ang shouted her guess. Often she came closer than the raving contestants, and Dad beamed with pride.

One of the last times Dad saw Keplani the crook was with my brother. "He is a bad man," Dad told Deepak. They were walking down Main Street, past the family-owned pizzeria and the Asian grocer who descaled fresh trout on the sidewalk. The Keplanis were having a birthday party.

28

Deepak, who was thirteen, didn't understand why a bad person got to have a birthday. But he didn't ask questions. When Dad told him to do something, he did it.

The party was not fun. While a group of men played poker at the coffee table, Dad and Deepak stood in a corner, keeping to themselves. Dad left the corner only to refill his tumbler of Johnnie Walker. They left early.

Back in 401, my big brother saw the light on in the bathroom. He approached it. Inside, Dad was on his knees, hurling into the toilet. The whiskey he'd had on an empty stomach came out much like it went in, only now thickened with bile.

"Keplani put something in my drink." Dad tried to explain away the scene to his son. "He poisoned me." But there was no hiding the fact. It was Dad—who kept clinging to ideas and people from the past—who'd chosen his own poison.

To migrate to America—to cross the Atlantic or Pacific Ocean or the Sonoran Desert—is the boldest act of one's life. You do it to be the hero of your own story. Only, God must have a sense of humor because, as every undocumented immigrant knows, you can't cross over and stand proud. You have to be invisible. That's safer than being seen by the wrong people. Invisible heroes. That was my parents, in a nutshell, until 1984.

In 1984 I went to kindergarten. It was also the year two men were running for president: a man named Walter, and another Ronald.

"OK class, we are going to vote today," my teacher announced.

Because we didn't know how to read or write yet, we'd raise our hands for our preferred candidate. I chose Ronald Reagan because he had the same first name as Ronald McDonald—a clown with red hair who skated on ice and gave children Happy Meals. Whenever we walked by McDonald's, and Ang and I looked at Mom pleadingly, she made it clear Happy Meals were well beyond our budget. I hoped Ronald the president could change that by making something called "the economy" better.

Dad was also a fan of Ronald because he said he would give "amnesty" to "illegal immigrants." He believed we should have "green cards." I knew those words because I heard Mom and Dad say them while talking in one of their other languages. While I was not interested in learning those languages, I was a sponge for any word in English.

Reagan won. Though we ended up getting our green cards another way. Mom's baby sister—who'd crashed their first date, married a U.S. citizen and moved to Queens—became a citizen herself. She and her husband sponsored us in a process some have derided as "chain migration," as if it were a bad thing. To me, the term is positive. Each family member is a link in the chain. The more links you add, the longer, the stronger, more unbreakable the chain is. Last I checked, strong families are a good thing.

It didn't take twenty or thirty years, like it would today. It took three years. When the green cards came in the mail, my parents didn't jump up and down like contestants on *The Price Is Right.* They sat together, taking deep breaths, feeling partial relief, like when you stretch a limb that's been contorted too long and the blood rushes back.

We would no longer have to cross the street to avoid NYPD. The Keplanis of the world couldn't hurt us anymore. We could put our name on complaint letters to the super when the heat stopped in the winter or the upstairs neighbor's shower seeped through the plaster and rained on us. These were considerable wins.

Still, the question of how we'd make a living didn't disappear. At their ages—middle-aged, too old to enroll in school or a great vocational program—Mom and Dad wouldn't suddenly have doors fling open for them. And—they saw this in our building—there were so many people with papers who were poor.

Not surprisingly, my parents had opposite takes on America.

"If you want to stay in this misery, you stay alone," Dad told Mom one day.

"*Kya*, dahling?" Mom didn't understand.

Dad was ready to do what millions of immigrants before him had done: pack up and go. We don't tend to hear this part of the American story. We know about the Ellis Island immigrants who poured in, not about those who then decided the winter was too cold, the city was too mean, and it was time to go back.

That was Dad's thinking. After his first business venture fell apart, he tried to pick himself back up. He went knocking on Broadway doors, asking for any work he could get. He got the most menial jobs, sweeping streets and shoveling snow. He would work a whole day and still couldn't put more than forty dollars in Mom's hand. And he longed for a country without snow—of which there are many. Paralyzing isolation and extreme weather—gross malfunctions of nature—are, for many immigrants, two of the most devastating features of America.

And while women are raised to know they will leave their own families to join that of their husbands, men are supposed to stay close to their parents and brothers until the end. That's what Dad grew up learning. Wasn't that another law of nature?

"Please," Mom tried to reason with him. "If you get a good job, we can move to a better place." By getting a green card, they'd just broken through a major barrier. Now was not the time to give up.

"You brought me here to slave away for you?" he said, the scorn of Dadi now dripping from his own tongue. *He'll kill himself slaving away for you. You don't care about him.*

"*Nah,* dahling." Mom shook her head. "We'll make it work. At least here we have our freedom."

"Freedom? What freedom is this?" Dad asked in earnest. What freedom could his wife possibly be referring to? The freedom to shovel snow for five dollars an hour? The freedom to have cockroaches crawl on the kids' pants while the kids were wearing them? The freedom to be far away from any familiar face?

"I'm leaving," he told her.

"Where are you going?" Mom asked.

Apart from Keplani the crook, Dad didn't have friends nearby. While she'd been making many friends among the neighbors, Dad kept to himself.

"Dubai," he told her.

"Dubai?" That's not what she expected.

All those times Dad was on the phone—on furtive calls with relations abroad—he was talking with his brothers in the Arab world. Dubai was not yet the Switzerland of the Middle East. It did not yet have an indoor ski resort or a shopping center bigger than the Mall of America. But migration is a bet. And Dad's brothers were betting their part of the world would afford more opportunities than his.

The little gold souk where his brother had opened a shop was growing. Oil sheikhs streamed in like petroleum at the pump. They bought rubies and diamonds and even blouses and belts crocheted from 18- and 22-karat gold. "Leave America," Dad's brothers told him. "Life is too hard there. It's not worth it."

Dubai wasn't exactly easy. It got so hot, the migrant workers imported from South India would slice potatoes paper thin, drizzle them with oil, and use the midday sun to cook chips for their masters.

Dad wouldn't have to come in that low on the totem pole. With his family connections, he could be a shopkeeper instead of a house servant. The heat and boredom of desert life would beat the frenzy of Flushing any day. At least, that's how he felt. It's how a lot of people would have felt.

But not Mom. "I won't go," she blurted to her husband, not able to control the words coming out of her own mouth. She was more determined to stay than she'd realized. "I'll never go."

Never?

"Then to hell with you," Dad blurted back.

In that moment, they were discovering the truth about each other. Despite pledging to be together till death do them part, they were growing apart. Dad wanted stability, and he wanted his honor back. A man is supposed to provide for his family. That's what makes him a man. New York had emasculated him.

"When will you come back?" Mom said.

He didn't answer.

Dad left with a suitcase in his hand and no return ticket. The elevator was not broken. It came when he pressed the button. Mom ran to block the door, a last-ditch effort to stop him.

"Dahling, don't do this," she begged. "For our children. Please!"

He shouted: "Move!"

Dad left, breaking his own cardinal rule. Never leave home angry. It's bad luck.

Mom was now in 401 with three children, on her own. It was an insane choice. Though it didn't feel like a hard one. She knew that America—far away from her husband's family—was the only shot at real freedom. And Mom had models, in our building, of other single mothers. Granted, they had college degrees and office jobs, unlike her.

32

But the fact that they existed gave Mom hope. *A woman can do it all,* she told herself, *so long as she's not afraid of hard work.*

Whenever I asked for Dad, Mom would say: *Oh, he's gone out. He's buying gifts for you. He's gone for a job. He was just here, but you were sleeping and he didn't want to wake you.*

Dad called her once a week, and each time they had a version of this curt exchange:

"Everything OK?" Dad asked. "How are the kids?"

"Hah," Mom said. "Everyone is good."

"OK."

"OK."

"Bye."

They were both angry at each other. Also, phone calls were expensive in those days. One minute abroad could cost a few dollars.

I didn't have a sense of how long Dad was gone because I was too young to tell time. I hadn't been alive that long, so a minute or hour for me was longer than it would be for an adult. That's the law of proportions. Also, time's increments—a day or a week or a month—bled into each other. They blurred, much like Dad's face and scent. It was becoming hard to remember the cactus prick of his moustache when he rubbed his cheek against mine or the smell of his Marlboro fingers.

That I had a father—somewhere out there—was a fact that did not fade. It was at the fore, easily provoked when I saw other kids with their dads or the dads on TV. Even when I could no longer picture mine, I missed him. He was ever present in his ever absence, the ghost of 401.

Though even without him, our home was still too small.

"Move," I screamed at my big sister.

"No, you move."

"Ang, you move." I gave a push.

"Mooooom! Aarti's pushing me!"

"No I'm not!"

Angelly and I were sitting on the toilet, together. Mom made us go number 2 at the same time. That way, she wouldn't have to come wipe us twice. When we sat with our legs on opposite sides of the seat and put our backs against each other—meeting right in the middle—we both fit. Ang was hogging.

"What is it?" Mom came growling. She didn't ask it like she cared. She asked it like: *I'm busy. What the hell do you want?*

Her boss at the bridal shop was kind enough to give her a Singer sewing machine so she could work from home. Dad's formica desk took up one corner of the Big Bedroom, and Mom's Singer another. We were interrupting her during business hours. It was the kind of moment where what we said really mattered. The wrong answer would get one or both of us a slap.

Ang must have felt that too, because when Mom repeated, louder— "WHAT IS IT?"—we both said in a whisper: "Nothing." My big sister moved her cheeks and gave me an inch.

Sometimes Mom would take Ang and me when she dropped off the wedding dresses.

"Uncle, uncle, it's my birthday," Ang told Mom's boss one time. My sister had a habit of yanking her hand away from Mom, running to his pant legs, and pulling, her cherubic face courting him, as if to say, *You can pinch, if you pay me.*

"Your birthday!" Boss Uncle pulled out his wallet. "Well, then, today you get five dollars!" He usually gave her one.

I couldn't believe Ang was so blunt about her material desires. She acted as if everything in the world belonged to her. I was serious, prideful. I refused to ask strangers, even uncles, for money.

Ang used the birthday cash to buy a Big Mac on Main Street.

"Angelly, my doll, why don't you get the regular hamburger? A Big Mac is too big for you," Mom tried to tell her.

"No! I want it," Ang insisted.

My big sister shared everything with me except food. Usually, it didn't bother me because I wasn't hungry. But that afternoon, I could smell the beef patty; I could see the mayo and pickle blending in each bite, sticking to the sides of Ang's mouth. I started to salivate. I wanted some.

"You can have a bite," she said. "But you can't hold it." She held it, keeping her fingers nearby the edge, letting me do no more than nibble. "It's *my* birthday," she reminded me.

Mom couldn't always take us to the bridal store, especially when she had to meet a client. She started leaving Ang and me home alone. *I hope they don't touch the gas,* Mom worried to herself. She put a latch on the kitchen doors, so we couldn't play with the stove. She left our food and bottles on the table in the hallway. Ang and I both used bottles—for different reasons. I wanted to drink from a cup but was still struggling, at age five, with hand-mouth coordination. My sister could drink from a cup but thought bottles took less effort.

Before bolting the front door closed, Mom would give Ang a pep talk: *Angelly doll, please make sure your baby sister doesn't get into trouble. Please take care of her—that she doesn't touch the gas, that she doesn't burn her hands. If she wants water, give her her bottle. If she wants toilet, take her to the bathroom.*

Sometimes I would use a chair to climb up and open the latch. Ang asked Mom, "If she climbs up, what can I do?"

"Don't let her pull the chair. Don't let her touch the chair," Mom instructed. It was nerve-racking, but it worked. We never burned the apartment down, not even once.

We also did not get poisoned—though that was no thanks to Mom. When she walked from her job to 401, she discovered bustling markets with all sorts of home remedies. Insect spines and magic mushrooms to cure the flu, ginseng for energy, and a special chalk in an orange box. It had a picture of a roach with a big X through it.

"Let's play! Let's play!" Mom came home with the special chalk and put a stick in each of our hands. We ran through 401, drawing lines on the edge of every wall, sticking our fingers under the refrigerator to mark up the linoleum tile beneath.

It didn't occur to Mom that the same poison that would kill cockroaches might also harm her children, whose lungs and brains were still developing. NYPD attempted to crack down on the magic chalk. They went door to door, confiscating boxes from the Chinese vendors. But demand was too strong to stomp out supply. When Mom went inside one of the shops—an empty orange box in her hand and a pathetic look in her eyes—the cashier pulled out the secret stash from under the counter.

Many aunties stepped into our lives to fill the vacuum Dad left. Auntie Ione made us bacon, eggs, and pancakes on the weekend, and she made Kevin share his toys, though he didn't want to. Auntie Gloria with the voice of a nightingale sang with us in the living room and took us on a road trip to Pennsylvania, where we passed giant rolled chapatis (they were bales of hay). Auntie Mireya took us to the Cloisters—though that was a small disaster.

The Cloisters, a monastery turned museum, is in Washington Heights, near the end of the A train. Auntie Mireya, a feminist professor from Cuba, was trying to expose Mom to some of the city's cultural gems. We'd done very little sightseeing. Mom told me we were visiting Cinderella's castle.

She grossly underestimated how important it was for me to meet Cinderella. I wanted to talk with her, girl to girl, about how hard it was to have sisters (mine wasn't as bad as hers, but still, Ang and I fought a lot). Also, Cinderella and I both didn't have dads.

"Where is she?" I kept asking Mom and Auntie Mireya.

"She's taking a nap" or "She just went into the garden" or "She's in the kitchen because her stepmother is making her work."

The lies went on and on, until finally I wailed like a banshee. Auntie Mireya, who had planned the perfect day and made notes for a guided tour, had to cut our visit short.

In Dad's absence, Deepak—who was barely a teenager—became our surrogate father. He showed early signs of leadership. He was self-grooming, shaving the thick moustache that so many Indian boys (and girls) grow before their time, and plucking the hair in the middle of his one extralong eyebrow to make them two. He taught Ang and me to fill balloons with water, tie them, and discreetly drop them from the Big Bedroom window when adults we didn't like were coming home from work.

He also engineered a way to stay cool in the summer. During the day, we could run over to one of the fire hydrants the bigger kids with wrenches had popped open. But at night, New York's blistering heat was so relentless, the latex paint on the walls melted, and so did we. Deepak took one of the saffron-yellow sheets made of Indian cotton, doused it in cold water, rang out the excess, and wrapped it around himself and us like we were caterpillars ready to be butterflies. And if it wasn't raining, we could move our cocoon to the fire escape and have a slumber party there.

36

When Mom was out, we weren't supposed to open the door to anyone but him. One day I didn't listen. I was bored, and when the doorbell rang, I leapt up.

"Oooz it?" I asked. I didn't know yet that "oooz it" was "who is it?" I thought it was two words that were a standard door greeting.

"It's Abe." That was my big brother's Egyptian friend. "D-pack around?" Deepak, whose name is pronounced dhee-PUCK, got turned into a name that rhymes with three-pack.

I let Abe in. I wanted someone to play with me. I knew he wouldn't be into dressing dolls or watching cartoons like Ang and I did. So I asked him to sit down and bounce me on his lap, like my big brother did.

We were just getting started when Deepak came home. At the sight of us, he looked like he might grab the nunchucks and ninja stars he was learning to use (he saw them in a Bruce Lee movie). Abe jumped up and beelined to the door.

As soon as he left, my big brother asked, "Did he make you sit on his lap?"

"No. He didn't make me. I wanted to."

"You sure?"

"Yes!"

This time, I was not in trouble. When I was in trouble—for not doing my chores or talking back to Deepak—he didn't hit me like Mom did. He used psychological warfare.

"You want me to sew your toes together?" He'd turn on Mom's Singer machine and, suspending me in the air with one hand, he'd hold my toes just inches from the needle with the other.

"No! Please no!" I'd beg through tears. "I won't do it again!" I could feel him press the pedal, hear the roar of the engine as the miniature dagger they called a needle thrust up and down, hungry for blood. In less time than it takes to hem jeans, it would pierce my nails and leave me with webbed feet like a duck.

One time, I broke free and ran out the door, down the hallway, to my Ethiopian big brother, Blene. "Deepak's going to sew my toes," I shrieked for help. Blene, who was Deepak's best friend, was a gentle giant. He bent down and lifted me into his arms, carrying me back to 401. As I clutched his neck, he pleaded with my big brother: "She's just a

37

little girl. That's not right." The boy-to-boy talk worked. Deepak stopped dangling me above the Singer.

One evening when we were having dinner, there was a knock at the door.

"Oooz it?" Deepak went to answer. Through the peephole he saw the comb-over he'd just as soon forget. It was Keplani the crook. My brother opened the door. He didn't feel he had a choice.

Keplani walked in as though he'd never stolen a penny and nothing had happened. Nothing except we were a family without a father.

Whenever Mom saw Keplani on Main Street, she'd turn the corner or run into a store to avoid him. Now there was nowhere to go. We were in the middle of dinner. He walked into our living room and stepped up to Mom—a step too close, my brother thought.

"It must be so hard with your husband gone," Keplani told her. He liked looking at her. Now he didn't have to hide it. And, taking another step closer, he reached into his pocket to pull out a thin gold chain with a small pendant.

"I can help you," he told Mom as he put the chain around her neck.

Mom and Deepak both wish that the second this poor excuse for a man stepped into 401, they'd put him in his place. But that's not what happened. Mom felt scared. Deepak felt hatred. They both froze. *We need Dad,* they quietly thought to themselves.

Keplani must have felt his power in that moment. It's easy to feel with people who are powerless. He walked out, smug as ever.

One afternoon, Mom went to get groceries at Western Beef. She could have taken Ang and me along. We loved to climb into the shopping cart and have her push. The wheels were so rickety, it felt like a bumper car inside.

But Mom was in a rush. She was always in a rush. She left us with Auntie Ione and then sprinted: down the stairs, down the sidewalk, over to the big intersection at College Point Boulevard. The light hadn't changed. She didn't wait, or get herself to the crosswalk, for that matter. The shortest distance between two points is a diagonal. That's the path she took.

Mom never made it to the other side. With her eyes set on her destination, she didn't see the car racing down the road. Her body ricocheted off the hood, and the driver—perhaps afraid of what harm may have happened—sped away. It was a hit-and-run.

When Mom woke up, she was in a hospital bed. Her hip may have been dislocated. In and out of sleep, not quite lucid, she did hear the doctors and nurses say "surgery" more than once. Mom knew she didn't have the money for surgery. When the car hit her, she was reviewing her grocery list, trying to decide if she could afford yogurt this time around.

She asked the nurse if she could use the phone. While Dad had every phone number memorized, there were only two numbers besides her own that Mom could remember: Auntie Ione, who'd become her building sister, and Auntie Nimi, her baby sister.

Auntie Nimi showed up with a teenage boy (he may have been a distant relative) and a wheelchair. Mom wanted to sign herself out before she got thrown in jail for not paying her hospital bills.

"Where do you think you're going?" A nurse stopped the teenager rolling Mom through the hallway.

"I don't want the surgery. I don't want the surgery." Mom repeated herself, giving the nurse the impression that she was afraid of doctors, not bills.

The nurse said all right, Mom could leave. But first she had to sign a release form, so that the hospital wasn't responsible for anything that may happen to her, including paralysis. "I'll sign anything," Mom said.

Auntie Nimi nursed Mom with Ayurvedic remedies, massaging turmeric and bay leaves on her back, spreading the crumbly paste down her vertebrae—where a bone or two now protruded. They prayed to Lord Ganesha, asking our elephant god to help the plants' cooling properties enter Mom's burning joints and snap them back into place.

Deepak and building aunties took care of us in 401. And when Mom was strong enough to be seen—it may have been a few days—Auntie Nimi brought us to her home. Usually, when I saw Mom after any period of separation, I charged at her like a puppy. This time, I stood completely still, dumbfounded at the image before me, my heart punching my throat. Mom—the woman who did somersaults in the grass and chased me up the staircase with groceries in her hands—was in a wheelchair, hobbling as she tried to lift herself with a cane. She couldn't carry her own weight.

"Come hug your mother," Auntie Nimi told me.

No, I thought. *This is not my mom. This is some older, crippled look-alike you picked up off Main Street.*

"It's OK, my doll." Mom eked out the words. Her voice wasn't even hers. It was air blowing through a cracked flute, all wind, no melody. She couldn't lift her arms to reach out and pull me in. Suddenly, I was cursed with this knowledge: her body and mine were not one and the same. We were two separate things, and I would lose her.

Mom was broken. Dad was gone. There was no one left to hold me. And soon there'd be no one left to pay the bills.

Shortly after the accident, there was another loss. Mom's boss passed away, suddenly. The bridal shop closed overnight. Mom had been having a hard time sewing since the car hit her. She'd lost her fine motor skills. Her right hand shook when she tried to thread a needle. Her boss had noticed this change, but he didn't have the heart to let her go. "Take your time, Nina," he'd tell her, and kept giving her work.

No one else had that kind of patience for Mom. She got odd jobs, sewing curtains and doing simple alterations, but no real job. When she could stand again—she said it happened because she prayed and God answered her prayers—she restarted her babysitting service for the neighbors' kids.

Mom's baby sister, convinced there was no way we would make it, decided to pick up a phone and call Dad. *"Bahu,"* she said, using the term of respect for your elder brother. "Your wife needs you. Your kids need you. It's been a few months. Please come back."

The day Dad returned to 401, he was carrying two heavy suitcases. I jumped all over him. He was not broken. He would not fall with my weight. We had someone who could protect us again.

He gave us presents from the faraway place he'd gone. I recall a camel figurine and chocolate. He also brought many, many beads. They were mother-of-pearl, threaded on long strings. "We can make the necklaces and sell them," he said.

Mom was overjoyed, and not just because Dad showed up. He looked genuinely happy to be back. His face glowed with seeing us kids. Even if the two of them were full of hard feelings, Dad loved us more than anything. He'd hated being far away. Together again with his children, Mom noticed, his eyes shone, calm but bright.

Dad went back to Broadway, and this time luck was on his side. He ran into another man from "back home" who ran a wholesale shop with electronics and garments. He gave Dad a full-time job inside the store, not outside, attending to customers from around the world, putting his many languages to use. Dad would be second-in-command. He only had to shovel the snow or deliver boxes of watches and calculators when other workers were out sick.

When Dad came home at night, the second the door slammed shut behind him, he would let out the longest, wettest fart you've ever heard. And he'd shout above his symphony: *tutageemahlah!* Loosely translated, it means: fart monster. It was gross, but it made us laugh.

I marveled at how long he could go on and sometimes counted along. A count up is more exciting than a countdown because the length of time is unknown. I wanted to write to the *Guinness Book of World Records* about Dad. But I couldn't write yet. I was just beginning to learn.

While Dad was a stranger of sorts—he didn't play with us or take us to the botanical garden like Mom did—he did let us kids tag along at the Off-Track Betting shop on Northern Boulevard. It smelled like a dive bar. Scruffy men with brown paper bags stood on line and gathered around TV screens to watch the horses sprint. Thick molecules of tobacco smoke pushed out all the oxygen.

Mom said Dad smoked three packs a day. He said it was just two. One time, influenced by him and a smoking camel on TV, Ang and I decided we would pretend smoke. Sitting on the brown carpet in the living room, we puffed away at plastic straws. Dad came in and lost it.

"You want to smoke?" He yanked the straw from Ang's mouth and shoved in the Marlboro dangling from his lips. "Smoke." She coughed and coughed. I got scared and hoped he'd let me off the hook. He was a softie compared with Mom. But he wouldn't. "Do it." He turned to me. It smelled disgusting and tasted the same.

There was blatant hypocrisy in Dad's lesson. He was telling us: *Do as I say, not as I do.* But it worked. Ang (who has no memory of this event) never smoked again. I (who remember it vividly) did not either.

While Mom no longer sewed dresses for a living, she did make matching outfits for Ang and me (and sometimes herself as well) for special occasions. They were usually Western wear. Though one Diwali—the Hindu festival of lights, which comes every fall—Mom stitched candy-striped kurtas.

I disliked wearing Indian clothes, and not because no one else wore them. Flushing was full of kurtas, *salwars*, saris, hijabs, ponchos, *hanboks*, Mandarin collars, and kung fu suits. "Ethnic" wasn't strange. It was normal. Still, I was self-conscious. I wanted to be supernormal. So when Mom put the kurta on me, I didn't do what I usually did: run down the hallway to show my Ethiopian big brother, the one who protected me from Deepak. I stayed inside 401 all evening.

Dad may have noticed. After we finished the *pooja* in front of our altar—which was one shelf over from the Johnnie Walker bottle on the particleboard wall unit—Dad did a rare thing. He started a conversation with me.

"You know what does it mean, your name?" he asked, pulling me on his lap.

I was a child who loved words: big words, small words, compound words, homonyms. The truth of "Oooz it" blew my mind. So did "days" and "daze." But my name—that is one word I hated. It was too hard to pronounce. My mouth didn't cooperate. I turned Rs into Ls: "ahl-tee." Mom asked me to say it when her friends came by, just so she could have a good laugh. Then Ang would show off how she could say it perfectly. I hated when my big sister could do something I couldn't.

"The meaning is very nice," Dad said. "When we do the *pooja* in front of the gods, and we light the *diya* in the tray, that is the *aarti*."

"So I'm the candle?" I didn't want to say the word "*diya*." It wasn't English.

"No, you're the light."

"You mean the fire in the prayer?"

"*Hah*," he said. "More or less, you can say that."

I was the fire in the prayer—a force of nature that, even as a tiny flicker, was the focal point of our connection to God.

After our talk, I ran down the hallway, eager to show my Ethiopian big brother the candy-striped kurta. Only, I didn't want to say that's what I was doing. So I took a cup and said Mom ran out of milk. Blene opened the door.

"You look very pretty in that outfit," he told me. "You should wear Indian clothes more often."

A working-class apartment building is different from a luxury building in that everyone knows their neighbors. It's hard to go long distances when you don't have a lot of money, so you become more interested in your immediate surroundings. And neighbors are the safety net—the people who provide emergency childcare when you're hit by a car or who loan you a cup of milk or sugar when you've run out. In 401, we borrowed from our neighbors all the time. Not luxury items, like yogurt or orange juice. Just the basics.

On very special occasions, Dad went to the Afghan butcher to buy fresh sugarcane and meat. His favorite was goat meat, which was cheaper with the hair still lodged inside the animal's follicles. So that's how Dad bought it: hairy. Ang and I would sit in front of the TV and use our nails to claw out the toe hair (feet were high in protein and collagen). Dad supervised. Anything we couldn't get, he'd wrestle out with plyers.

One Thanksgiving, we didn't have to clean goat or borrow food. God delivered bags and bags of groceries, through our Christian cult.

Flushing is the birthplace of freedom of religion in America. Back in the 1600s, the dictatorial Dutch governor ordered English Quakers to stop their quaking worship. They fled to northern Queens, finding sanctuary on the property of a wealthy landowner.

The governor, outraged that a rich man acted above the law, sent his minions to arrest the landowner from his home (which happened to be right by the playground where Ang and I played seesaw). The arrest sparked a movement. It laid the groundwork for the First Amendment. And it left a local legacy. Flushing has more houses of worship than an amusement park has rides, from every tradition: Old Testament, New Testament, Sutras, Talmud, Koran, Vedas, Tao Te Ching, and the more contemporary "Divine Principle"—the holy scripture of the Moonies.

Reverend Sun Myung Moon, the Korean founder, was a former prisoner of war who claimed Jesus Christ anointed him to create heaven on earth. His Unification Church created unity by arranging marriages across nationalities: Nigerian with Chinese, Guatemalan with Swedish, Californian with Canadian. The world would converge into one culture, he said, and "Blessed Couples" (as we called them) would be at the van-guard.

Mom became a Moonie because the church gave her a community to socialize, and she liked seeing different races come together on Sunday morning. But she wasn't exclusively a Moonie. Our native religion, Hinduism, doesn't make people choose one god, like Christianity does. We can worship as many as we'd like. I liked the Flushing Moonies for their diversity, too. Though I didn't believe the stories they told about human creation—especially the part where a woman comes from a man's body.

My favorite was the Buddhist temple, where monks taught meditation. It's a practical skill that takes discipline and training, like running. And when you build meditation muscle, it's not that the world suddenly becomes calm, or "zen," as the marketers like to say. It's that you can observe far more clearly, aware of how your own prejudices and emotions cloud vision.

When our 401 doorbell rang Thanksgiving night, we didn't expect a Blessed Couple with bags of roasted turkey and pork, ham, gravy, fruits, pies, and potato salad. Ang and my eyes lit up. It was a real Thanksgiving—just like we saw on TV. We began peeking inside, calling out what we planned to eat first, second, third, pushing each other out of the way to see.

Instead of helping us place the food on our own table, Mom took one of the trays of meat and headed out. She wanted to share with the neighbors. Ang followed. Mom meant to go to the specific people she was closest to or knew needed the most help. But in the packed elevator, people inhaled so loudly, Mom started handing out cuts of meat like a McDonald's cashier. She may have given pork to a Muslim—though she told everyone it was turkey.

Ang and I thought it was right of Mom to share, but she should have given us the first bite. We were her children, after all. Mom disagreed. She believed that when we have generous hearts, God provides. Dad and Deepak were quiet on the matter.

Mom started and was voted president of the Tenants' Association. She'd only finished seventh grade and wasn't comfortable with writing. Her fellow Moonie, Auntie Chemis, who'd finished college, typed up the documents needed to make the group legitimate in the eyes of the super. While many neighbors still didn't have papers, they wrote down their names on the list because they trusted the Tenants' Association, and Mom.

As part of her leadership, she began to turn our birthdays into building events. She didn't stop to ask if we kids would prefer five guests or a hundred. In 401, while there was not space enough for the five of us to live, there was space enough for all God's children to party.

Mom pulled it off on a shoestring budget. The cabbage and mint salad that my grandmother threw against the wall in Casablanca was a big hit in Flushing, and cheap. Three dollars could make thirty servings. When Western Beef had a sale on C&C cola, Mom stocked up. She wasn't financially reckless. Just emotionally so—like on my sixth birthday.

Ang says it was her birthday. But I know it was mine, because I was the one Mom humiliated. My sister and I were wearing matching princess gowns Mom stitched from a floral cotton print. She added a black sequined flower at the waist, which clashed (or popped like statement jewelry).

The kids our ages came first. Then some of the Building Boys—who were too cool to play with us—walked in with a boom box. They were blasting either Hot 97 or a mix tape. I thought, *Oh no, Mom is going to get angry and cause a scene.*

My worry was misplaced. Mom eyed the boys and flashed a smile that was exuberant, a tinge of crazy. She left the party. "Where's Nina?" adults began asking. Mom returned dragging an enormous cardboard box behind her.

"I got this from the dumpster," she told the Building Boys. "Help me make a dance floor."

The petite Indian immigrant who had three children, spoke too many languages, and shouted at them for loitering was suddenly cool. A cool auntie.

One boy stepped into the middle of the living room and moved the throngs of guests against the walls. "Everyone step back." He motioned like a security guard. Another boy flattened the box and laid it down. It covered practically the whole brown carpet.

Turns out, the Building Boys were B-boys, and we had the perfect makeshift floor for break dancing. One of them cranked up the boom box, full blast, and dove right to the center, hands first. He stood and then walked on his palms. The circle clapped on the beat and then roared when he dropped onto a single shoulder, spinning like a windmill. Another kid went. Then another. We were intoxicated—collective pride in their artistry. So much so that Mom, taken by the spirit, jumped to the middle of the floor.

Is she going to break-dance? I thought. *She can't! She broke her back in the car accident. Please be careful, Mom.*

Again, my worry was misplaced.

"OK, everyone," Mom shouted above the music. "Now let's see what the birthday girl can do! Aarti, my *pichikery*, come show us!"

The fantasy life of this grown woman was nothing short of remarkable. She imagined that somehow her baby girl, who was still working on pull-ups at the monkey bar, could do hand hops because she willed it to be so. It was the same magical thinking that got Mom to cross the Atlantic and stay. Only now, I was the victim of it.

"C'mon, Aarti," she egged me on, clapping and commanding the circle to keep clapping, too.

Lord Shiva or Jesus or Reverend Moon help me. I stood there, eyes fixed on the collection of gurus on our wall unit, legs trembling, and burst into tears.

That night, when Dad got home, I wanted to be a tattletale on Mom. If he knew what she had done, he'd give her a scolding in a way I could not.

Only, I kept quiet because our building life was a secret life. Dad didn't know about the parties and meetings—which were usually a lot of fun—until one day he came home and a cameraman scolded him.

"Will ya watch where ya goin'!" the cameraman said as Dad stepped over a coil of black wires.

"This is my home," Dad replied, in his usual calm, his attention drawn to a large white beach umbrella propped up in the living room.

"It's to diffuse lighting," the cameraman explained. "You're just in time for the interview."

The Shahanis were being featured on ABC News. Dad did not know.

"A hundred years ago, twenty years ago, yesterday they came. Today and tomorrow they will continue to come in search of their dreams," host Roz Abrams began the one-hour special on diversity. "If America can make her experiment work, she can be the beacon for true equality and joy in our world. But how can we move in the direction that will bring us together?"

My family was a small part of the answer. Dozens of people filled our living room and hallway, every color and creed, a postcard of what makes this country great. Dad could not pull Mom aside—there was no empty corner—so he smiled politely as he asked in our ethnic language if she had lost her mind.

Mom, in a peacock-blue dress—that was her favorite color—smiled demurely and tugged Dad's hand, making him lurch to the floor. They'd sit together, a united couple.

"Sharing curry and cultures with their neighbors is what the Shahanis do in real life," the host announced.

Mom pointed to the sofa piled with friends: "They're pretty used to coming to my house." This was news to Dad.

She'd thought about telling him beforehand. But he'd forbid it. And she wasn't having the cameras come for self promotion. It was for pro moting brotherhood and sisterhood in America. *Even if he gets angry,* Mom thought, *it's better to ask forgiveness than permission.*

That night, she didn't end up asking him for either. When the last of the neighbors cleared out, Dad sat in a quiet rage, burning through cigarettes more quickly than usual. Mom pretended not to notice. It was their version of agreeing to disagree.

Though, increasingly, they just disagreed outright. Mom began doing something in 401 she wouldn't have dreamed of trying in Casablanca: she was talking back to Dad, using her freedom of speech. Regularly.

"*Chaa kichero hai?*" Dad would call the meal Mom made garbage if it was pasta or another bland American food.

"This is dinner!" she'd retort. "If you don't like it, make yourself something." Or instead of asking if she could go to one of her community meetings, she'd assert, "I'm going!"

Dad wasn't used to this. He didn't like it. But he was also a pick-and-choose-your-battles kind of guy. "Be home by seven thirty." He'd give Mom a curfew. She'd nod in agreement. It was a reasonable balance between her duties at home and her passions outside. And besides, she could blame the Q44 bus if she was a little late.

On one point, however, there was no middle ground.

"You say you'll quit smoking, and you haven't. When will you quit?" She wept. "You don't respect me."

"I've just come home from work," Dad said. "Why are you talking such stupid things?"

"*Kya?*" Mom pushed back. The health of the kids was not a stupid thing.

"*Hah.* OK. I will quit," he'd appease her. "Soon."

This was the fight they had on repeat. A fight without resolution. Dad smoked to cope with real-world pressures. Mom hated cigarettes because they killed. Where one saw life, the other saw death. The fight drove Mom out of the Big Bedroom and into the living room. This time, Dadi wasn't getting in the way of Mom's sleeping with her husband. It was the Marlboro Man.

One night, when my parents began to recite the familiar script, Mom changed the final scene. She headed for the door.

"Where are you going?" Dad asked.

"Away!" she shouted as the door slammed behind her.

The pep talks her building sisters gave her were starting to sink in. *Why do you put up with him? Where's your self-respect?* they asked. Mom used to say (or think), *Even if he's set in his ways, he's faithful to me and loves the kids. Every relationship takes compromise.* Now she was questioning how much compromise was too much.

Mom didn't come home that night, or the next, or the next. When Dad was at work, she'd slip into 401 to see us kids after school, feed us, and leave dinner for him. I thought she took off in the evenings because we were not good kids. If we behaved better and helped more, she would stay.

When Dad came home, I went to the kitchen to make his *paaper.* In *Little House on the Prairie,* the girls started cooking very early. I figured I could, too. I didn't use my bare hands, like Mom did, to roast the paper-thin chickpea cracker. I was afraid of getting burned, so I used tongs. My *paaper* caught on fire. I blew as hard as I could, and when it didn't stop, I doused it in water. It took a few tries, but I finally made one that was mostly not charred.

"Thank you, my doll." Dad stroked my cheek when I brought the plate from the kitchen.

We sat quietly and ate. There was nothing to say to each other. Usually, Mom made the conversation at dinner, asking each of us what we learned that day or sharing some gossip about a neighbor. Dad was too busy being lost in his own world.

I couldn't eat. My world was coming to an end. First, Dad was gone. Then, Mom was broken. Finally, they were both back and things were normal. I wanted my home to stop falling apart.

The phone rang. *Is it Mom?* It was one of Mom's friends. Dad was rude: *No, she's not here.* Click. He didn't like people calling after 8 P.M., when it was family time.

The phone didn't ring again.

"Did *mumuh* call?" Dad asked Deepak.

"Yeah. She's with Auntie Mireya."

Dad suspected that Auntie Mireya—the same woman who pretended I would meet Cinderella—was a lesbian who was trying to sweep Mom off her feet. He must have sat there thinking to himself, *Why the hell did my wife bring me back to this country if she was just going to leave me?* and, *Is she going to leave me for a woman?*

"Daddy, let's call her?" I begged.

"No." He wanted to deal with it by ignoring it. Avoidance.

I wouldn't let him. "Pleeeeeaaaaaase."

"I said NO."

He rarely spoke to me like that. I started to cry, and he lifted me onto his lap.

"No, my doll. Don't cry. Don't cry."

He couldn't bear when we cried. Sometimes, I put on tears just to get my way with him. This time, I tried to stop but couldn't. The tears came from a deeper place than I could reach to turn off. I buried my head in his chest, my face and his shirt soaked.

"OK," he relented. "Let's call her."

Dad dialed the number. He didn't need to walk over to the kitchen wall, which Mom turned into her phonebook, writing directly on the latex paint. His photographic memory had seen and remembered.

Auntie Mireya answered the phone. Dad didn't want to speak with her. He hastily shoved the handset from his mouth to mine.

"Is my mommy there?" I asked. Usually, I was excited to hear Auntie

Mireya's voice because it meant we were going somewhere new. She made our worlds bigger. This time, I just wanted my world to be small and safe. She put Mom on.

"Mommy, when are you coming home?" I sobbed and sobbed.

Dad's brother—the one who helped us escape Dadi and board a plane for America—had given Mom a call, too. "You and Namu have been through so much," he reminded her. "Namu leaves and calls you every week. You leave and cook his dinner every day. You both have love for each other. There's no sense ending your marriage."

Divorce lawyers were cheap. Mom had looked. But in the end, she decided to come back. The details of her return escape me, except for one: how we embraced. The memory is physical. I wrapped my legs around one parent and my arms around the other, squeezing my limbs as if to seal our pact to stay together.

While it's true Mom and Dad had grown further apart, they'd also grown closer—not unlike veterans out of battle. The move from Casablanca to Queens was the biggest bet of my parents' life. It came with wounds: betrayal by loved ones and poverty in the greatest country on earth. There was chaos in the upending of norms—what it means to be a husband or wife, how many countries can fit into one building. Being undocumented was the greatest threat from without, and opposing reactions to a strange new culture the greatest threat from within.

My parents often saw what was supposed to be the same journey very differently. So different, at times, it felt impossible to share it. It took them a while to finally reach the same conclusion: life was more impossible apart. Call it true love or migrant economics. Mom and Dad stopped leaving each other.

ACT 2

We Made It

A DAUGHTER PRESENTS, TO a man, an existential crisis. He's spent his whole life learning there are differences between the sexes. Because that story has often worked in his favor, it's in his self-interest to reinforce it. But it's also in his self-interest to see his offspring leap as far as possible, to achieve the dreams he could not.

Dad's was a life of dreams beyond reach. A lifelong migrant, forever set back and starting over, he had no firm ground to stand on. Yet he was a truly ambitious man. He knew how to spot ambition in others. He admired it. And it confused him when it turned out that in America, his most ambitious child—the one getting the highest grades, determined to leap the furthest—was not the eldest son (as it was supposed to be). It was the youngest daughter. Dad came to learn this when it was time for me to go to high school.

Every nerd in New York City public school takes a test to get into the top three high schools: Stuyvesant, Bronx Science, and Brooklyn Tech. I did that, and was over the moon to get into each. But I also got tapped to walk through a secret door.

It happened because of dumb luck. My eighth grade chemistry teacher's maiden name was the same as mine: Shahani. She paid special attention to me—asking how my weekend was or if I enjoyed a certain problem set. This kind of attention is not normal in a class with forty-five students. One day she put a brochure in my hands: "A Better Chance"—a program that takes smart kids of color from public schools, gives them some tests, and shepherds them into the best private schools in the country.

Well, talk about underselling and overdelivering. The program should have been called "A CRAZY Better Chance." It changed my life overnight.

The Brearley School is an all-girls school on the Upper East Side of Manhattan. It goes from kindergarten to twelfth grade, and current tuition is $49,680 a year. That's about one Tesla luxury sedan a year, for thirteen years. That's more than my parents made jointly in any year of their work. But we didn't have to pay it. I was a scholarship kid.

Brearley was like nothing I'd ever seen before—and I don't just mean because it was nearly all white. Though we can start with that. When girls filed into the building around 7:30 A.M., I was hit by a tsunami of white bodies. I'd never seen so many before. I mean, sure, on TV. But not in real life.

"Oh my god, you look greeeaaaat! Where'd you go this summer?" They sounded white. So white. In public school, I was the whitest-sounding kid in class. My teachers and friends didn't know how I got that high-nasal pitch, why I used words like "perhaps" and overenunciated every syllable as though life were a drama class. At Brearley, every girl did that—some even better than me.

And the places they went. The Swiss Alps. Santorini. Paris. They were like kids out of a movie.

All I did over the summer was catch a couple matinees and comb through the racks at Bang Bang—a store I thought was the pinnacle of fashion because it cost more than Conway (where Mom made us shop).

I also read the required summer reading. In public school, you're not expected to read over the summer. At Brearley, they assume you're inhaling literature. Some girls did a book a week—which means they read more books in one summer than I'd read in my lifetime. The ninth grade summer assignment was *The Adventures of Huckleberry Finn*.

My parents had no way of knowing whether this prep school business was a big deal or not. It could be a scam. Dad, a skeptic, doubted that such a great education could come to me for free. "Nothing in life comes free," he was fond of saying.

Truth be told, I wasn't sure myself. Two data points convinced me.

First, the admissions test for Brearley and the other Upper East Side prep schools felt like a rectal exam compared with the standardized tests for public school. There was a personal essay, where I had to explain, as an eighth grader, my role in community leadership. *My mom and I are trained in nonviolent conflict resolution. At the Quaker center in Flushing, we help different nationalities get along by talking to each other face-to-face.* I also disclosed my dreams: *I'd like to be a prosecutor when I grow up.* Though I didn't make the full disclosure: *I plan to run for office to become a U.S. senator like Hillary Rodham Clinton.* I wasn't sure if they'd think I was aiming too high.

Second, there was a celebrity name in the mix: Donald Trump. His daughter went to the prep school across the street, Chapin, which I also got into. That fact spoke volumes to Dad. If his favorite character from the *New York Post* sent his kid to one of these places we'd never heard of, they must be special.

For Mom, it was location, location, location. When she took me for my interview, she saw the building was on the waterfront—the East River reflecting the sun's rays into the library. The interviewer told us Gracie Mansion was up the block.

"What's the Gracie Mansion?" Mom asked.

"It's the house of the mayor," the interviewer explained.

"Oh my god." Mom squeezed my hand. "I can't believe how far my baby has come."

On the first day of class, I went into culture shock. It started with the term "country house"—meaning, a house that is not your primary home. It's a place you go to on the weekends. Having grown up in 401, the concept blew my mind. While my siblings and I were fighting with each other and the roaches over who got to use the closet shelves opposite the bathroom, there were children in this building who had their very own closets in multiple homes.

I also found it strange that Brearley girls changed in the hallways. The bell rang, pants dropped. They didn't seem to care if a male teacher walked out of the elevator—Mr. Karb or Mr. Harrison. When I asked about that, a classmate told me that the men are mostly gay, so it doesn't matter.

Brearley girls' bodies looked so different from mine. I don't just mean skin. I mean bones. Stacey pulled off her top and her rib cage protruded, like those impoverished skeletons in the Save the Children commercials—only she had pale, ghostly, translucent skin, blue blood pumping just beneath the excessively sheer surface. Taylor's biceps was just a bit bigger than my bony wrist. Quite a few of these skinny girls had dried-out hair—brittle like the straw of a broom. No one said the words "anorexia" or "bulimia" out loud. I wouldn't have known what they meant yet. But that's what was in the hallway. An epidemic of eating disorders.

It looked grotesque to me. In Flushing, girls wanted curves. Tight waists, sure. But size D breasts and big butts—these were life goals. It's what we saw in the hip hop video "Ice Cream." Raekwon didn't feature a bunch of marathon dieters. I was ecstatic when my flat chest blew up to fill a C cup. I was well on my way to the body I assumed was beautiful—and was beautiful outside the towers of Brearley. I wore a skintight Lycra shirt the first day and probably every day thereafter.

"Oh my god! Does she own anything besides Lycra?" I heard a girl whisper to her friend as I walked down the hallway. "What a ho."

Ho! Bleach blond Blair from *The Facts of Life* just called me a "ho." Freedom to dress the way I liked was why I chose Brearley instead of the rival prep school. At Brearley, girls did not have to wear uniforms, starting in the ninth grade.

If I were in Queens, I would have grabbed a girlfriend or two and gotten in her obnoxious face. Here, I was outnumbered. And, interestingly, it didn't nag at me the way things usually did. I didn't replay the scene over and over in my head, concocting a fantasy movie where I brought street justice to preppy Brearley. It just kind of fizzled. Too much else was going on.

My summer "buddies"—assigned to make sure I felt at home my first week—were two terrifyingly nice and lanky blondes. (They looked naturally thin and naturally blond, not forcing either.) They'd come find me in the hallway or cafeteria just to "check in." I thought people "checked in" at the doctor's office before getting a fatal diagnosis. Apparently "checking in" is what the hyperelite do for a wide array of situations that could cause mild discomfort.

"I'm good," I'd tell them. I wasn't doing badly. I was just, well, confused. Bursting with questions—mostly about my classmates: *Who's rich?*

Who has a scholarship like me? Until what age does one have a "nanny"? Does everyone have a million extracurriculars? I didn't feel I could ask those questions.

So people became little mysteries to me. One girl, Margot, had spectacular legs—long, lean but not skinny, the quad and calf flexing with each graceful step. *Is she training to be a professional athlete?* Turned out she played in tennis tournaments. I played handball on the brick wall outside our building. *Did that count as an extracurricular?*

No one caught my attention more than two black girls who were attached at the hip. They weren't black like the girl on *Clueless*—with green eyes and a butterscotch complexion. They were black black, dark-chocolate black. One was petite and the other was curvy. Both were gorgeous and brimming with confidence. They walked around like they owned the place. *How do they feel so at home here?* I was too intimidated to even say hello to them.

History class had eleven students. That was full attendance— and not even the smallest of my classes. (Latin had six.) One day the bell rang and Ms. Leonard called my name: "R-D, can you stay for a moment?"

R-D was my Americanized name. It's kind of like a Starbucks name. I got it in kindergarten. Mom and Dad made me go, against my will. My teacher read from the roster: "Aaaar-T? R . . . D . . . Is there an R-D here?" She surveyed the room for a little boy— assuming my name was short for Arthur—and was surprised I was a girl.

It soon became self-enforcing. When an Indian elder would ask my name—*"Aapka naam kya hai?"*—I'd say: "R-D."

"Kya?" What? They didn't understand.

"R-D," I'd repeat and spell it. "A-a-r-t-i."

"Oooooh! AHR-thee!" followed by a burst of laughter, as if I were a circus animal.

At Brearley, Ms. Leonard was free to design her own course of study. It wasn't dictated by the Board of Education. She dedicated an entire curriculum to Vietnam. She was a pacifist. Even with World War Two, even against the spawn of Satan, Adolf Hitler, she felt she would not have sent America to war. I found that to be an extreme position, particularly because her own origins were Jewish.

You always hear about the hippies who turned into baby boomers and lost their soul in the suburbs. Not Ms. Leonard. It's like she aged in reverse—becoming more leftist, more idealistic, more impractical.

She introduced me to the term "Ms."—as opposed to "Mrs." or "Miss." I quickly made up a story about why: this liberated woman couldn't find love, and, shackled in her solitude, she spun a sophisticated argument to hide the fact. I was wrong. She was in love, happily married to a legend in the literary world. But, she took the time to explain to me, "We call men 'Mister' because their marital status does not matter. Single or wed, a man is 'Mister.' Why should it be any different for a woman?"

Ms. Leonard went above and beyond for me. Homeroom was divided into two sections. Even though I wasn't in hers, she'd "check in" with me in the hallway or join me during lunch.

When she asked me to stay after class, I was afraid I'd done something wrong. That's a feeling that's chased me since childhood. Whenever an authority figure reaches out, I go into apocalyptic panic: I've messed up badly and my life is about to fall apart. I thought maybe Ms. Leonard was going to tell me that the teachers met in the faculty lounge and agreed I was not Brearley material. She was nominated to deliver the news—which was barely news because it wasn't a hard call.

"Sit down, my dear." Ms. Leonard called me "dear." "I want to talk with you about your writing."

"My writing?" Phew. I wasn't getting expelled.

"You see, in class, when we discuss the readings—if we analyze graphs to look at the data for patterns—you know exactly what you're talking about." She said the word "exactly" with exactitude. Such a crisp T. "You make very sound observations. But in your homework, you don't do the same. You don't write how you speak."

Write how you speak. That sounded nuts. Nobody's supposed to do that. The spoken word is where you get to be yourself. The written word is where you pretend to be one of the dead white men whose picture is hanging on the wall. And to do that, you're supposed to use mellifluous, capacious, anachronistic words, even if hackneyed. In other words, BIG words. In public school, bigger was better. It meant higher grades.

"So this writing-how-I-talk thing," I leveled with her, "isn't that too casual?" I could ask Ms. Leonard questions I couldn't ask my classmates.

She smiled and had me take out the last day's assignment. A sheet of paper with a hideous B+ at the top. In public school, I never got a grade that low. It hurt my feelings. I was trying harder here than I'd ever tried in my entire life, and I still wasn't good enough.

"Let's talk through each question," she said.

We went over the charts. They may have been about rice cultivation from a USDA report on Vietnamese agriculture. To get full credit, I had to state a clear fact: production plummeted in 1965. Then I had to offer a possible reason, not evident in the chart, but which I would draw from other readings, like: 1965 is the same year the United States sprayed herbicide, in a bombing campaign to destroy Vietnamese crops.

I found that answer jarring because it was so short. It left empty lines on the page—ugly, angry gluttons demanding to be fed with anything I could spew out.

"I see," I tried to take it in. "So even if I don't fill the whole space, I won't get penalized for that?"

"Not at all," she said without judgment. "Just say what you mean, R-D. You have no problem saying what you mean in class . . . all the time." We both laughed.

Ms. Leonard liked that I was so talkative. A new kid—and scholarship kid, no less—didn't tend to be that way. I wanted to hug her. (That's another thing Brearley girls did: hug.) In fifteen minutes, she gave me a crash course that would change my entire life. And the central lesson was counterintuitive. I felt that to get ahead, you had to stuff your mouth with flashy words, pretend to be what others wanted you to be. And here she was saying, Be yourself; don't pretend. That's real power.

While I was becoming Nerd Girl, Dad was becoming Casio King.

The boss who gave him his first big break on Broadway—entrusting Dad with customer relations—ending up breaking a promise. The boss did not make Dad a partner. Dad did not take it sitting down. He left and opened his own store—one block away, a direct competitor. He would do wholesale electronics, too. Like so many of New York's immigrant entrepreneurs, Dad got his startup capital from abroad. His brothers in the Middle East invested.

This store was the greatest accomplishment of Dad's career. And it had tremendous symbolic power. It was on the very street where, a decade earlier, he shoveled and swept for other men.

And his store was bigger than theirs: floor-to-ceiling windows facing one of the busiest avenues the earth has ever seen. Two stories high. Dad would use the ground floor as his showroom, placing watches, calculators, keyboards, and CD players under fluorescent spotlights. In electronics, it's crucial that glints of metal catch the eye.

Upstairs was storage. Dad had, what he called, "a good name." He wasn't a Rockefeller or a Ford or a Kennedy. He came from nothing. His burden was not to live up to a reputation, but to build one from scratch, which he did. Distributors trusted him. He could get bulk merchandise from them on credit, keep it on premises to fulfill orders quickly, and pay back when he got paid.

We all went to inaugurate the store with a *pooja*. After praying and eating *mithai* (we offered the sweets to God first), Dad made his shocking announcement.

"I have given a lot of thought to what shall be the name of the store," he told us and his three workers, all gathered around a glass showcase we'd turned into an altar. My heart skipped a beat. *Dad is going to name the store after me*, I thought. *I'm his most studious child.*

"*Hah* dahling," Mom said, her brow furrowed. She did not know he'd decided on a name.

"I have decided to call it Roopa Enterprises."

"Roopa?" Mom said.

"Who's Roopa?" I wanted to know. So did Ang. My big sister, Dad's favorite, the "happy-go-lucky" one (he liked to call her), looked more hurt than I did.

Turns out, Roopa was a first cousin we did not know existed. We had more than thirty first cousins scattered across four continents. She was one of the few still in India. Dad believed she was lucky for reasons I could not understand. "She was born under a good star," he said. He had consulted astrologers.

There was no debate, no vote. Only our dejection and Dad's fiat. In no part of the world was he in charge. Here, that would finally change.

Dad's hours at work became longer and longer. He went from working six days a week to working seven, from getting home by 8 P.M. to sometimes 9 P.M. His footwear changed, too, from dress shoes to sneakers. He was starting to understand why America's working men need to be so casual.

The grueling schedule didn't beat Dad down. He was energized, having fun.

"Guess who came to the store today?" Dad said one night, starstruck.

"Who?!" we kids said.

"Amitabh Bachchan!"

"Who's that?" I asked.

"Maaa ji bohli." He rolled his eyes. His Americanized kids were so clueless.

The customer was only the biggest star in all of India, Bollywood's version of Michael Jackson. He bought a watch and posed for pictures. Throngs of fans on Broadway—who were all better Indians than me—surrounded the store, eager to get a look. Dad was beaming.

I didn't like visiting the store. Open the door, cross the threshold, and it was a tear gas attack: a Marlboro jet stream vaporizing my lungs, baking into my clothes and my very big hair. I put a lot of effort and hairspray into that hair.

I had no passion for electronics. The latest and greatest cutting-edge hardware from Sharp, Samsung, Toshiba, Sony, and of course Casio—it was lost on me, a junkyard of copper wire and plastic casing.

The glass showcases were so wide, and so many customers packed the narrow corridor, I had to push through on my tiptoes sometimes to reach the backroom. There, the water dispenser was splattered with instant coffee and dollar store creamer. Gross. Too many men in a hurry to chug Nescafé before the next shipment deadline.

Shipment—the science of packing, unpacking, and repacking merchandise—was the core of the business. On a rare weekend or evening, I'd have to come in to help.

"Little sister, you take each Casio watch out of the box," either Sanjay or Abdoul, Dad's workers, started the lecture. "You put the watch in the bubble wrap and then lie it nice and neat, side by side, in this empty carton." I nodded. I missed Brearley. "Then you put the Casio box—the one the watch came in—into this other carton."

"How many do we have to do?" I asked, staring at a giant box with two hundred watches, hoping we wouldn't have to do them all. This task wasn't as bad as plucking toe hair from a goat, but it wasn't a whole lot better.

"Ten thousand," Dad's worker said. *Have mercy*. Maybe it was as bad.

Sanjay was a lean Indian who came to the United States in his twenties, lived in Queens, and picked up white women at the yoga class he taught on nights and weekends. Dad worried he was a bad influence on us because he had an earring and a dating life. Either way, Sanjay was a disciplined worker.

Abdoul was a broad-shouldered Senegalese man who wore bright dashikis and a kufi on his head. Every afternoon, the back room became his prayer room. He rolled out a small rug and turned east to Mecca. Abdoul was our Africa liaison, bringing in fellow nationals and the Nigerians, Ghanaians, Kenyans, and South Africans who visited the wholesale district. It would be incorrect to call them "countrymen." So many of them were women—women who, back home, wouldn't have had permission to be entrepreneurs like they were on Broadway.

This was the 1990s, before smartphones took over our hands and eyes and ears, before it was possible to stream an audiobook or podcast. I felt my brain decay with each new Casio watch I packed and unpacked. But it had to be done.

And, you could say, it was a public service, a leveling of the global playing field. New York's financial sector is well known for economic globalization. But the wholesale district was an unsung hero in that same process.

Around the so-called Third World, we were known as *the* place to go if you wanted to bring cutting-edge consumer technology to your country. High-end, official channels cost too much in import taxes and shipping fees. So buyers took the merchandise, stripped of all the name brand boxes; put them in suitcases; and carried them as checked bags on regular flights. The seller, like Roopa Enterprises, would send the boxes, empty of any contents, through a far cheaper service. Watch and box would reunite—in Dakar, Johannesburg, Mexico City, Bogotá—and land in the hands of a happy customer.

Without this drudge work, the rising middle classes of these countries would have to absorb the cost of shipment, which would be too expensive. So we were helping the little guy.

I tried to get myself excited by this story. But it was forced. Brearley parents were surgeons, judges, media moguls. My dad was a shopkeeper. The path to his store wasn't lined with evergreen hedges. It was piles of broken-down boxes waiting for the garbage truck to come by and a couple guys running a three-card-monte hustle on the corner.

Like any shopkeeper, Dad had to deal with nuisance and criminality. When a local homeless man wobbled by in a drunken stupor, Dad or one of his workers ran up to block the door. When word got around that Broadway customers carried cash, Dad had to watch out for the gang of teenagers who'd come by on weekends, using screwdrivers and knives to mug people in broad daylight (he didn't see guns).

Then there was the ketchup trick. This one was devious, the stuff of organized crime.

Our store and many others banked at Broadway National Bank, around the corner. One day Abdoul went to make a deposit. Dad trusted him with money. He came back with ketchup splattered on his back pocket.

"Abdoul, what happened to you?" Dad asked. "You stopped at McDonald's?"

"No, boss." Everyone called Dad "boss." "A strange thing happened. I was standing on the line. A man behind me said I had ketchup on my pants. He wanted to help me clean it off. I said it's OK. I'll deal with it later. I don't know how I got it."

"*Hah.*" A lightbulb went off for Dad. "Come with me back to the bank."

"Why, boss?"

"We have to report it," Dad said.

Dad had heard of this trick before. Another shopkeeper went to the bank with a briefcase. A man in line told the shopkeeper he had ketchup on his back. When the shopkeeper used both hands to clean it off, the man grabbed the briefcase—which was full of cash to deposit—and bolted out the door. The shopkeeper didn't realize until it was too late. His money was stolen.

Dad took Abdoul back to Broadway National, pointed to his ketchup butt, and asked the Korean tellers for the manager. A white man in a suit came out and listened attentively to the debrief. "We'll keep an extra

61

eye out, Mr. Shahani. Very sorry for this inconvenience." The manager didn't call Dad "boss," but he knew him by name.

The business was going so well that Dad came home one night with dreadful news: we were moving to New Jersey.

Mom and I were stunned. Flushing was home. It's the longest Mom had ever lived anywhere. She was active in so many groups that valued her. And, she suspected, that was why Dad wanted to get away. All the people piled up on top of one another, helping each other raise kids and petition for exterminators: what was community for Mom was slumming it for Dad. He wanted space, to not be packed in like the roaches we kept chasing with shoes and outlawed chalk.

The move would give me the commute from hell. To get to Brearley, I'd have to take four trains and one bus—leaving home by 5:45 A.M. on the typical day to get to the Upper East Side before the bell rang at 7:40 A.M. And that wasn't the worst of it. I would face a brand crisis. People would call me a "Jersey girl."

Ang, on the other hand, couldn't wait to start saying she was from New Jersey. She was the only native New Yorker I'd ever met who pretended she wasn't from New York.

"Dad, do we have to move?" I pleaded with him. "I hate New Jersey. We're from Queens."

"*Kya*, you hate New Jersey? Uncle Amin is from New Jersey."

Dad had a point. Uncle Amin was the dear friend from Morocco who drove Mom to the hospital when she went into labor with me. He married a nice Jersey lady. We visited them during holidays. That was our family vacation.

"But can't we look for a home in Flushing?" Mom chimed in. "I've seen so many houses for sale here."

"No!" Dad was not interested in her research. "I'm done with this place."

Dad was running on emotions. We happened to land in one of the crummier buildings in the neighborhood. But there were far nicer ones. And Flushing was becoming a regional hub. Turns out, people gravitate to highly diverse, multiethnic neighborhoods with incredible fast food and mass transit. They are convenient and fun. Home buyers choose it over and over, and it shows in the climbing real estate values. A home in Flushing could have been a great investment. Dad was too scarred by 401 to think like an investor.

Our first house was a lovely colonial perched on a small hill of a front lawn, with a driveway the length of a Fashion Week runway, a two-car garage, and a backyard big enough for soccer (which none of us could play). The house rattled whenever the New Jersey Transit train pulled into Roselle Park station.

We had four bedrooms. For the first time, Mom and Dad didn't have to share with us kids. They even had their own bathroom. I got the pink room (the walls were painted pink). Ang got the blue room. Deepak, who had just graduated from college, got his own room, too.

My big brother went to Boston University. He was the first in the sprawling Shahani clan to get a bachelor's degree. He majored in engineering—stepping away from Dad's footsteps and chasing opportunity in the American labor market.

Deepak also had a Filipina girlfriend and pierced his ear. Dad was afraid my big brother had gone astray. He insisted Deepak come back to live at home after graduation. The eldest son should stay with his parents, Dad said.

Deepak—whose experiments in wet beds included water-drenched sheets in 401—decided to get a water bed. I backed the choice whole-heartedly.

Water beds get a bad rap. Yes, the man who founded *Playboy* reportedly had one, king-sized, which he covered in Tasmanian possum hair. And, yes, the popular advertising slogan went: "Two things are better on a water bed . . . One of them is sleeping."

But look beyond the hypersexualization and what you find is an engineering feat. The bed is its own cooling system, the thick rubber mattress chilled at all times because of the water inside. With a water bed, there's no need for an air conditioner. That's hundreds of dollars in savings, and a reduction in carbon emissions. Water beds can reverse climate change.

We also had a five-foot television. That was a team choice. Five feet is small adult–sized. If we held Mom across the TV, the length of the diagonal, she and the TV would be equal. We Shahanis did not tend to splurge. For us, fine dining was all-you-can-eat at the Chinese buffet; live entertainment was Ang and my running commentary as we binge-watched sitcoms. Divide the TV's discounted wholesale price by total minutes used, and really it was a steal.

Our first Jersey winter included our first snowman. Making one is much harder than it looks. The Christmas commercials are false advertising, zooming in on the small child patting the last fistful of snow into place, not the icy grind it took before that wistful, iconic moment.

After a near-blizzard, Ang and I got to work, each shoveling fresh snow into a pile.

She broke the silence. "This is taking too long." I was relieved she said it first.

"Yeah, but we can't stop." I tried to sound determined.

Deepak came out with a giant cardboard box, sliced open the top and bottom, and stood it up. It was taller than us. "Snowman-sized!" He smiled at his clever hack. He took one of the shovels and, without grace, barked at Ang and me: "Move!" He began to toss heaps of snow from the ground into the box.

Mom and Dad came out to watch. Deepak offered Dad the shovel—deference to the head of the household. Dad, with a Marlboro dangling from his mouth, shoveled with joy for the first time in his life.

"Hold the bottom so it doesn't open, stupids," Deepak told Ang and me. We didn't usually listen to him. But the sight of Dad enjoying himself made us care less about our big brother being a jerk.

"Better than shoveling snow on Broadway, *hah*, dahling." Mom said what we all thought. Dad didn't laugh. It was still too raw.

Once the box was full, Deepak sliced the side, unfurling it to reveal a snow cube his height. Mom got to work, shaping it into three spheres—a bottom, a top, and a head.

The snow was littered with maple leaves. We hadn't thought to rake all fall. "Can you girls pick those out?" Deepak barked some more.

"You mean like your pimples," I said.

"Stupid, don't talk back to me. I'm your big brother."

"Watch your mouth," I talked back. "Don't call me stupid."

"Papa, *hee chaa hai*?" Deepak whined to Dad. Because Deepak spent a decade in Morocco, he spoke five languages.

"Aartiiii," Dad said in a stern voice.

"What? He started!" At Brearley, I saw kids talk back to their parents all the time. I couldn't believe my ears at first. Then I liked it. A lot. I decided to give it a try at home.

Dad hissed.

"OK, OK, let it be," Mom tried to de-escalate. "See what a beautiful snowman we're making."

Even with the leaf pimples, it was a sight to behold. Mom used pebbles for eyes and twigs for a mouth. And then, glancing at her husband, she couldn't help but ask, "Dahling, should we give him your cigarette?" Maybe Mr. Snowman wanted to be a chain-smoker, too.

Dad did not laugh at that either. The rest of us did.

Family is all about give-and-take—a steady stream of extraction. Jersey was a concession to Dad. The time had come for him to concede to us.

For years we'd asked for a dog. Dad cited space as the excuse to say no. Now we had all the space in the world. Our first floor alone was almost twice the size of 401.

Wrinkle Shahani got her name because, in the beginning, she had wrinkles. Her coat was loose, piled up like folded towels on her forehead and thighs. She was just a few weeks old. We didn't pick her for her looks. It was her personality—how enthusiastically she rubbed her wet nose against our palms, licked between our fingers, demanded her belly be rubbed. She was demanding love—a real Shahani.

"Can we have her? Can we have this one?" Ang, Deepak, Mom, and I all agreed. We were at the North Shore Animal League—the shelter we kept seeing on our giant TV.

"*Hah.*" Dad said yes. "She matches the carpet." That was his only requirement, that she be sandy like the living room rug.

I spotted Wrinkle first. She was so soft, I couldn't let go.

"Give your sister a chance," Mom told me.

When I handed the fur ball over, she instantly plummeted from Ang's hands to the floor. My sister, who was afraid of crushing Wrinkle's newborn bones, had dropped her. She crashed head first.

"She slipped," Ang yelped. "It was an accident."

My sister's skin is much lighter than mine—what Indians call fair and lovely. She was pink turned red, on the verge of tears.

Which was the cue for my brother to taunt. "Oh no!" Deepak said. "You gave her brain damage. Now she'll be stupid like you."

"It was a mistake," Ang cried. "She's fine. Look, she's fine."

Dropping the puppy sealed the deal. Family is supposed to hurt each other—and then not let go. It didn't feel right to let Wrinkle go after what we'd put her through. And she was fine. Turned out she was quite smart when we tested her.

Of everyone at home, we couldn't believe Ang was the one to housetrain Wrinkle. At first, none of us had the heart to do it. So we laid newspapers all over the kitchen floor.

"We leave rats in one kitchen and now you're turning this one into a toilet for the dog," Dad complained to Mom.

"When do you ever enter the kitchen anyway?" she talked back. "Are you suddenly making your own food?"

Still, he had a point. Ang took the reins. None of us knew she had it in her. She was terrible at following instructions, waking up early, cleaning—that is, the things one must do to housetrain a dog. She did extensive research (for the first time). She learned that if you lock the dog's crate at night, it will learn to hold its urine because it doesn't want to soil its home. Ang jumped out of bed at 1 and 2 A.M., letting Wrinkle out to pee as the puppy built her stamina for waiting.

While I was motivated by achievement—that's how I got up for Brearley before dawn—Ang seemed motivated by something totally different. She simply loved Wrinkle. In five days, our puppy was fully housetrained. And then, while Dad and I were in Manhattan (he at work, me at school), Ang and Mom started teaching her tricks.

If you said "Wrinkle, act funny," she would spin in circles, chasing her own tail. If you said, "Wrinkle, *Jai baba*," she would sit on her hind legs and bring her two front paws together in prayer. This was key.

When Dad came home, Mom brought Wrinkle to join him in his worship of Guru Nanak—a sage from the fifteenth century. A gigantic rock-star poster of the guru hung above the fireplace. He looked like

Santa Claus, only brown-skinned and wearing a turmeric turban instead of a red jumpsuit. Dad put his hands together; Wrinkle, her paws.

Dad began to call Wrinkle on his own. At first, he was afraid of her. When he sat in his chair and she ran by, he'd raise his legs up to his stomach and scream: "*Ohp, ohp, ohp!* Get her away from me! Away!" Through prayer, their friendship blossomed.

The one problem with Wrinkle (it shocked us to learn this about our pit bull mutt): she was a racist. The first hint of it came when Kevin (our little brother from 401) visited. "Movin' on up!" he said proudly. "We got the house, the dog." Only, when he bent over to pet Wrinkle, she growled and flashed a canine, reminding him she was made to kill. "OK." He backed off. "Not gonna touch you."

One time does not make a pattern. But when the growls and teeth came out again and again, like clockwork when we walked by the one black family across the street, Ang and I knew.

"Well, she's not the only Shahani," one of us noted. "There's Uncle Ratan, too."

Uncle Ratan was Dad's little brother who'd moved to Casablanca with Dadi and who then moved to New York to help us run the family business. We sponsored him, his wife, and their son for green cards. He was my least favorite family member. What he did to Wrinkle gives a window into why.

We had to get Wrinkle spayed. While the procedure was routine, the recovery was brutal—sorrow for which no vet prepared us. Deepak carried Wrinkle in his arms, cradling her like a baby. He laid her gently on a corner of the velvet sectional, where she barely moved. After a few days, she rallied the energy to go upstairs. She didn't want to "act funny" or do "*Jai baba.*" She wanted to be alone.

My stuffed animals began to disappear. I went searching, and then a small teddy bear strewn on the floor led to the closet where Wrinkle had been hiding. There, she was curled up, quietly nursing a litter of stuffed animals. They were the babies she was meant to have, had a scalpel not gotten in her way.

Mom cried. Ang and I, too. Who knew a dog could feel so much? Would we ever feel that way about babies?

Dad must have told Uncle Ratan, because his little brother stopped by to see for himself. He removed his shoes at the door and bolted upstairs. I followed, to show him the closet. And the moment my uncle saw this sight—a young would-be mother grappling with her lost motherhood—he snatched one of the stuffed animals from Wrinkle's litter to get a rise out of her.

"GGGGGGGGGRRRRRRRR." She jumped and didn't just flash a canine this time. The hair on her spine stood in a sandy-brown mohawk. She was ready to sink her hulk jaw into his calf.

Do it, I thought to myself. *Do it*. I wanted her to draw blood, put him in his place.

But at that moment, Dad came in and shouted his little brother's name. Like an obedient dog, Uncle Ratan dropped the toy and heeled.

You're not supposed to say this out loud: my family felt small-time to me. They lived in a dusty world littered with Styrofoam cups, held together by packing tape and dull box cutters, and populated by knuckleheads. My Brearley world was big—a place where we debated the great questions of our time with the great leaders, like the Notorious RBG.

It was the beginning of tenth grade when my class at Brearley took our civics trip to Washington, D.C. Ours was a special trip. We were going to meet the Supreme Court Justice Ruth Bader Ginsburg. She had just been appointed by then president Bill Clinton, and she was a Brearley mom. Her daughter and granddaughter had attended our school.

Our trip was happening during the historic trial of a mass shooter. The man boarded the Long Island Railroad with a handgun and 160 rounds of ammunition. He opened fire just outside Queens, killing six and injuring nineteen. The murderer lacked an iota of remorse or humility. He fired his defense team and said he'd represent himself. He wanted to be the man at the podium, cross-examining the survivors who had to play dead on the train to escape his bullets.

"They should give him the death penalty," I told one of my classmates.

"What? That's *sooo* wrong," she said in high-pitched, liberal indignation. "How can you believe in the death penalty? You design a system for the averages, not the extremes."

By that she meant that, even when some lunatic (she said "mentally ill person") is caught red-handed, we as a society are all better off not having the electric-chair option because, inevitably, innocent people will get sentenced to death, too.

I rolled my eyes. I'd wanted to be a prosecutor since I was seven years old because I knew what it was like to grow up in a building with crime. My Brearley classmate didn't. She grew up in a nice building, in a nice part of town.

I almost blurted out "rich girl." But that would not have been right. She wasn't one of the rich girls. She was one of the nerd girls. Her parents were academics. While the daughters of CEOs kept the lights on at Brearley, it was the daughters of professors who lit up the classroom. With cerebral debate and obscure references to books that weren't even assigned reading on our already massive syllabus, the nerd girls were as much a part of my education as Ms. Leonard. I hated to admit it, but whenever they spoke, I was taking notes.

I hadn't been to the nation's capital before. As the Brearley bus pulled in, we saw an inordinately long obelisk, gleaming white, thrusting into the sky. "That's the Washington Monument," our teacher snickered on the loudspeaker. "They don't call him the father of the country for nothing!" Gasp. She made a sex joke—which was OK because it was highbrow.

Skylines are like altars. They tell you what a city stands for, in what it bothers to frame, display, honor. The New York City skyline—steel towers competing for the glory of being tallest or sharpest, squat brick buildings in their shadows—is an altar to the gods of global trade, who feed off inequality. I imagine people who see my city for the first time might have the same mix of awe and unease that people who came upon Constantinople or Peshawar felt in their heydays.

D.C. is an altar to the gods of nationalism. And its skyline looked, to me, incomplete—like there could be yellow tape around swaths of city blocks that read "we're working on it." America is such a young country after all. We haven't finished figuring out who deserves a tablet or a monument. It'll get settled through dialogue or shouting matches. Either way, I hoped that in twenty or thirty years, the tiny lady we were going to visit would have a monster of a statue in her image.

When my class filed out of the bus and into a Supreme Court conference room, a hush fell over us. There was no space for words in the enormity of what RBG represented—a future without glass ceilings, because she was determined to shatter them. We were inspired.

And we knew it was in the realm of the highly possible that one of us could be sitting where she was sitting one day. We're Brearley girls, after all. We are destined to run the world, I kept hearing. Even those of us on scholarships felt it.

After a brief introduction, RBG invited us to ask questions. My hand shot up. I wasn't even sure what I wanted to ask. It's just that my mouth worked so fast, I didn't need to overthink. I could move my lips, and 80 percent of the time something decent would come out.

This time, however, we were solidly in the not-good 20 percent.

"What do you think of the LIRR gunman representing himself?" The question rolled off my tongue. I was happy with it. Current events. Close to my heart. First question from the class. And maybe RBG will say something I can use in that unfinished debate with my fellow nerd girl. (It was unfinished because I had not won—at least not yet.)

Justice Ginsburg responded, "What do you mean by 'what do you think'?" She sounded unimpressed. "What do I think about what?"

Uh-oh. She was not going to make this easy. I'd assumed she'd find the hook for me. But the guardian of the Constitution made it clear that it wasn't her job to go fishing in my kiddie pool of outrage. She doesn't pontificate on any matter that pops up, like politicians do. She lives to interpret what the amendments and prior precedents say about unsettled matters of law that are well defined, not sprawling.

"It's just that, it seems like a mockery of justice, of due process." I searched for words and defaulted to courtroom TV. I sounded like Judge Judy.

Justice Ginsburg could tell. She turned to her handbag and retrieved a small pamphlet. It was a pocket-sized copy of the U.S. Constitution. "I strongly encourage you to read this," she said as she handed it to me. "Next question, please."

Her words stung. She was implying that I hadn't read our nation's founding document before. If I were really American, I'd know and wouldn't ask nitwit questions. At least that's how it felt—because I knew

I was at Brearley representing a group no one thought needed representation.

While students and teachers consumed politics, their America was divided between the white majority and the African American minority. The foreigner was an issue, not a constituency. They debated immigration if it came up in the State of the Union address, but they didn't talk to immigrants—not the ones who served our food in the cafeteria or took kids home after class. Those were my people, and I let them down.

When I was humiliated at Brearley, it wasn't because someone was trying to make me feel like less of a person. It was because I didn't rise to be the biggest person I could be. At home, it was the opposite. The message there was: you're smaller than you think you are.

On Saturday nights, while my classmates were out living their lives—at concerts, on dates, building their "extracurricular" bona fides at a city shelter—I was stuck at the Shahani compound. It was Dad's time to feel he still had the world he'd left behind, the one where your family is your primary social life (the way it's supposed to be, he thought).

The men and boys sat in the living room—playing carrom board, munching on samosas, drinking whiskey or soda. Mom and Auntie Shanta, the wife of Uncle Ratan, were in the kitchen, putting the last touches on a meal we would serve the men and boys (before eating ourselves).

We were in Uncle Ratan's home. He bought a place down the road from us. I was sitting on his carpet, half watching his five-foot TV. There may have been a story about a religious riot or political rally in Mumbai (they looked alike). It was Indian news, not even ABC.

"*Chuhree!*" Uncle Ratan barked at me. "Why are you sitting there, looking like a fool? Go help your mother in the kitchen."

Chuhree. That favorite word of his. Crazy girl. I couldn't tell if he was being Third World playful, or if he was serious. He had a trace of a smile.

Either way, I wasn't in the mood. When I was younger, if an adult told me to jump, I wouldn't even stop to ask, "how high?" I'd just jump as high as I could, hoping to surpass expectations and gain approval. Now that I was getting older, I wanted respect. I ignored him.

"*Chuhree*, did you hear what I said?" He repeated himself, harsher this time. The trace of a smile was gone.

"They don't need help," I told him. "I already checked."

"Then go stand there and learn how to cook."

He was trying to break me in. Back when Ang was in sixth grade, Dad ordered her to take cooking lessons from Auntie Shanta. My big sister didn't get top grades. Dad wanted to make sure she would at least have good marriage prospects. He didn't force me. Ang thought it was because my grades were strong. I thought it was because, unlike her, I'd put up a fight. Dad didn't like to fight.

His little brother did. "I said go to the kitchen," Uncle Ratan repeated himself.

"NO!" The single syllable shot out of my mouth and pierced his eardrum.

"What did you say?"

I couldn't believe it either. But I wasn't going to take it back.

Our eyes locked. I wished they hadn't. I don't know how to avoid eye contact. We were in front of an audience—Dad was right there—and I had defied my uncle directly, out loud. His manhood was on the line.

"What did you say?" he repeated.

"I'm going downstairs."

I got up to head to the staircase. There was another TV in the basement. I could find a sitcom about a happy family. Uncle Ratan blocked me. Standing inches from my face, the vein on his temple pulsing, I smelled the stench of his breath. It always smelled like rotten eggs.

No longer speaking but shouting, the grenade of his temper came straight at me. "Go to the kitchen, or I'll break your mouth."

"Lay a finger on me, and I'll have you arrested," I said. "This is America."

My legs trembled. But even if it meant a black eye or a broken tooth, I would not lose this fight. Chalk it up to Brearley training or my inherent nature.

Uncle Ratan thought about it for a moment. I could see the wheels in his mind churn, creak, his jaw clench (maybe his fist, too). He stepped away.

As I headed downstairs, I saw Mom standing still in the kitchen. She looked frozen in time. Moving to the suburbs did that—stripped her of friends, left her in an empty house with just her memories. Was this moment bringing her back to one before my birth, when she questioned a direct order? Did the protracted, intergenerational battle over who belongs in the kitchen follow us from the past to the present?

I caught a glimpse of Dad, too, his face pale behind the wrought-iron bannister, his eyes fixed on the floor. I couldn't tell if he was ashamed of me or his brother. No matter. *A man threatens your child and you sit there, you coward.* I was ashamed of him.

My family's double standards taught me early on: the rules are how people with power keep their power. Maybe that's why I liked to break them, and was drawn to other rebellious teenagers, like Corinna.

A magnetic force pulled me to her instantly at Brearley. She was my first white friend. And, I have to confess: she's the one who taught me to dance. Yes. I learned to dance from a white girl. This detail is key to our adventures in rule breaking.

Corinna was the smartest human being I had ever met. She breezed through chapters in our history textbooks so quickly, I figured she was just skimming. Then in class she'd remember the exact dates and names of military excursions, and where the relevant passages were. That must have meant she wanted to be a historian, given how good she was at my favorite subject. But no, she planned to be a medical doctor. She was that good at all subjects.

The Franklins lived in the Episcopal seminary in Chelsea. While it was a ten-minute walk from Dad's store, I didn't invite Corinna to our family business. It felt too small compared with her family business—which was to staff this elite Christian institution that took up an entire city block. Her father was a professor, in charge of training future ministers.

Their stone house, set against a long, green pathway, looked like a fairy-tale castle. It was four stories tall, neo-Gothic—the only thing missing was a watchman's tower. Corinna had her own floor, her own bathroom, and her own fire escape.

Our music tastes were different. Corinna loved Nirvana and Pearl Jam. Eddie Vedder—whom I saw as disheveled—was her heartthrob. She ate up his lyrics—which, sure, were more clever than the ones in my music, but also so morose. I listened to LL Cool J, Boyz II Men, En Vogue, and Salt-N-Pepa. When "Shoop" came out, I sang along every time. It never got old.

That said, my body couldn't move to the rhythm. Corinna's could.

"Damn girl, where'd you learn to move like that?" I'd ask her.

"In the fields, between tipping cows," she'd say. She grew up in Minnesota and liked to make fun of how provincial New Yorkers are about the rest of America.

Sometimes I slept over at her place. While Dad didn't want any of us to stay over with friends—he thought that was another bad habit in America's overcasual culture—Mom made the case that Corinna's home would cut down my brutal commute and let me study more.

Corinna and I turned the lights out but couldn't fall asleep.

"Do you think Mister Spock has sex?" I asked her. I had just watched *Star Trek* with my brother.

"He has to have sex," Corinna said. She said everything with certainty.

"What if he's a warrior monk? Or like Jesus?"

We went on like this for a bit. She may have explained her recent obsession with fractals and chaos theory. Then, finally, one of us mustered the courage to say what we were really thinking, "Do you wanna go clubbing?"

It started in the ninth grade and continued well into tenth—made possible by church and state. The Limelight, which was three blocks away, was an Episcopal church that had been converted into a nightclub. In Manhattan, these acts of sacrilege happen. Our mayor was still David Dinkins. The city was still fun. His successor, Rudolph Giuliani, had not yet come in and obliterated our underage clubbing with his quality-of-life campaigns.

In the dark, Corinna and I tiptoed to her closet to sift through her clothes, she fishing for a plaid shirt (her farm wear, I called it), and me for anything tight, black, and short. We slowly pulled up the window and stepped out onto the fire escape, two thieves in the night.

Once past the seminary gates, we were in the clear—like any other kids in the city that never sleeps and that's full of perverts. The pervs hanging out on crowded, well-lit streets were not scary. The ones at the Limelight (also nicknamed the Slime Light) were.

"Wanna drink?" An old guy, maybe thirty or forty, came up to me within minutes of my getting in. He waved a plastic cup in my face.

"No thanks," I said. "I'm not old en—uuuh, I don't drink." He was probably too drunk to understand words. Still, I didn't want to blow my cover.

"Here, have a taste." He tried to shove his cup to my lips.

"Nah, man." I pushed him away, a little shaken by how close he got. It hit me for a split second that someone in here could hurt me.

Rebellion is not a monolithic desire to break every rule. It's more nuanced than that. I wanted freedom against the dictates of Dad, my uncle, and even my big brother. Deepak had started acting like Dad—lecturing me about how I dressed and how I wasn't allowed to go out at night. He said he was doing it for my own good—to protect me from the lowest of the low. I thought it was pure hypocrisy. He drank, dated, wore whatever he wanted. One time when we were still in 401 and our parents were away, he threw a party. He locked Ang and me in the Big Bedroom. We couldn't go out to use the bathroom—until the police came and broke it up.

My rebellion was controlled. I knew I didn't have a security blanket, like my Brearley friends. It wouldn't take much for my life to unravel. I lived standing on a cliff: the tiniest misstep, and I'd lose my scholarship and my future. And yet I couldn't stop visiting that cliff.

Corinna and I kept climbing out of her fire escape, going out clubbing, until one night we got caught by Dr. Franklin—not her dad, the theologian, but her mom, the Italian immigrant. She came to America at age sixteen not speaking a word of English. The next year, she got a perfect score on her SAT and admission to Radcliffe—the sister college of Harvard, back when Harvard didn't take girls.

Dr. Franklin was up, sitting at the kitchen table. Our steps down the fire escape, past her bedroom, had woken her.

"It wasn't her idea," Corinna said to her mom. "I made her."

It was the noblest and stupidest thing to come out of this brilliant girl's mouth. She shimmied the skintight black dress onto my unwilling body. She was trying to protect me.

"Sure, child," Dr. Franklin said. She called Corinna "child." Even though it's a blunt monosyllable, when she said it, it was singsong, like an opera.

My mind raced with thoughts of Mom, who so earnestly lobbied Dad for my right to sleepovers. "For school, for her future," Mom would tell him, believing I couldn't betray her trust. What hell she would pay for this.

Dr. Franklin turned to me. "I'm not going to call your parents," she said, reading my mind.

"Thank you, Dr. Franklin."

For a split second, she stopped being the erudite professor of Latin who taught at Columbia University. She became a fellow immigrant, a confidante from the Old World who knew what happens to girls like us when we step out of line. I was grateful for her protection.

Being a girl was not all downside. It afforded me freedom in a key way: because my father did not expect me to have a career, he did not pressure me to follow in his footsteps. My visits to his store were infrequent. Even though he could use a lot more help, he didn't call on me that way.

That meant when I turned sixteen, legal working age, I could forge my own path. With help from Brearley, I set out to get the summer job of my dreams.

The Fred F. French Building is an art deco skyscraper on Fifth Avenue. The entryway is dipped in gold: revolving doors, mailbox, elevators, radiators—every corner is like an Indian bride's neck.

I was here for my first job interview. It wasn't for manual labor—cleaning floors or serving food (though Mom, who'd done that work, would have been very proud). It was a job that came with a desk, a computer, and a view. I hit the gold button for the 22nd floor.

"Welcome to Squadron, Ellenoff. How may I help you?" the receptionist greeted me. She was black, the only dark face I spotted besides mine. This place was the adult version of Brearley, with even fewer people of color.

"I'm here to see Elliot Sagor," I said, unsure if I was supposed to hand her my résumé. She nodded for me to have a seat in the waiting area.

"I'm here for a job." I offered this detail she didn't ask for.

A jolly-looking man with a towering yet soft physique arrived in minutes. He was not handsome. He was clean-cut with a functional face—his long nose tempered by full cheeks and a mop of thick silver hair.

Mr. Sagor reached out his hand to shake mine. "Firm," he said of my grip. "Good."

I liked him. He affirmed me.

He was the husband of my English teacher. She taught my class on American literature and often brought homemade scones and jam for us to munch on while we dissected Faulkner. That was Brearley: a top-notch teacher with top-notch pastries. I didn't care much for Faulkner. Stream of consciousness seemed like one of those elitist ploys to call something "art" because it was incomprehensible. But I loved her orange scones.

When she asked in class if anyone wanted a summer job that paid twelve dollars an hour, my hand was the sole one to shoot up. That was a lot of money—nearly triple the minimum wage at the time. Only at Brearley would no one else jump at it.

"You're my wife's student," Mr. Sagor seemed to remind himself, and then he flattered me a bit more. "She says you're a very good student. Very hardworking."

I panicked. *Would he quiz me on* The Sound and the Fury? I wasn't prepared.

"Can you type and write shorthand?" he asked.

"I'm a very fast typer. We have a computer at home, so I've practiced a lot." I spoke quickly, as if there were a timer running and the speed of my mouth was a proxy for my typing. Dad bought us an Apple Macintosh and, while he didn't use it, he enjoyed watching us master it. I wasn't sure what "shorthand" was—if it was a specific way of taking notes—so I hoped that line of questioning would go away. It did.

"When did you start at Brearley?" Mr. Sagor asked me.

"In ninth grade."

"That's pretty late, isn't it? Don't most of the girls start in kindergarten or first?"

"Yes. I was in public school before, in Queens. I came in through a scholarship program." As soon as that detail left my mouth, I wanted to shoot myself. This is not the food stamp office; it's a job. If he knows I don't come from money, he'll know he can pay me less.

I was being paranoid. Mr. Sagor hired me on the spot and didn't try to nickel and dime me. In fact, he added that when I worked overtime, the hourly rate would go up 50 percent to eighteen dollars an hour. I was floored. By my estimate, I would be making more in my first job than Uncle Ratan's son made. He worked at the store.

The only hard edge in this softball interview came at the end. My soon-to-be boss asked that I come to work wearing "appropriate attire." We both tried not to look at my V-neck leotard from Bang Bang.

I was so eager to share the news with Dad, I nearly took the R train to 28th Street. The store was minutes away. But Dad would not have approved of my top either. So I went home to throw on a sweatshirt and wait. It had been so many years since I was excited for Dad to come home. I felt like a little kid again.

The second he walked in, I blurted out, "I got the job!"

My announcement did not disrupt his routine: remove shoes, hang coat, stand before the poster of Guru Nanak, do *Jai baba* with the dog.

"Hah." He kissed my forehead when he and Wrinkle were done praying. "Tell me."

I recapped each detail: my English teacher, the golden skyscraper, my firm grip, and, finally, the bombshell of details. "Twelve dollars an hour. Eighteen overtime."

"HAH?" His eyes widened.

"Yes! That's my starting wage." It was a slight embellishment. I wasn't sure if or when it would go up.

"Do they provide lunch?" Dad asked, searching for facts to make this implausible dollar figure more plausible.

"No, Dad." I shook my head. "Professional offices don't do that." I was now briefing him on the professional world.

"Hah, doll," he said. "It is very good. God bless you. Always."

I was speaking to him in his religion. To call Dad a "workaholic" would be to put in anemic, clinical terms a phenomenon rooted in his spirit. "Work is worship." That's not what Dad said, at least not out loud. It was the mantra on his keychain, always in his pocket, a heavy bronze medallion with the Lord Vishnu and his four hands etched in—Dad's reminder that through labor a universe is born.

This night, Dad didn't show excitement. He showed focus. His eyes were with me, not somewhere faraway like they usually were. On her first attempt, his baby girl shattered a ceiling in America that he could not reach in his first several years of trying.

ACT 3

Breaking at the Seams

UTOPIA WAS SO CLOSE, I can still see pixels of what should have been: Dad and his brother should have kept selling Casio watches until the mortgage was paid, then retired to poker games and samosas. I should have leapt into glory vis-à-vis college and law school, fulfilling my dreams and Mom's. We Shahanis should have had the most food- and fun-filled Diwalis and Thanksgivings, where I—more accomplished and powerful than any male in the clan—should say without saying: I told you so.

"Should" is a red herring. Treacherous. Never trust it. Scan each unfiltered sentence. Look for where it's hiding. Wherever it is—right there, in that spot, is a seed of misery. Dad and I, who saw the world so differently, came to agree on this when things that should *not* have happened did.

Dad and Uncle Ratan were already home when I walked up the driveway. *That's strange,* I thought. They were standing in the backyard with everyone else: Mom, Deepak, and Ang; my uncle's wife and his son, Babo. Oh no, they found out about Georgetown.

I had recently gone to visit my boyfriend. He and I met at an interschool dance. He was two years older than me, and I liked to think of him as an older man. A tall, dark, handsome nerd from the Bronx, he taught me to ride a bicycle on the Grand Concourse. (I'd only done tricycles until then.) Then he graduated and went off to college.

When I wanted to visit him, I didn't ask for permission. I wasn't allowed to have a boyfriend—just like I wasn't allowed to go to dance parties or wear short skirts (I got around that by keeping one in my backpack). I got in the habit of improvising. I told my parents I had to go to Washington, D.C., to debate. "There's a Model Congress tournament. It's for school."

I knew the lie had caught up with me. My family had gathered to confront me. My pace slowed; my heart raced. *My boyfriend is black,* I thought. *They're gonna be so pissed.* According to my uncle, Indians aren't supposed to be friends with black people, let alone date them.

Everyone heard my steps and turned to me. I couldn't go inside the house and hide.

"What's happening out here?" I said as casually as I could.

"Aarti . . ." I noticed the tears in Mom's eyes as she called my name. *Oh no. She's in trouble, too. She's always made the case for my freedom to study. I've betrayed her.*

"The police came today." Deepak said it, quietly, as I joined the circle.

What? Interracial romance is no longer a crime. "Came where?" I asked.

"To the store."

"Oh." For a split second, I felt relieved. But then I stopped to think about what he said. "Wait—WHAT? Why?"

It was after lunch, about 1:45 P.M. Sanjay and Abdoul may have been in the back room packing; Dad, on the phone with a supplier; Uncle Ratan, talking up a new line of calculators to some North African regulars. Then the police came in. Not just one. Several officers.

"Who owns this business?" one of them asked.

"I do, with my brother," Uncle Ratan told him.

The officers began asking questions about a specific customer—another one of Uncle Ratan's regulars, from Colombia.

Uncle Ratan gave details. "He calls to put in the order—what products he wants, how we should ship it."

"He tells you how to ship it?"

"Yes. It could be Continental, AIA Cargo Express, RB Express. The customer faxes us the order. We follow the instructions."

"How do they pay you?"

"They deliver in cash."

Customers cleared out. Officers walked up and down the length of the store, getting fingerprints all over the glass showcases, going behind them in search of something.

"Where's the last payment?" an officer asked. "Didn't they drop off a hundred thousand dollars?"

That threw off Uncle Ratan. *How could this man know the exact amount of the Colombian's last purchase?* They asked to see the money. He didn't know what to do. He felt he had no choice. He walked them to the back and opened a cardboard box, where it was wrapped with rubber bands in brown paper bags. It had just arrived, so he hadn't taken it to the bank to deposit yet.

"Is there any more cash here?" the officer asked.

Uncle Ratan hesitated a moment, then pointed to a videogame box, where there was more. The officers took all the cash and left. Dad and Uncle Ratan closed the store early and came home.

"How much cash?" I asked.

"Four hundred thousand," Dad said.

Four hundred thousand dollars. U.S. currency? That was mind-boggling. It was more than enough money to pay off our house and Uncle Ratan's. We'd be set for life.

"How do we have that much money?" I asked.

"It's not our money." Dad huffed. "It's the suppliers' money. We have to pay them for the merchandise we took on credit." About eight percent would have been our profit.

Dad was in a bind. His good name was at risk. But I felt everything would be OK. It's not like anyone got arrested. The police probably just needed to run the cash through a police machine and they'd return it in no time. Our store wasn't shady. It was like all the other stores on Broadway.

"Why are we standing outside?" I asked. The sun had set. It was getting cold.

"We don't know if the house is bugged," Babo said. "The police might have wiretaps. Maybe that's how they knew the Colombian customers."

Wiretapped? I plunged back into my depths of despair. *Have they heard me talking to my boyfriend? Are we part of some DA's file?*

Uncle Ratan and his family went home. My family went back in the house and sat in front of the five-foot TV. In its soft glow, without a word, we ate dinner and slept it off.

By the next morning, when I headed out for my killer commute, yesterday's news was just that: a distant memory, more dim with each transfer. Four trains and one bus later, I was sure Dad would get the money back and no one would find out about my boyfriend.

Ms. Leonard asked if I wanted to cat sit. What that really meant was, Did I want her four-story brownstone on the Upper East Side all to myself while she and her husband vacationed in France for the summer? It was a tough call, but I said yes.

It was the summer before senior year. The Leonards' was my dream home: walking distance to Central Park, wall-to-wall books (I'd hoped to read that many by the time I was my teacher's age), a garden with overgrown ferns, and the burble of a fountain drowning out the neighbors.

I planned to attend SummerStage and Shakespeare in the Park. New York offers world-class live entertainment, free of charge, and puts it in the heart of the wealthiest neighborhood. I was a borough kid who'd finally see how Manhattanites lived.

My Manhattanite job was not as glamorous as I'd hoped. Turns out, Mr. Sagor had a temper. He'd been through a spate of secretaries and assistants. He was the white-collar version of my uncle, only worse because Mr. Sagor also shouted at his elders. I winced whenever he got on the phone with his poor mother.

Our own honeymoon period ended quickly.

"It's all wrong!" He slammed a document on my desk one day.

I flinched. "Are you sure?"

He glared. "Am. I. SURE?"

I shouldn't have spoken. It made him angrier. Mr. Sagor said I screwed up the edits on his legal brief. My idiocy could cause real harm to real clients.

I looked at the printed page as he walked away. It just didn't make sense. While I had strong opinions about his clunky writing (he needed a Brearley crash course), I wouldn't make up edits or even venture to guess if one dot of his chicken scratch was a comma or a period. I would ask. But the original markup had disappeared from my desk. It was gone.

Until, that is, I rummaged through a stack of papers on Mr. Sagor's desk. Right there, in red ink, I found the proof of my innocence. When he got back from lunch, I showed him. He didn't say "sorry." He just said, "OK."

"Who does that?" I asked my father. I was so angry, I went home in search of comfort. I wanted Mom's food and affection. And it seemed I wanted Dad's affirmation. Maybe because one man tore me down, I needed another to build me back up.

Dad sat, unmoved.

"Well?" *Be my ally, please.* When he gave me nothing, I consoled myself. "I guess at least the pay is good."

Dad's eyes widened, a restrained smile. *Nothing in life comes free,* he said without saying.

That was probably our last heart-to-heart—well, his version of one—before Dad's life turned into a case study on that point. A few days later, maybe it was a couple weeks, my pager went off. Mom bought it for my sixteenth birthday. iPhones did not exist yet, and regular cell phones were still too expensive. I was out of the house so much, she wanted a way to get a hold of me.

"What's up, Mom?" I called her back. I was at work, making overtime. My wing of the law firm was empty.

She was sobbing. "The police came."

"Came where?"

"The store. Daddy's in jail."

"WHAT? Why?"

Police officers raided the store, this time guns drawn. They threw Dad, Uncle Ratan, and their accountant against a wall, read their Miranda rights, carted them off.

"Why?" I repeated myself.

"I don't know, doll."

Of course, it was that cash. That cash had something to do with it. I never found out if Dad got it back. It was such a big amount. He was so shell-shocked the day it was taken. I didn't want to know. So I ignored it. The police did not.

Dad was in Queens, in a jail right by the airport, Rikers Island. A whimsical summer on the Upper East Side was not in my cards.

Rikers is on a tiny spit of land. You can see it when you fly in or out of

LaGuardia, though from the sky you can't tell that you're looking at hell on earth; that inside the rows of gleaming white barracks, there are men slicing each other's faces with any sharp edge they can find (say, a torn piece of a plastic bucket); that someone is being gang-raped as an officer looks on; that officers are ramming the heads of handcuffed prisoners against a concrete wall, causing concussions worse than a football game. On Rikers—a city of roughly twenty thousand back in 1996, when Dad landed there—violence was how the law kept order.

In public school, we had jokes about Rikers. "He's going to Rikers," we'd mock the boy in detention. Honors kids can be cruel.

Up to three of us could visit Dad at one time. I went with Mom and Deepak. We got the first taste of what was inside on the Q100 bus, when the moms and girlfriends of other inmates crammed in. It was nearly all women and their children. *Do men visit each other or their women who get locked up?*

"Bitch, get out my fuckin' face." One passenger pushed another, who pushed back.

Mom, who'd handled her share of bullies in 401, and who'd more than once instructed young mothers on a public bus how to handle their toddlers, did not scold anyone. She shrunk. So did I. I'm pretty sure Deepak's adrenaline was rushing; he stood guard in front of both of us.

There were checkpoints and more checkpoints. At the first one, a corrections officer shouted at us to empty our pockets. He wasn't doing customer service. We weren't taxpayers and voters worthy of respect. We were animals, just like our loved ones inside.

By the second checkpoint, laminated posters reinforced that message: a young man with a red gash from forehead to jaw; another with an eye so beaten and bloated, it looked like puss would push the eyeball out of the socket.

What are we doing here? My head was spinning from the "art"—or was it the ammonia? It smelled like a toilet in there. *We don't belong here.*

Three hours later, our thirty-minute visit began. We were in a large hall with high ceilings and no sharp edges, rows of tiny tables lined up like an elementary school classroom. A guard escorted Dad, who was in an orange jumpsuit, to our table.

"No touching," he shouted when we hugged. A security measure, to make sure no visitor slipped an inmate a razor blade. Distance was for everyone's good.

"Papa, hee chaa hai?" Deepak began in our language, trying to lighten the mood. "What are you doing here? You took a wrong turn?"

Dad let out a sigh, as if to say in all of his crossing of worlds—a child in civil war, a tenant in 401, a street cleaner on Broadway—only now had he learned what rock bottom really looked like.

"We'll get you out," my brother went on, sounding so certain that it was all some misunderstanding.

The aspiring prosecutor in me wasn't so sure. *What did you do, Dad, to get yourself into this mess?* I wondered but didn't ask. That was not my only question. *Where are all the white criminals?* I didn't see a single one in that enormous room.

Dad leaned in and spoke in French and Sindhi to my brother, a grave look forming on both of their faces.

"What? What happened?" I wanted to know. I didn't understand.

"Last night," Deepak whispered into my ear, "another inmate went to Dad's bunk and said he'd cut off Dad's finger if he didn't give him his wedding ring."

I looked at Mom, who was crying silently.

"I shouted loud." Dad tried, in a hushed voice, to mimic the shout. "NO! NO! NO! I said over and over. The guard came and said, 'Anything wrong?' The *lagaar* said, 'Nothing wrong' and walked away. Never before I've seen a place like this."

Deepak said something in French. Dad lowered his hands below the table and began wrestling the wedding ring off his finger. He hadn't taken it off since his wedding day. The ring had gotten tighter over the years, the flesh underneath indented. Deepak looked left and right for guards and then reached under the table, too. Dad slipped him the ring, unnoticed. Deepak put it on and then wrapped his arm around Mom. She couldn't hold herself up anymore.

When Dad called that night, he needed to talk to Mom. "Why didn't you tell me to keep the ring on?" he asked her. "You should have told me, Don't take the ring off."

"It's just a ring," Mom said.

"But I felt you were with me. Now I feel alone."

I was desperate for a silver lining. Maybe that's why I told myself that even if Mr. Sagor was a jerk, God must have put him in my path. His practice was dedicated to defending businesses that got in trouble for crimes like insider trading, securities fraud, tax evasion, and money laundering.

Because Dad and Roopa Enterprises were much smaller than Mr. Sagor's standard client, I thought he could swoop in and clean up the mess. I had been a very good worker. Two secretaries applauded how long I'd lasted—more than two months so far—and he was asking me to do overtime regularly.

The sun was setting when I walked into Mr. Sagor's office. It felt hauntingly quiet. I asked if he had a moment to talk. He did.

"May I close the door?" I asked.

"Go ahead, R-D."

All day I had planned what I would say, the precise words I could use to frame the problem as manageable. I would not say, "My father is in a place where men gang-rape each other. Can you help him?" I would say, "The state has started a white-collar case against my family business, and I'd like your guidance on the matter."

Well, that was the plan. The door closed and tears fell.

Mr. Sagor extended his hand across the table to pass me a box of tissues.

"Oh, that's why you have those." I tried to make a joke. I wanted to stop being so melodramatic, to get a grip and get to the point. It took a while, but I finally eked out some version of an explanation and handed him the indictment, which listed the counts against us. He leaned back in his swivel chair and read it page by page.

"Do you have your notepad?" he asked.

"Yes."

He'd told me to never come into his office without a notepad.

"I want you to take down this number. 2-1-2 . . ."

Mr. Sagor gave me the contact for his good friend, a talented lawyer who could help. I wrote it down with mixed feelings. I knew I was sup-posed to feel grateful, for being shepherded into capable hands. But I actually felt disappointment. I knew what it looked like when an adult passed the buck.

"Thank you so much." I led with gratitude and left his office.

My big brother became the liaison between this lawyer and our father. A family friend found another lawyer for Uncle Ratan. They were not allowed to share counsel. They each had to have their own.

We all went to the first hearing. Deepak drove. And Mom drove us crazy.

"Where are you going?" one of us asked her in the courtroom.

"To talk to the Chinese lady," Mom said.

"NO!"

She didn't listen. The prosecutor, a petite East Asian who could have been one of our 401 neighbors, was sitting in the front row. Mom wanted to talk, woman to woman.

"Talk to your lawyer. You can't talk to me directly." The prosecutor shut Mom down immediately.

The hearing was far shorter than I'd expected, and my family's crime far more serious. According to New York State, our electronics shop was a front for the Cali cartel, the transnational drug family headquartered in Colombia, in the city of Cali.

The cartel was founded by two brothers, around the same age as Dad. They started their trafficking outpost in New York quite casually, putting bricks of cocaine on a ship that sailed to the Queens shore. The crew threw the bricks overboard. Colombian swimmers would pick them up and sell them at bars.

Over the years, the Cali family cultivated relationships with the Italian mob, learned from them, and began using Queens apartments as stash houses. When a local journalist investigated Cali, they opened fire, killing him in a restaurant in Jackson Heights.

The cartel used and sold to children. There was so much drug money, they bought an original Picasso and a $100,000 dining table. They were the epitome of the forces of evil that Mom and other tenants fought to kick out of our building in Flushing.

I couldn't look at my father. Guards brought him and Uncle Ratan in handcuffs and jumpsuits. Their accountant, also there, had been trying to make them laugh back in the holding pen, singing Hindi songs and saying, "This will soon be over."

What a fool. *Was he a hardened criminal too?*

The prosecutor read the people's charges against my family. The Shahanis were no longer part of "the people." The indictment had thirteen counts. Most of them related to alleged cartel members. Three named our family and our store, Roopa Enterprises.

From about October 1995 to March 11, 1996, the charges read, my family took more than ten thousand dollars in drug money—"monetary instruments which were the proceeds of the criminal sale of a controlled substance"—and knew it was from drugs.

For the first time, I met the lawyer Mr. Sagor recommended. I noticed when Alan Kaufman had to speak to the whole court, he spoke in a normal voice. But when he pulled us to the side, for a private conversation, he talked louder—the way Americans sometimes do when they're traveling abroad and don't know the native language, as if volume would make up for it. Only, there was no language barrier. We were all fluent in English.

Is our lawyer being condescending to us? I wondered if we'd made a mistake hiring him. He was way out of our league. His clients would be the dads of my rich Brearley classmates. My family was too small to matter.

I pushed the thought aside. He's the best. A Brearley connection told me so. And he and our other lawyer got us bond. Dad and Uncle Ratan could fight from outside, not inside Rikers. *Everything will be fine.*

Everything was not fine, though, on my transcript. The first semester of senior year, when I was supposed to put on the strongest performance of my life, go for the gold, I let myself go.

"R-D, please have a seat."

Mrs. Gardiner was the college counselor. Tall with a silver coif, she looked like an older model from a Talbot's catalog. We sat at her small meeting table.

The width of her smile was a precise measure of a student's chances of getting into Harvard. In our first meeting, which was before Dad got arrested, she smiled nearly ear to ear. I wasn't a shoo-in, but I was a "very strong" candidate. I had "adjusted so quickly" for a scholarship kid who came in the ninth grade.

Now the counselor's lips rested as flat as the earth before Columbus sailed to America. I knew why.

"You've gotten into some very fine schools." She nodded politely, pointing to my acceptance letters, which did not include Harvard. "It's too bad you didn't apply for early admission."

Early admission is a strategy. When a student applies to only one school, early on, she signals full commitment to attend. That improves her chances of getting in because the Ivy Leagues, who accept students, want to get accepted back. They're competitive with each other about their "yield rate."

If I had applied early to Harvard, the college would have seen my nearly perfect transcript (straight As except for one B+ at the end of junior year), not my nearly straight Bs now. I had been cutting class. My grades dropped.

"I don't see any way to petition for you," the college counselor said.

I didn't realize one could "petition." This was yet another secret door. Brearley had a direct line into every elite university in the country. When a Brearley girl or her wealthy, powerful parents were unhappy, our counselor could call the admissions office to lobby, to explain how the rejection must have been an oversight. These kinds of calls have gotten many Brearley girls into the Ivies who've rejected them.

"Are there any new extracurriculars we can point to?" Mrs. Gardiner asked me.

"No," I said.

The only new extracurricular in my life was watching my dad decompose. He'd lost weight, hair, a couple teeth. Mom told me she thought he might try to kill himself. I was furious at her. *Can't you keep any of your problems to yourself?*

"Your parents are not alums of these schools," the counselor continued. "They haven't been contributing like so many of the other parents have."

I already knew I was not a "legacy kid," who, by virtue of being the child of an Ivy graduate, was far more likely to be admitted. I didn't need the reminder.

Brearley wasn't feeling as perfect anymore. In part, life outside went dark. But also, the college process showed me an uglier side of my limousine-liberal classmates.

White students with the same anxieties as me—will I get into the best school?—started to debate the merits of affirmative action. Legacy kids were, in their opinion, perfectly fine. That kind of extreme preferential treatment was fair; promoting racial diversity—which benefits the white kids, exposing them to cultures in our global world—was not.

These students did more than debate. They sabotaged.

Two black girls in my class decided to run on the same ticket for student body government. We had a copresident system. The two were the same two who caught my eye on my first day at Brearley—the supremely confident, stunningly pretty best friends. Turns out, each was a superstar in her own right. One was a scholarship kid from Brownsville who came to Brearley through a program called Prep for Prep. She started one of the first community gardens in East New York and spent a summer at Oxford University. The other was the daughter of a man who led efforts to recruit black students to his alma mater, Harvard Business School. She was bookish and engrossed in art. Both were varsity-level athletes.

I assumed they'd tag-team and win. That win would be a shot in the arm for college. Though even if they didn't win, they were so stellar, they'd still go wherever they wanted.

One afternoon I walked into homeroom and saw a few girls huddled, talking about our presidential race.

"They're always getting everything."

"Alexis didn't even get here till middle school."

"I mean, they're not a diverse team."

Not diverse? The two candidates represented the elite and the working class; the deeply scholarly and the wildly charismatic; active citizenship in school and out; Brearley old and new. One started all the way back in kindergarten; the other came years later.

They were diverse in every way but one: the color of their skin. It's when I heard that last line—said in such a prim voice—that I noticed: the huddled group was all white.

Soon, an opposition team formed: the white team. Their picks for copresidents were two girls who were kind, in my estimation, but did not stand out as leaders of the pack. One looked like she was recovering from an eating disorder—a telltale sign of a severe lack of self-esteem. The other had begun to take up environmental issues, though had not yet established a track record.

I thought they didn't have a chance. I was wrong.

Homeroom started to feel like a segregated lunch counter. Because I was not black or white, I could float between groups, eavesdrop on conversations as long as I was discreet.

One white student had made a shortlist of who was most likely to get into Yale. If the black team won, each winner would be stiffer competition, diminishing this white classmate's own chance at a coveted spot. The white team was not Yale material, she'd calculated; winning the presidency wouldn't get them in. She campaigned fiercely for them.

Also, it turned out, more than one of my black classmates disliked the well-to-do black candidate. She grew up in a building with a doorman and had a country house. Her privilege raised the question of whether she was really black.

Election Day came. The votes were cast. Team White won.

"Tribal" is a word I used to associate with National Geographic documentaries. It became a word I'd associate with Brearley. While the school was easily the best education I'd ever have—with teachers I wish everyone could have—it wasn't free of the same blind spots and land mines that littered the real world.

Because I applied to college from Brearley, it softened the blow of my Bs. One of the best schools in the country, the University of Chicago, offered me a generous scholarship. I got federal aid, too, and I'd been saving my legal salary (I stayed at the firm and was promoted from Mr. Sagor to other pieces of work).

"My doll, I'm so sorry we can't help you." Mom was guilt-ridden. My parents had no money for tuition or my plane ticket to the Midwest. Whatever they had, it had gone to the case. Deepak was paying the mortgage. Ang had gone off to Mount Holyoke—an all-female college I'd lobbied her to attend. (I saw at Brearley that when boys aren't around, girls let themselves be as smart as they really are.) My big sister took out bigger student loans to pay for her school.

While there were plenty of things to worry about, my tuition was not one of them. I told Mom that prep school connections made everything fall into place. I was genuinely in great shape and asked her only to work on getting the name right. She kept calling it Chicago University.

Though that was better than Dad. He was so distracted. I'm not sure he could remember where I was going at all, if my step forward felt in any way like he was stepping forward, through me.

Moving is a great way to push the bad thoughts away. When I landed in Hyde Park, my family became the distant background, and my foreground was parties (this time, no need to sneak around) and "shopping" for classes. I'd attend a dozen and pick my favorites.

Also, I regained the ability to read. After Dad's arrest, I could not read. I mean, I could tell you what the word was on the page, but not what the sentence had said. Nothing stuck. On campus, my brain synapses fused back.

UChicago is the fairy tale I'd longed to live in: at its entrance, a large arch draped in ivy; a cathedral where a hunchback must have been hiding; and regular sightings of gargoyles. These stone statues of dragons, demons, and monster bulls perched above doors, hiding in corners, told me the ancients had an eye for the tragedies that befall man—either that or a great sense of humor.

At orientation, adults impressed upon us the Nobel Laureates and world leaders who'd sat in our seats years ago and how the future was ours. It was euphoric.

While I sat in the hall of giants, writing the script of my own life, Dad was in Queens Criminal Court, reading the one handed to him.

"[Your lawyer] tells me that you wish to plead guilty to the Class E felony of money laundering in the second degree." The judge addressed my father. "Is that what you wish to do?"

"Yes, sir," Dad said.

The judge did not ask why Dad came to that conclusion. Everyone knew the answer: a trial was too risky.

Our defense lawyers told us that if Dad and Uncle Ratan went along with the state and didn't put up a fight, each man would serve eight months in prison. (The sentence was one to three years, but they'd get released early on good behavior.)

If they went to trial, the lawyers said, they could get slammed with fifteen years for the exact same crime. That's because of the "trial penalty." People are penalized, severely, for exercising their constitutional right. And if my family won at trial, a disgruntled prosecutor in

Queens could go to the federal prosecutors and have them start a new case from scratch.

For nearly every defendant who goes through the system, pleading guilty isn't a decision so much as an inevitability.

The judge prompted Dad to read his carefully worded confession. "Tell me what it is that [you] did that constitutes the crime of money laundering." The truth is never scripted—except for in the twilight zone that is the justice system.

"My store—" Dad stumbled and started over. "My store, Roopa Enterprises, I think did business with customers in South America in which we sold them merchandise consisting of electronic products and the customers paid for the merchandise in cash." His hands shook as he held the statement his lawyer gave him. "We were given reasons to believe that cash was the proceeds of the criminal conduct. We deposited over ten thousand dollars of that cash in Roopa bank accounts." Dad wrestled with the last lines. They were heavy on legalese. "I'm informed that such deposit constitutes the exchange of cash for the equivalent property under the statute."

Uncle Ratan read a similar plea. Each of their lawyers felt out the possibility of pinning the crime on just one brother. *Is there an argument to make that your brother did all this?*

Dad and my uncle stayed loyal to each other. And when the prosecutor insisted on prison time—he would not consider giving probation and extensive community service—Uncle Ratan asked if he could serve his brother's sentence. The state said no.

But the state also made a puzzling counteroffer. The two men didn't have to serve their sentences right away, at the same time. Uncle Ratan could go first—and before going, he could take a few months to hand off his customers to Dad. Dad could go after his kid brother was done. That way, one man was out at all times, free to run the family business.

Usually, when a business is a front for a drug cartel, the prosecutor doesn't bend over backward to keep that business alive. *If we're just a Cali operative, why not send both men to prison at the same time, to decapitate the store, ensure it crumbles?* The plea deal didn't make sense. The prosecutor structured it so that our business could survive.

That was my impression, from a distance. I intended to keep that distance.

I could not stay silent, however, when it came to the colossal mistake my big brother was about to make.

"Please don't do this." I was visiting home on a break. "Please. She's such a weirdo."

Deepak had agreed to an arranged marriage. "Just because she's not a know-it-all like you and Horse Face doesn't mean she's weird." (He'd taken to calling my brilliant Brearley friend Horse Face—which she was not.)

For three years, our parents had been nagging Deepak to wed a Good Indian Girl. It was Dad's idea. Uncles from overseas called in, to warn the eldest son that American girls, who had no family values, would cause his demise.

Deepak was a catch in the *shaadi* market: he was a U.S. citizen (Dad pressured him to naturalize for this reason), and he had a college degree and washboard abs (he'd been working out and plucking his unibrow). While he'd agreed to meet potential brides, he kept saying no to marriage offers.

Until, that is, Dad landed in Rikers Island. The American criminal justice system did what my Indian clan could not: guilt Deepak into being a dutiful son. When he and Ang went to visit Dad one day, the conversation took a very dramatic turn.

"Take care of the family," Dad told Deepak. "What I have to face, I will face."

Dad looked so down and out, Deepak wanted to put some fight back in him. "No, Dad. We'll get through it! WE! You have to come out and be there for my wedding."

It was such a grand gesture, Ang was stunned. *Deepak's getting married? Does he know something I don't? Is Dad going to hurt himself in here?*

Dad patted Deepak's hand. "God bless you always, *puti*." And thus the matter was settled.

The bride to be was twenty-five, a year younger than my brother. Her lineage is what got Dad. Anisha grew up in the same town where Dad's family fled after Partition. She was the niece of Dad's old boss from Morocco. The boss reached out—which was flattering. He said Anisha's parents, Makshi and Ashok, had requested a meeting. Their daughter was very fair-skinned. That became her standout qualification. (Indians are the most color-conscious people on earth—far more obsessed with skin color than America is. They run commercials for vagina whiteners, to get the lips down south as light as possible.)

While Dad droned on about how Anisha came from a "good family"— I was put off by the contents of her character.

"Do you work in India?" I asked during an obligatory phone call.

"Yes, I've done volunteering, to take care of needy children." Her voice oozed with sweetness. Saccharine sweet.

"I mean a career," I pressed her. "Do you plan to work in America?"

"Oh yes. I'm very interested in child psychology."

She was years out of college, without a job or clarity about what building a career entailed. And she peddled in Indian Bride Talking Points. "I love children so much," she proclaimed to Mom. "I am learning to cook your favorite dishes," she told Dad and Deepak.

It made me nauseated. Yes, her skin was nice and white—as illustrated in any number of photos she'd sent. Personally, I was a fan of her cheekbones, which were high. But that didn't make her a fit for my family or my country.

America is much harder to live in than many parts of the world. This point is not well understood. The middle class in developing countries, like India, don't have to do their own laundry, ironing, cooking, cleaning. They hire "servants." That's what they call their dirt-cheap human labor. Anisha's family had servants. Here, she'd have to do manual labor for herself.

I thanked the heavens when her family dumped us. Again, it was the criminal case. Mom and Deepak told Anisha about the mess we were in. Deepak told her that for the foreseeable future, the newlyweds couldn't move out. He was our primary breadwinner. She agreed and told him she loved him as well as "Mama and Papa." (She was already calling them that.)

But then she broke off the engagement, after her dad came to visit us. He was acting as emissary, scouting his daughter's future digs. One day Deepak took him to meet an Indian couple in Queens (he did real estate, and they were thinking of buying property back home). In the couple's living room, my brother and Ashok Uncle (I called him "uncle") both discovered that we Shahanis were the talk of Little India, in a bad way.

"What's happening with your father's case?" the wife asked my brother out of the blue. Deepak had no idea these strangers knew about our problems. Her husband quickly changed the subject.

After that visit, once Anisha's dad flew back to India, the family stopped all communication. They wouldn't so much as return a phone call. *Good riddance*, I thought. *Deepak doesn't have to martyr himself with some phony.*

But then, a few months later, Anisha reappeared, this time with a transnational-love-letter campaign. In four back-to-back, weepy, rambling letters, she begged Deepak to take her back. She blamed her dad, who'd encouraged her to break off the engagement. "Yes, in some way he probably was being overprotective," she wrote in one six-page ode to their true love. "My dad didn't mean to come in the way of our happiness."

I suspected she tried to land a better option (she mentioned other suitors, and we heard our share of rumors); and when one or multiple offers fell through, she may have freaked out. Though in her version, she had a spiritual awakening.

"I forced myself to join a meditation camp," she wrote in another soliloquy, nine pages long. "I had stopped my voluntary service at the orphanage for quite some time, but I signed up at a blind school where I taught English to kids . . . being there for those unfortunate children who life had taken away the most precious gift that is light, it amazed me to see them so very unaffected by this reality, they just seemed so happy and always had something to offer me in their own small way . . . I realized what I had done to myself and you."

Through the blind, she could see again. Sure.

Mom and Dad fell for it. "Take her back" and "she's so sorry" and "everyone makes mistakes," they panted.

Have my parents lost their minds? I wondered. Maybe the criminal case had made them so insecure about their place in society, they'd eat up any morsel of acceptance. We were not a "good family" in the eyes of our community. Or, rather, their community. It wasn't mine.

"She's not a catch." I tried to warn them. I didn't expect Deepak to go for a nerd girl like me. I knew he couldn't handle that. But my brother, whom I often felt was a knucklehead, was fundamentally an honest and hardworking man. He should have a wife with those qualities—not someone who says anything and everything to get from point A to point B (and uses too many words to do it).

Dad rolled his eyes at me. His old boss was a rich man. Anisha's lineage was excellent. Dad had married up. He wanted the same for Deepak. Mom morphed into Traditional Mom (which she did selectively). "You don't understand the culture, Aarti." Mom didn't either. She was never Indian enough. Her own imposter syndrome and guilt over Dad's problems in this country were driving her to endorse a marriage that was even more traditional, even more arranged than her own.

My sister agreed with me. But she wouldn't speak up. I wished Ang weren't so conflict averse.

"Why her?" I pressed my brother.

"Because she's not a big mouth." He smirked. "She'll listen to what I say."

He was doing what men so often do: play down how scared he is; twist the facts to make it sound like he's in control; tell himself the adoring woman he barely knows is the pliable goddess who'll serve his every need—cook dinner, raise kids, raise depressed father's spirits, look sexy while he pursues his goals (in this case, saving his family).

How I wished my brother and parents would heed Dad's lesson. *Nothing in life comes free.* Didn't that principle apply to brides, not just bosses? I walked away, disgusted.

Though I didn't walk too far. We had a wedding to plan. On the eve of Uncle Ratan going to prison, to begin the sentence he and Dad would each have to serve, the Shahanis were going to party. All of Dad's brothers, who'd been scattered around the world, flew into town. It was the first time they were in the same room since Dad's childhood. Deepak's promise at Rikers was fulfilled. Dad came back to life.

Ang and I met Anisha and her little sister, Kavitha, for the first time. They were even scarier in person than on the phone. They treated each other so, well, cordially. Kavitha, a tall teenager, had a pip-squeak Mickey Mouse voice with an Indian twist. It was her real voice. She used it to dote on Anisha incessantly. "*Didi,* shall I get you *pani* or make you chai?"

"Don't get any ideas," I told Ang, whom I refused to call *"didi,"* a term of respect for the big sister.

The marriage festivities included a poetry recital. The Indian Disney teen stood in front of our five-foot TV. At her parents' prompting, she began reading an original work that went something like:

Mommy and Daddy are great;
they don't arrive late;
they get me from school every day;
then we go out to play.

Mom was the only Shahani whose applause was genuine. Ang—so repulsed it intrigued her—blurted out to the room: "Another! Let's hear another!" Dad scowled. He wanted to watch the television our young poetess was blocking with her broad shoulders.

For the *mehndi* party, we hired a couple of girls to draw henna tattoos on the bride's hands and feet and the hands of female guests. ("Ew! I hate the smell," my sister complained.) For the main ceremony, we rented an event hall. While we could not afford a horse for the groom's entry, we did pay for a belly dancer. Her sultry artistry was hard for me to appreciate because it also highlighted the hypocrisy of the men in my family. While it was not OK for me to wear provocative clothes, it was OK for them to wave dollar bills at a woman dancing in her bra.

When the Hindu priest recited the rites, I listened intently for the moment he might ask if anyone objected. I'd hoped to raise my hand. Only, he didn't. Our ceremony wasn't like a Christian one. The rings were exchanged, the matter settled.

It appeared I was wrong. The arranged marriage did bring profound joy back home. Less than a year into their union, Deepak and Anisha got pregnant. A baby—the first Shahani to be born in America—was on the way.

Anisha made it clear that it was a difficult pregnancy from the outset—so difficult, she could not work. Her professional experience in the United States was as extensive as I'd expected. She delayed looking for a job for many months. Then, a couple weeks into working at a preschool as an assistant aide, she called in sick. Her home pregnancy test came up positive, and she quit. "You can keep working—I mean, if you want," Deepak told her. She didn't feel strong enough to.

Akshay Deepak Shahani was born with a unibrow—which is to say, he was one of us. The baby avoided coming out for as long as possible. Doctors induced labor. It was the beginning of summer. Ang and I were both back from college, living at home and working at the same law firm. I got her a job there as a paralegal.

"Be nice." Ang pulled me aside one day.

"What do you mean?" I played dumb.

"You know what I mean."

I found Anisha to be needy and self-righteous. "Will you thread my eyebrows?" she'd ask me more than once, right after I got home from a long day. (I'd taught myself threading to help manage the Shahani unibrows.) She also lectured me about how good I have it as a girl in America—to which I pointed out she was in America, too.

Ang told me to put my pettiness aside. After a long spell, the drought had ended. The criminal case had zapped my parents of life. Now, bathed in the light of their first grandchild, the anxiety lines smoothed away; a soft glow replaced the dull yellow of their skin. Deepak was giddy.

"Look, look, look!" He came up to me one evening. The baby was fast asleep in his arms. But the moment Deepak held Akshay closer to his bare chest (he had no shirt on), the baby opened his mouth in search of a nipple.

"He thinks I'm his momma." Deepak laughed his hyena laugh, reveling in the small miracle that is human instinct. He moved the baby in and out, the infant mouth opening and closing each time, the baby beginning to get irritated.

"Ew." I was grossed out. "He's gonna choke on your chest hair. Don't do that."

"Deepak, you're being so silly." Anisha trailed behind, giggling, and then turned to me. "Do you want to hold the baby?"

I nodded. As my brother slowly moved his son into my arms, both parents gave a litany of instructions on how exactly I should position myself.

"You know, I've held a baby before," I felt the need to say. "I babysat when I was little."

"Can you stop being such a know-it-all and just listen," Deepak shot back. *Be nice, Aarti. Be nice.*

Akshay was small and soft like Wrinkle when we first got her. Only, he didn't wriggle around or lick or cuddle. He just laid still. *Maybe I'll feel more of a connection to him when he's older.* I kept the thought to myself.

A few moments in my arms and he began bawling. "You still need to work on the mother's touch," Anisha said as she rescued her child from my clutches.

I'm nineteen, lady; don't plan on needing that touch anytime soon. Again, I kept the thought to myself.

While our house was enormous compared to 401, it was starting to feel cramped. Anisha's family had practically moved in. Her mom and little sister arrived from India two months before the baby was due. Her dad came right after the birth. No one showed any sign of leaving.

"When are they going back?" I asked Mom. "It's been four months already."

"Aarti, you know we can't ask them."

While Americans value transparency, Indians value hospitality. In the United States, if a person plans to visit a friend or even one's own blood, it's normal to set a departure date *before* arrival and make it known. Indians, however, leave that date shrouded in mystery—as though the depth of the secret is a measure of the bond shared. And, sure, hosts may complain about guests behind their backs, but not to their face.

"Can I ask them?" I snickered. "I'm American."

"No, Aarti!" Mom didn't find it funny. "Don't disrespect us that way."

"Fine." *Be nice, Aarti. Be nice.*

I'm not the one who had to sit around at home with them, anyway. Mom was. Ang, Deepak, Dad, and I were out at work all day. I assumed Mom was on cloud nine. She loved looking at and holding the babies of complete strangers. And she'd been studying how to give infant massages—walking her fingertips around Akshay's belly button, drawing larger and larger circles clockwise.

That's not how she passed the time. "They're not letting me touch him," Mom told me one evening when I got back from work.

"What do you mean?"

"They spend all day upstairs. They don't come down. I'm sitting here like an idiot by myself."

Now that she mentioned it, I had noticed a frostiness from Anisha's family. They were making less eye contact and less physical contact. One day after work, when Dad asked to hold Akshay, Anisha said no. The baby just wants his mother.

An American might consider that a completely reasonable response.

Among Indians, however, that was unequivocally disrespectful. The paternal grandfather is the head of the pride. Others say no to him sparingly. Anisha breached a rule she knew far better than we did. Everyone in the living room noticed. Dad said nothing.

Poetess Kavitha had stopped offering recitals. Before the marriage, her verses flowed like nectar. Now the fruit had dried. I was too relieved to make anything of it.

"Don't worry, Mom." I downplayed her concerns about Anisha. "It's her first kid. And she's the mom. Give it a bit. When her parents are gone, you'll get more quality time." My maturity pleased me. *You're being nice, Aarti!*

I was glad to be out of the house. The law firm was so much easier than it used to be. I'd been promoted to the Help Desk. It was my job to write macros in Microsoft Word—short lines of code to automate the work that fellow secretaries and I had been doing by hand.

When I wrote it right, in just one click the table of contents for an entire three-hundred-page contract would appear like magic; the font for each and every heading would go from Times New Roman 12 to Arial 11 without the tedious work of editing one by one. There's so much elegance in efficiency.

"Can you guys get this fixed for me?" A lawyer swung by one day. His document didn't update correctly.

"I can do it," I volunteered.

"Huh." He paused and had to ask, "What's with your accent? You don't have one of those, ya know, accents."

"You mean . . . from India?" I was surprised he was surprised. Then I remembered, I'm sitting in IT and I'm brown. "No, sir. I'm from here—from Queens."

"Oh. OK."

The geek squad didn't make me want to change my career path. While working with computers was a big step up from doting on a maladjusted boss, it wasn't sexy or exciting. My friends had internships at magazines, youth programs, political offices. Only, they were unpaid internships. I couldn't afford that. This law firm was the entire reason I was getting by. With overtime, I'd take in more than eleven thousand dollars in a summer.

Dad and I didn't talk about it, but I knew I was bringing in more than he was. That fact made me feel bad for him, not proud of myself.

The store wasn't doing well. He had to downsize from our two-story shop on Broadway to one of the drab offices on a side street. Uncle Ratan was still in prison, which was confusing because I'd thought he would be out already. Maybe I'd misunderstood. I didn't pry. Whenever he was released, it was Dad's turn to go in. That made me nervous.

Though the baby really took the edge off. Whether Dad got to hold Akshay for a moment or just stare at him across the living room, I saw glimmers of pride. Dad agreed to smoke only outside. It looked as if he was smoking a few less cigarettes so he could linger around his grandson longer.

One evening I got home from the firm and half the family was out—Anisha's half.

"They're with friends in New York," Mom told me.

Oh, thank God. It felt great to have the house so empty. I rested my head on her lap and dragged her hand onto my face. "Massage me." I had a bad habit of clenching my teeth. Mom had learned a way to pry her fingers into the muscle, stretching me like a rubber band along my jawline. It was so relaxing, it put me to sleep.

"Guys, I don't know where they are." Deepak came running downstairs.

"Who?"

"Anisha. Akshay."

It was past 9 P.M. Deepak didn't like that she had the baby out for so many hours. She didn't call to say she was running late. Whenever one of us would be home late, we'd call.

Deepak stared at the clock. By 10 P.M., they still weren't home. They must have lost track of time. By midnight, Deepak began dialing friends she may have met.

"Chaa tho chee?" Dad asked what the friends said.

"No one met her today," Deepak replied, confused.

"Chaa?" What?

The friends hadn't seen or heard from Anisha. Deepak called the police: "My wife and son are missing."

When the officers came to our home, we were all sitting there.

"They left late this morning," Deepak started to explain. "I don't know if something happened to them in New York City."

"Now, did you and your wife have any argument?" an officer asked.

"No. I mean, nothing outside the usual."

"Is there anything missing from the home?"

"No. Just them."

Only, a strange item was missing. Mom had noticed all her plastic grocery bags gone, the ones she shoved in the broom closet and reused for trash. There had been dozens of them. But that didn't seem relevant.

"Look, they could just be out taking a walk. It's a beautiful summer night. I know you're worried. You're a new dad. Just wait it out," the officer told him.

Deepak had been a dad for two months. His worst fear was that his wife and child had been harmed. Anisha didn't know Manhattan like he did. She could've taken a wrong turn and got knifed. He'd have to wait a few more hours to file a missing persons report. He was going stir-crazy. None of us knew what to do.

"You know! I can check online." If a mugger got Anisha's ATM card, there might be a withdrawal—which would give a clue about location. He ran to the computer upstairs to check his account. It had gone from $7,977 to $77. That was all we had—the money Deepak used to pay the mortgage, utilities, groceries. It was gone. Did a thief hold Anisha at gunpoint and force her to a bank?

Then more clues trickled in. All the photographs of Akshay were gone. So was his birth certificate and the records of his immunization shots. Deepak's U.S. passport was gone, as well as his citizenship certificate, his wife's Indian passport, and the copy of her green card application. Mom's jewelry was missing. Suitcases from the attic were missing. Cash—$3,100 that Ang and I gave Mom to help pay the bills—was no longer under Mom's mattress.

"They kidnapped him?" Deepak said the words out loud. He'd put the pieces together.

"No, no. It must be some misunderstanding," Dad said.

I couldn't be nice anymore. "Dad! Get REAL. It's like these people took everything they could get their filthy hands on and ran. That's not, Let's talk. That's, Screw you."

Mom grabbed my forearm, pleading with me to stop. It hurt too much to hear. Ang's eyes were wide open, in disbelief. When Deepak agreed to get married, my sister had asked him to send her a picture of the happy new couple. She'd been trying to believe in his and our parents' choices.

The next morning, we'd learn Anisha wrote herself a check to empty the bank account. A few weeks before taking off, her family went on a shopping spree, charging the Citibank Visa at a few baby stores, as well as stores that are for adults, like Lane Bryant, Modell's, and Foot Locker. They'd applied for Akshay's U.S. passport twenty-seven days after Anisha's father arrived in the country and had it mailed to a neighbor's home. Anisha, the baby, and her sister and parents boarded an Air India flight from JFK to Mumbai.

In the face of these facts, Deepak saw certain conversations in a new light. Before the marriage, when Anisha was writing him love letters, her mom wrote to our mom, confessing that her husband's real estate business had come to "a total standstill" and they were in dire financial straits. Repeatedly in their year together as a couple—up to their last night together—Anisha asked Deepak to send money to her parents (she said her dad was drinking and becoming violent), to sponsor her sister and parents, to pay for her sister's college and purchase a separate home.

Deepak didn't say no. He said, "Not now. I need time."

It appeared her requests were more like demands, and the baby was her ransom. Those times I'd grilled her about career plans, they were staring me straight in the face. Anisha was trying to milk my brother for what he was worth. That was her version of being a dutiful daughter.

We hired an attorney, who ran into court. We got a court order for the baby to be returned to the U.S. immediately. When we mailed it to Anisha, she had her own lawyer respond with a letter that was a sob story. She claimed that she was tortured by each one of us and our dog Wrinkle and subjected to slavery, poisoning, and physical abuse. And, if we attempted to come to India for the baby, we'd be subject to criminal and civil charges.

Dad's brothers—the ones who pressured Deepak to get married—didn't offer to fly on our behalf to play negotiator. We toyed with the idea of hiring kidnappers to get the baby back, but decided that would put his safety at risk (and be very, very illegal).

And so the first Shahani born in America was taken from his homeland. Dad sat as he always sat, saying nothing. Only this time, he knew he really was guilty of something: forcing his own child into a toxic union.

The life that the wedding and a grandchild had given Dad was gone. There was no solution, for now.

When I flew back to Chicago for junior year, I had all I needed to shut out home and plunge into the life of the mind: eight hundred miles of distance, friends, and a picturesque setting. The autumn leaves turned their golds and crimsons, and lifted by the winds of the Windy City, did cartwheels down the Midway. Mother Nature's reminder that there are seasons, and seasons change, was comforting.

I'd strong-armed my way into a lecture hall, where a popular new professor dedicated an entire book to proving one simple line: migration does not just happen, it is produced. I repeated that line over and over, out loud, to myself, to my roommate. The course set me on a hunt for any and every class that explained what a "nation" and "nation-state" were—not in emotional, felt terms (that I knew for myself), but in historical terms. While we treated nation-states like the natural order of things, they were, in fact, a novel human experiment.

I had what every college kid dreams of—a line of study that makes you feel like you swallowed the red pill, stepped out of the matrix. And still, the horror of the summer chased me. To exorcise the demons, I tried something new. On the eve of my twentieth birthday, I sat down and wrote two letters.

The first is simple enough to explain. It was to my big brother. He was not talking about what happened to him. He was working long hours and, when he wasn't working, he was clubbing. I felt he needed to slow down and let himself mourn—which was much easier to say on paper than out loud.

"I look at Dad and see a man who has suffered but not allowed himself to know it," I wrote. "He's gone through a spiritual death for years, perhaps a lifetime, and I don't want you to have that same life . . . Your family—with your wife and child—was torn apart. I know that tears you apart."

The second letter requires more explaining. Akshay, my nephew, was not the only member of our family missing. The uncle I did not like was missing, too.

Uncle Ratan had served well over a year in prison. I thought he was supposed to be out already. I'd decided to suck it up and ask why.

"What's going on with Uncle Ratan?" I turned to Mom.

"Sweetie, I really don't understand it. Can you talk to your father about it?"

"Dad, what's up with Uncle Ratan?"

"He is having problems getting the release."

Uncle Ratan went before two boards: one that decides if a prisoner gets work release, the other that decides parole. Either is a form of permission to return home and work, under the watch of an officer who keeps tabs and can order you back to prison. My uncle got denied both.

"Did he do something?" I asked Dad.

I could easily see Uncle Ratan trying out one of his racist jokes at his interview: *Do you know why Chinese have slanty eyes? They eat so much rice, they have to squeeze real hard when they take a shit.*

Maybe the parole board wanted to protect society from his sense of humor.

I was wrong.

"He has no fights, no discipline against him." His wife, Auntie Shanta, spoke with me on the phone. "He graduated from the GED." Uncle Ratan hadn't finished high school and so (I didn't know this) he'd been taking classes. That would make him a better candidate for release. "He's working in the kitchen," she continued.

The kitchen! The last frontier of my family's culture war, a place he'd never set foot in. Prison really had broken him in.

"Can you ask him to call me?" I said.

"*Hah.*" She agreed. "How come?"

"I dunno. Maybe there's something I can do."

I did not enjoy getting on the phone with Uncle Ratan. He sounded like himself again. "Have they told you why the fucking *behnchods* are keeping me here?" ("*Behnchod*" means sister fucker. It's equivalent to "motherfucker.")

"That's what I'm trying to understand, Uncle."

"The lawyers screwed up my case."

The lawyers. Every convict blames the lawyers.

I listened to his account with a dose of skepticism: before he was sent to prison, his defense attorney spotted an error in the paperwork. His presentence report—the document that summarizes his crime—pegged my uncle as a member of the Cali cartel and included details of the cartel's extensive distribution network throughout New York City.

But my uncle was never convicted as a cartel member. In the indictment of more than a dozen counts, he accepted one: he was the shopkeeper who took money from a source he believed could be involved in crime. He did not plead to drug trafficking. He was not convicted as a cartel member.

In court, in front of the judge, the prosecutor agreed to have any and all mention of the Cali cartel removed. Only, that never happened. The state did not keep up its end of the plea bargain.

Uncle Ratan had no way of knowing this. Six months into his sentence, when he was up for his first release interview, the panel accused him of being a drug dealer. He sat there, apologizing again and again, not denying anything because that's how fellow prisoners coached him. "Show remorse" is the prisoner mantra.

"I said I am sorry. I said I would not do it again. I said I had learned and have the remorse," he told me. "Your mother's always saying how smart you are. You get scholarships to the best schools in America. Look at what's happening in my case."

I decided I would. And it turned out, every detail he gave was right.

That's how I wrote Letter Two, the letter that turned me into the Shahani family lawyer. I tried to get hold of the prosecutor, and a person at his office told me it wasn't "appropriate" for me to reach out. So I went to the top. I wrote directly to the judge in the case, Joel Blumenfeld. And I was pissed:

I would like someone to explain to my family and me what justifies the relation between my uncle and one of the most notorious drug families in the world; why the attorneys have not yet followed the corrective order you gave them [to] redact the pleadings; how the State and my uncle's attorney can fail to rectify a mistake that keeps a good and unarguably harmless man in jail . . .

The denial of his parole, what the attorneys attribute to "administrative error," is a crime against my uncle. If he were a fluent English speaker, or wealthy, he could lobby for himself against this crime. But he is neither, and because the attorneys involved have illustrated their indifference, I turn to you.

The letter wrote itself. The words came right out. I only double-checked the details against the notes I'd been taking since that first phone call with my uncle. At the post office, I sent it certified mail for $3.09.

Then I went with a friend who was drinking age to get booze. While I didn't drink in college—it felt like a risk I didn't want to take—I'd decided to break that rule for my twentieth birthday party. We got a keg. I danced till my feet hurt. And I ended the evening—which may have been the morning—doing my first and only keg stand.

I lived above a fast-food restaurant, in a large apartment, where my share of the rent was two hundred dollars. A total steal, I thought, until a roach crawled into my bed. My mattress was on the floor. The roach was two or three inches long—much bigger than in 401. *Will I ever have a home that's not roach-infested?*

My roommate knocked on my door. "There's a letter for you."

"Really?!" I was happy. *My big brother is getting his feelings out,* I thought. *He must have written back to me.*

"It's from a judge," she said.

"Oh!"

I did not expect that letter to get a response. That's why I paid for a delivery receipt. I assumed it would be the only proof I'd ever have that my message landed in human hands.

Judge Blumenfeld wrote back himself. He didn't hand me off to a clerk or paralegal. He promised he would get the transcript of the court hearing, where he and the lawyers talked about the error. (Apparently, he was so busy sending people to jail, he had no memory of it.)

I was satisfied, except for this one line of his: "If your uncle is dissatisfied with his attorney, your family can always hire a new one." Sure, judge. Because we're swimming in cash. That's why my mattress is on the floor and I sleep with roaches.

Not long after, the judge called an emergency hearing in Queens. He ordered all the lawyers to show up, and the prison upstate to "produce" Uncle Ratan. The judge wanted the prisoner in the room, not phoning in. He didn't give me an order, but I flew in from Chicago because the cost of not being there was too great. If the adults screwed up again, I would have to fix it.

I didn't know court could be so fun. Finally, it was the stuff of John Grisham novels. In my front row seat, I watched the man in robes seethe, accuse, pounce. How could the lawyers be so negligent? Why was he hearing about this from his new "pen pal"?

Me! That's me! I was his pen pal.

The lawyers scratched their heads. *So strange about this slipup in an otherwise perfect system.* The prosecutor's office would get to work. Uncle Ratan would be released soon.

I glanced at Uncle Ratan, in an olive-green jumpsuit, flanked by guards. I hadn't seen him in a very long time. He'd changed. He was no longer a chubby Indian uncle, whiskey gut bulging through the buttons of a multicolored rayon shirt. He'd been working out. His traps protruded, an upside-down V behind his neck. Biceps, too, probably from pull-ups. He'd shaved his head bald.

I approached the divider to say hello when the hearing ended.

"You're looking really fit, Uncle!" I tried to sound light and breezy.

"*Hah.* Thank you, Aarti. Thank you." His eyes were wet. He pulled me into a hug before they put the handcuffs back on. He was heading back to prison, and I to university.

My uncle's wife and son began preparing for his homecoming. A parole officer came to survey their house—a very good sign. They wouldn't send an officer if it wasn't real this time. My cousin started looking into short vacations that he, his mom, and his dad could take before jumping back into the grind of Broadway.

Uncle Ratan—who accepted his guilty plea because he was told he'd serve eight months—ended up serving two and a half years. That's 375 percent more time. It happened not because he messed up, but because the state did. And the state doesn't have to pay for its mistakes.

If only that were the worst of it. It wasn't. It was about to get worse. On the day my uncle was set to be released, he disappeared.

"Where is Uncle Ratan?" I asked Dad on the phone. Autumn leaves had long passed. It was nearly the end of my junior year, almost summer again.

"Doll, we don't know still."

This is the exchange we had for one, two, three days.

The prison didn't allow us to pick up my uncle in person. They would load him, shackled, in a bus back to Queens. The drop-off could happen in the middle of the night. He would call once free, and we would get him. He never called.

My imagination ran wild. *Maybe someone stabbed him for his wedding ring and left him for dead in a ditch.*

There was no counselor we could talk to. The parole officer didn't know what was happening. Finally, on day four, my phone rang. It was Dad.

"They took him. They took him," he said.

"Who took him? Who's him?"

"Ratan. Immigration took Ratan."

"Huh? What are you talking about?"

"For deportation."

That last word sent a shock wave through my body. Deportation was an abstraction to me. It's what the Nazis did to the Jews in the lead-up to the Holocaust. It came up in American history, too—when we imported Mexican braceros to work the farms and then deported them in a sweep of more than a million migrants—but school hadn't taught me that example. And while I grew up in a zip code that was mostly immigrant, no stories came to mind of anyone I personally knew taken away.

"Are you sure, Dad?"

"*Hah,* doll."

Dad was breathing heavily. Not smoker's breath. Another heavy. Heaving. *Is my father crying?* I hadn't heard him cry before.

"Dad, it's OK. It's OK. This must be some misunderstanding. Uncle Ratan has a green card. That's permanent. It's in the title. Permanent residency."

"Then why would they take him?"

"I don't know, Dad. Do you know where he is?"

"*Hah.* He called me and told me this number to find him."

Dad tried to stifle the tears so he could dictate a toll-free hotline. He then told me to write down something else—the "Alien" number printed on his little brother's green card. I'd need to enter that in the automated system.

"Dad, everything is going to be fine."

"*Hah,* doll."

"This is America," I reminded him. "There's no double jeopardy in this country. Uncle Ratan already did his time—more than his time."

"I'm sorry to trouble you, my *pichikery.*"

"It's not a trouble, Dad."

In the world Dad was born into, a man turns to the men in his tribe for help, not to his baby girl. Now—after so many twists and turns that could not exactly be called his choices (too many of them were not choices)—he lived in a new world. He stopped trusting his old reflexes. I was the first person Dad called.

I sat alone, trying to wrap my mind around what he just told me. If it was true, if my uncle was in fact being taken away, that meant Dad would be next.

What would that mean for the rest of us? Would Mom have to go? She was a U.S. citizen. She'd put in the papers to naturalize. How about Deepak? And Ang? They naturalized, too. Ang applied when she got to college, and it took nearly four years because the government lost her paperwork.

The only ones who hadn't naturalized yet were Dad and me. We never got around to it. Dad was too busy working. I was too busy doing Model UN and Model Congress. Sure, those are excuses. But how could that matter? We had green cards. We didn't know "permanent" meant impermanent. And there's nowhere else on earth my family belonged. For God's sake, I couldn't pronounce my own name. I was "R-D."

Life doesn't tend to change in a single moment, but in that moment, mine did. I felt a complete metamorphosis. All the shame that had built up over the years—of my family holding me back, of my parents not being enough, of my father being arrested—it shattered like cracked glass from a windowpane. And now, the shards gone, I could see clearly. I knew, deep in my bones: enough is enough. We've paid the price. This is my country. That means it must be my father's, too.

Uncle Ratan was locked up, yet again, this time at 201 Varick Street by SoHo. The address meant nothing to me until I got there.

201 Varick was a post office, with a hidden prison above it. It happened to be right across the street from SOB's, Sounds of Brazil, my favorite club in the city.

SOB's was one of the places I went underage dancing. It's where my taste in music evolved. I went from strictly 1990s hip hop to Latin, discovering Celia Cruz, Marc Anthony, Héctor Lavoe, and Shakira (back when she was an edgy Colombian brunette, before she became a blond pop star). SOB's is where I learned salsa with laid-back Puerto Ricans and strict Cubans. "Communists bring a whole lotta rules to the dance floor," I told a man leading me one night. (I thought I was funny. He didn't.) SOB's is where a Dominican woman taught me to use my shoulders and butt, not just my feet, when moving to a bare-bones four-step bachata. "Honey, ju gotta put it all in." And SOB's was home to Basement Bhangra—*the* party that introduced New Yorkers to the most popular music in Mumbai. I took so much pride in that party. The DJ who started it was, like me, a girl from Queens.

Now, it turned out, while one set of immigrants was dancing, the other set—our relatives—was locked up right across the street, on the fourth floor, about to get tossed back to the same countries whose music we imported, mixed, and sold.

When I got to the visitation line, it was short—unlike Rikers Island. I didn't see a single white person in it—very much like Rikers.

"Uncle, I'm so sorry," I said as we sat down together.

"These ASSHOLES."

I opened my eyes wide, warning him to be careful. We were divided by glass, speaking through phone receivers. Maybe the government was recording.

"I don't care." His body shook. He couldn't stop the shaking. "Let them hear me. I want nothing more to do with this country."

"Uncle, we're going to find a good lawyer—"

"Don't find anyone. What we do won't matter. We won't win."

"I get you're upset," I said. "But we have to try."

"The officers—they came to me and gave me the papers to sign. They said, 'If you want to get out of here, you can sign out.'"

"Sign out?" I asked. "What do you mean sign out?"

"For the deportation."

That couldn't be. The government wouldn't put a man with a family and a mortgage on a plane, without a hearing. That's what they do in those failed states, on the other side of the globe. Not here.

My uncle was right again. That's how this legal system worked. A few other detainees decided to sign out.

"Did you sign out?!" I asked.

"No. Not yet."

Relief. He was of two minds: kicked down, yet willing to get back up. I left promising him I'd be there for every step of this fight.

I wanted to find the best lawyer in the city (though I didn't know how we'd afford it). I was still researching when Uncle Ratan's family hired someone else. Of course they did. I didn't tell my auntie and cousin what I was up to. And they weren't going to sit around and do nothing.

The lawyer told them all the things we'd want to hear: Uncle Ratan, a first-time nonviolent offender and lawful permanent resident, would be released on bail soon; he would not have to fight deportation from behind bars; he would get a pardon because kicking him out would cause hardship to family members who are U.S. citizens and green card holders.

Turns out, every single one of these statements was false. We all attended the hearing. It was on another floor of 201 Varick that was turned into a courthouse. The hearing lasted a few short minutes. The immigration judge scoffed at our lawyer. *This man's an aggravated felon. He doesn't have a single argument for bond. He's not eligible for relief. Next.*

An "aggravated felon." The term was so stark. I didn't know what it meant, but it ended the conversation before it could even begin.

Outside the courtroom, the lawyer summarized the hearing as if we weren't sitting right there, hearing it for ourselves. "OK, so the judge says Mr. Shahani is not eligible for relief. But we are able to appeal. That is his right."

I didn't trust this man. It sounded as if he'd given this rap a thousand times—and there was a piece of the story missing.

"What is an aggravated felon?" I asked him.

"It means the most serious crimes—like murder and rape," he said. "Nothing your uncle has done."

It was a comforting answer. Again, he was speaking to common sense. But then why would the judge call my uncle an "aggravated felon"? We'd sorted out the Cali cartel mix-up.

When I went home and looked it up for myself, I discovered the lawyer was either ignorant or lying through his teeth. An "aggravated felony" in the immigration law meant a giant pool of convictions which were neither "aggravated" nor a felony. The term included many misdemeanors. Once an immigrant is an "aggravated felon," that pretty much seals the deal. Short of proving you'd be murdered or tortured back home at the hands of the government, there was no way to stay in the United States. Having a green card or family members who were American citizens didn't change that.

The lawyer, who got two grand out of my cousin, had taken us for a ride. Though we had to waste our money on someone. In deportation, there is no public defender. You either hire a lawyer or represent yourself.

When Auntie Shanta went to visit Uncle Ratan later that week, she couldn't find him, again. He was no longer at 201 Varick Street. He had been transferred to another jail, in Maryland. There, he slept on the floor because there were not enough beds. He could not get aspirin for a deep cavity that he'd planned to get treated as soon as he was out. The pain got so bad, he held his own mouth open as a fellow detainee yanked out his rotted tooth.

Uncle Ratan was put on a plane a few weeks later. It was weeks, not days, because the immigration agents got him to the airport too late. He missed his flight and spent more nights in detention, on the taxpayer dime. His wife and son left America to join him. He was not allowed to return to the United States ever again. It was a life sentence.

Dad was next.

INTERMISSION
Reporting the Case

IT'S TIME TO TAKE a break from the past and step into the present day, to get a bird's-eye view of the criminal case that spiraled into punishments well beyond the criminal sentence. Twenty-two years have passed since Dad's arrest, four years since that chance meeting in the judge's chambers. While I wasn't ready to be a journalist about the case then, I'm ready now, no longer worried that the act of looking back will trap me inside a world I was desperate to leave. It's amazing, the confidence you can feel, when you fix your credit score.

I decided to go off my Silicon Valley beat and report *New York v. Shahani* like any other assignment: get the paper trail, call some experts, track down key sources. For too many years, I'd been lost inside the microscopic details—how it felt to live, crushed under the thumb of state prosecution—but had not seen what it looked like from the outside.

Our case is a fascinating little footnote in the history of globalization, New York City, the war on drugs—take your pick. Petit bourgeois immigrants from the Indian subcontinent, rendered stateless in an independence struggle against the British, landed in Queens, and became foot soldiers for a notorious Colombian cartel. Or so the state's story goes.

Back when Dad got arrested, he said more than once, "We're doing what everyone else is doing." I didn't care, because I was angry at him. But the reason that line stuck with me all these years is because of the ketchup trick.

Remember the ketchup trick? Thieves would go to Broadway National Bank, the local bank where the wholesale district kept accounts. The thieves would squeeze ketchup on a person's back, hoping that as the victim used both hands to clean up the mess, they could snatch the briefcase or duffel bag left on the floor. This crime only worked if the thieves could count on that bag to have cash in it—that is, cash was the industry standard, not just the Shahani family standard.

I thought I would have to hunt down former employees of Broadway National. I'd get them to talk with me "on background." It's a common practice in business and political reporting. Informants tell the seedy truth of how things really work (humans are human and have an existential need to talk). The reporter prints that truth, but not the names who provided it, and adds a line like "sources declined to be named for fear of losing their employment."

Turns out, there was no need to hunt. When I googled "Broadway National Bank," I found that America's most famous prosecutor had already done the work for me.

Shortly after Dad was sentenced in New York City, James Comey of the U.S. Justice Department prosecuted a case against the bank. He charged that it was a front for money laundering to the Middle East, Latin America, and other regions. The case was in federal court, Southern District of New York.

NPR had sent me to Manhattan for work. I decided to run down to the federal courthouse, literally run, weaving through the Lower East Side and Chinatown. It was drizzling but not yet pouring, the kind of humid afternoon that makes everyone's hair puff out a quarter inch.

"Ya like running?" the security guard at the court asked. He was chatty. "I'm a big runner too."

"I bet," I said, glancing at his belly.

"I mean, I *was* a big runner. Now I'm just big." He laughed at himself.

It's wonderful coming home. New Yorkers are unfiltered. Sparring is our language of love. California is achingly polite—the dramatic natural beauty of redwood forests and Pacific Coast bluffs such a stark contrast with the uniform, socially enforced positivity of everyday conversation.

In the records room, a clerk pulled out the file. I assumed it would be several accordion cases thick—an all-out litigation bloodbath between dogged prosecutors and corrupt businessmen. It wasn't. The entire file was about a dozen documents, no thicker than a book you'd grab for the beach.

"You sure that's all?" I asked.

"I'm surprised, too," the clerk said. "These cases are usually a lot bigger."

I sat in a cubicle beside a fake green shrub, made in China. The plastic leaves were dusty.

I pulled out each document one by one, smirking, shaking my head, rolling my eyes at the details: Broadway National was accused of laundering $123 million through 107 bank accounts. A consultant they'd hired warned bank executives to clean up. An employee hired to help clean up turned around and tried to help his own son withdraw money from an account at the bank that had been frozen because of fraud.

My hands trembled as I unfolded one document in particular—the one that would solve the mystery of just how guilty the Shahani family was.

Aarti, it's just a story, I had to remind myself. *Don't take it too personally.*

It was a large spreadsheet, dozens of columns, each one the name of a business on Broadway. Our store—Roopa Enterprises—was there. So was the store that used to employ Dad—where the boss promised to make him a partner and then reneged. So were fifty-three other businesses.

Underneath each account, there were rows and rows of deposits in cash. According to this data—I had data now, not just wishful thinking—many of the businesses deposited more money than we did. We were nowhere near the top. Some months, we were near the bottom. Dad was right.

The bankers handled the legal attack a lot better than we did. Broadway National paid a fine of $4 million, and no bank executive served a single day in jail. In fact, while the case was still going on, the CEO of the bank was celebrated for his contributions to this country. He received an Ellis Island Medal of Honor—alongside leading American politicians John McCain and Eliot Spitzer.

I recalled an argument I once had with my uncle about this country. *"America is corrupt just like everywhere else,"* he had said. *"If you have the money, you can buy your freedom."* I told him he didn't know America like I did. Now, I wondered.

That evening a friend of mine from California was in town, a brilliant woman who sold her lingerie company to Calvin Klein. At age forty, she could retire. But she liked working so much, she was looking into opportunities in biotech. That's right. From bras to genes, not jeans—a totally different line of work.

This is what I love about Silicon Valley—such a high concentration of people who don't put themselves in the same boxes the rest of us do. They can think in terms of the core skills they have—fund-raising, brand marketing, data mining—and apply it to any sector they want. It's the ultimate freedom of movement.

I hadn't seen my friend in months. I was now part of the high-flying world, where neighbors only manage to meet while traveling in other cities, in hotels instead of living rooms.

"The Library at the NoMad could be good," she texted me. "I'll call today and make a reservation."

While I'm the one from New York, I have the tastes of a borough kid. I like cheap immigrant holes in the wall, not *Sex and the City* happy hours. I followed her lead—which, you could say, led me back home.

Google told me that "NoMad" is a high-end boutique hotel, right across the street from my family's old store. The entire neighborhood was now called NoMad—one of these realtor rebranding tricks to make rich people feel invited and regular people uninvited. *I hate those places,* I told myself on the way there.

Two doormen held the heavy doors open as I stepped into a dimly lit atrium with pillars wrapped in leather. This used to be a hallway leading to small offices where Dad's friends had their shops. Residents of the nearby welfare hotel used to come around, pestering the shopkeepers to sell one or two items at wholesale prices.

I walked into the restaurant, winding through tables of designer clothes feasting on raw carrots that cost sixteen dollars. To be fair, the carrots were presented beautifully on a bed of shaved ice.

I headed to a secret back room called the Library, lined with unread leather-bound classics and open to hotel guests only. My friend was connected.

I was early and cold. Manhattan buildings have the terrible habit of blasting the air-conditioning in the summer.

Mom and Dad on their wedding day in Morocco. This near-mouth action was risqué for the time and place. Dad was being bold.

Guests at the wedding. Mom and Dad didn't have plans to move to the United States. They thought, for a while, that Morocco was home. All three of us kids were born there.

My big sister, Angelly, holding me weeks after I was born.

Mom made Ang and me matching dresses a lot. In many (if not most) of our child-hood pictures, we are wearing her homemade clothes.

We came to the United States when Ang and I were toddlers. Deepak, almost a decade older than I, had to be our surrogate dad at times.

Flushing was the site of the 1964 World's Fair, and was nearly home to the United Nations. We could walk to the globe from our home and see it every time we rode the 7 train into Manhattan.

Apartment 401 was our first home in America.

Mom organized many parties and community meetings in 401, with guests from all over the world. My upbringing was a working-class United Nations.

My fifth birthday. Am I old enough to be holding a serrated knife?!

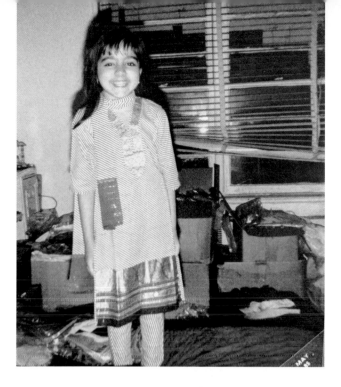

Mom stitched this cotton candy kurta for Diwali. After Dad convinced me to like it, I posed for a picture in the big bedroom— which was also Mom's sewing factory and Dad's office.

By my seventh birthday, I was definitely old enough to hold a serrated knife. Auntie Gloria, fifth from left, led the singing. She was a soprano who sang solos for her church choir.

In 401, Dad taught Deepak to shave. Later on, Deepak taught Ang and me to pluck our unibrows.

Wrinkle Shahani joined our family shortly after we moved to New Jersey.

Journalism is my second career. Before I sat in a studio and spoke through a microphone in Silicon Valley, I shouted through a bullhorn on very rainy days in New York City.

My first love, Subhash, with me, my siblings, and guests, dancing and cutting cake at La Linea in the East Village. He threw me a surprise party.

This is pretty much how my siblings and I get along wherever we go—not just at surprise birthday parties.

Akshay was the first member of our family born in the U.S.A.—in a hospital in New Jersey. Sadly he is too young to know who Jon Bon Jovi is.

When Ang got married, we had one of the best female DJs from the Bronx spin hip-hop, and a Punjabi group teach everyone how to bhangra.

Dad on the day
I graduated
from Harvard.

Visiting Dad in a
hospital in Pune,
India. I did the
twenty-six-hour
commute from
San Francisco,
in an emergency,
when doctors said
he'd pass away at
any moment.

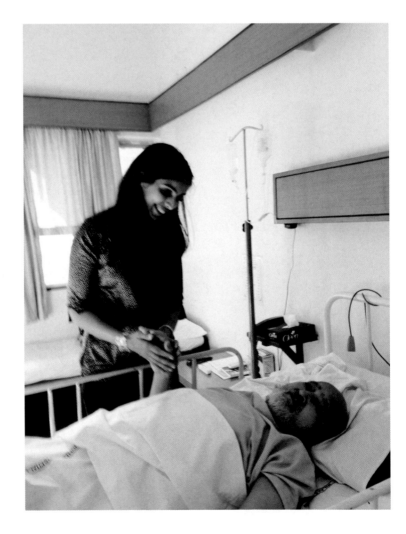

"You don't by chance have spare coats here, do you?" I asked the waiter, half joking.

"Lemme see what I can do," he said and made a dramatic turn, like a stage actor. Minutes later, he came back with a black pashmina shawl—real pashmina. "Here you are, honey." He draped it around my shoulders.

My friend was running late, so I struck up a conversation with him. That's another reporting trick. Talk to locals to get a sense of place. I hadn't been on Broadway—or NoMad—in years. I could see for myself the clash of civilizations: high-end globalization (like this hotel) colliding with low-end globalization (like my family). What did this waiter—himself working class or, as Americans like to say, "middle class"—make of the small businesses that were surviving at the periphery of his fancy employer?

"I hear they're all money-laundering fronts." He gave a devilish look, aroused at the thought of danger lurking in our midst. "I mean, I dunno, but they *look* shady as hell."

Shady. This young man was white. I am not. I wondered if "shady" is how he'd describe Dad, back when my father was pushing hand trucks down the block.

"That's exactly what they are." I attempted to take his observation and recouch it, defining money laundering not according to criminal code, but real-life economic function. "These small businesses, cash businesses, are how poor people managed to buy homes and send their kids to college. They're how a bunch of immigrant newcomers climbed their way into the middle class."

He paused and gave it a quick thought. "Go immigrants!" he said with gusto, flashing his Dentyne smile. "That's awesome!"

When my friend arrived, I wanted to pull out the spreadsheets I'd copied in the courthouse, to tell her what the rows of data meant to me. But I had to remind myself: this was not the time or the place. We ordered the sixteen-dollar carrots.

So now that we know cash transactions were, as Dad claimed, the industry standard—our store was not exceptional—we still have an outstanding question. Why did the infamous Cali cartel shop with us? Of all the stores on all of Broadway, why'd they have to come into ours?

119

I didn't buy Mom's explanation: "Dad was such a great business-man—he was so much better at languages and talking than everyone else—he attracted the biggest customers." A victim of his own success. It was too flattering.

I thought it might be more random. Maybe a parking spot happened to open up right in front of our door. Maybe it was pouring rain and a Cali foot soldier needed to dry off. Or maybe Dad did have a secret life.

There was one man who would hold all the answers: El Burro, the donkey.

My father, my uncle, and their accountant were not the only defendants named in the criminal case. There were seven men total. The others were invisible. They didn't come to court with us. Their hearings were on different dates.

El Burro was the linchpin of the case—the crucial link connecting the cartel to my family. According to the indictment, he was the man who dropped off the duffel bag with hundred-dollar bills, and the man who'd call my uncle to talk about the latest line of scientific calculators. Prosecutors knew about the money because, as my family had feared, they were running a wiretap. While so much Cali cartel activity had shifted to pagers and fax machines, El Burro spoke with the Shahani brothers on the phone—and the government listened.

I was open to whatever information El Burro would give me. And I was prepared to fly to Colombia to get it. I assumed he had been deported after his eight-year sentence.

It turns out, he wasn't. He was right here at home.

"Hi, can I speak to Mr. Jose Camacho please?" I used his legal name.

"Yes, he is speaking," he said politely.

"Is this Jose Camacho?" I repeated.

"Yes, I am."

I'd been sitting on his number for months. I got a student at Queens College to go to the courthouse and copy every defendant's file. This cell phone was handwritten on an appeal filed by El Burro, *pro se*—defending himself. I'd taken that as a clue: he was dog food for the Cali cartel, not a higher-up worth the cost of a legal team.

"Hi, my name is Aarti *Shahani*." I emphasized the last name. "You don't know me, but years ago you were involved in a criminal case that my father was in also. And I got your number from court records. How are you?"

I didn't want to hide the fact that I'm a journalist. But I just blurted out the affiliation that felt the most relevant.

He said nothing. I wasn't sure if the signal dropped or it was a language barrier.

"Usted habla español también?" I asked if he spoke Spanish, and his voice reappeared.

"Sí. Dígame." He asked what I wanted to know. *"¿De qué quieres del caso?"*

Sometimes I talk so fast, I swallow my words (the habit annoyed Dad as much as when I left hair in the shower drain). Now I was speaking slowly—exaggeratedly so—when I asked if he recalled two gentlemen by the names of Namdev and Ratan Shahani.

"No, yo no recuerdo." He said he did not.

That answer made no sense. He had to know them. He was the linchpin. They were criminal co-conspirators.

"I don' lie. I dunno this people. I NEVAH know ju family," he repeated, adamantly.

"You didn't know my family?" It struck me that I never asked my dad or uncle about the other men listed on the indictment.

"No, I don' know nobody. They make up the case. I never in my life—I, I give you da phone numba for my lawyah. Ju can call him."

"Uh-huh."

My head went foggy. Whatever he might have to say about how he met Dad, I didn't think El Burro would deny that meeting ever happened.

Also, his accent confused me. In Spanish and English, he dropped the *t*'s from the ends of his words and pronounced "you" like "Jew," so he sounded Dominican. He was supposed to be Colombian. After all, why would a Colombian drug cartel employ someone who was not their own?

"Sir, would it be possible for us to meet?" I asked.

He agreed.

I happened to be in New York when I made this call, on another work trip from Silicon Valley. I wanted us to meet on Broadway, where my family's store used to be, to search for slipups or clues—if El Burro seemed familiar with the block, if he unintentionally pointed me to the halal fast food when I asked for a lunch spot. The phone gives you a person's tone; the meeting his body language; and the place, if well chosen, the secrets he forgets to hide.

El Burro and his lawyer insisted on their home turf—a small rent-controlled apartment on the Upper West Side. I didn't argue over it. That may sound needlessly risky: to walk into the home of a stranger who'd been in prison a few years.

But the meeting felt fragile—a teeny opening in the tunnel that could easily collapse if I pushed too hard. And there are commonsense ways to go to unfamiliar places. I'd have a trusted contact—in this case my brother or sister—track my smartphone location with a time-limited GPS pin and call the police if I didn't check in regularly.

Thankfully, I didn't need to take the security measures. The night before our meeting, El Burro changed locations to City Diner, a big diner with comfort food that takes up half a block on the Upper West Side. It's a well-known landmark. I passed it all the time in high school. Maybe he realized I'd feel safer there.

When I arrived, the hostess pointed me to a booth at the far end. There was a man hunched over a bowl of soup. *That can't be him,* I thought to myself. He was wearing a gray sweater vest on top of a baby-pink dress shirt. Small rectangular glasses with a wire metal frame sat on the bridge of his round, wrinkled nose. He looked like a grandpa.

"Mr. Camacho?" I walked by and backtracked.

"Sí, sí. ¿Misses Shahani?"

"Yes, please call me Aarti—*como artista.*"

We shook hands, my grip firm and his tenuous. He'd brought his "lawyer"—an irritating specimen of a human being whose identity kept changing over the course of our meeting. He was, at varying moments, also or instead the "private investigator," the "cousin-in-law," and the "ex cousin-in-law."

According to El Burro, he was at the wrong place at the wrong time. He was a gypsy cab driver, dropping off a passenger he'd never met before in the Bronx. When the passenger got out with two bags, NYPD stopped him and found thirty-five kilograms of cocaine. Both men were taken to the precinct. Five weeks later, the passenger pleaded guilty and the case against El Burro was dismissed entirely. The court even returned his bail money—which he took to mean he'd been exonerated.

But—this is the twist in the story—the case reappeared in Queens a few weeks later. Prosecutors in that borough filed new charges, citing the exact same date and time as the Bronx arrest, only now claiming that El Burro had the drugs and that he was connected to my family's store.

"I lost eight years of my life." Camacho's face grew flush. "My wife left me. I live alone now."

"Don't get excited. Don't get too excited," his "lawyer" interrupted him. "Just listen to the questions and answer."

Only, when Camacho did that, his "lawyer" still interrupted. Our meeting lasted nearly three hours because of this third wheel, and also because of Camacho's speech impediment. He had a hard time stringing words together. The man who'd call my family store to place orders did not, according to my family, have a speech impediment.

"I have an accident when I younger." He turned and showed me his left ear. (I'd been seated to his right.) The cartilage, scarred, bent forward. "I have mental problem. I slow." He'd written this line in his appeals. He didn't include proof of mental impairment—though that's a catch-22. If you're impaired, it's hard to know how to prove it.

"My back is broken." He pointed behind his neck.

"May I feel?" I asked him.

Camacho began trying to lift his shirt, so I could get a good look.

"No, I mean above your shirt." I wanted to be discreet. We were in a diner. "May I touch your back?"

He nodded. My fingers walked down his vertebrae. Three bones were raised. Again, the accident.

I left with more questions than answers about Jose Camacho's case, and the sense that he, too, had fallen prey to the same plea bargain system that ensnared my family.

The system got us good—and not just by threatening to put my dad and uncle away for longer if they exercised the constitutional right to trial. The government also separated the defendants, making them invisible to each other, so that the pieces of the puzzle didn't need to fit together to secure multiple prosecutions.

I called up our defense lawyer, Alan Kaufman—the fancy white-collar litigator who came so highly recommended from my first boss. He had very little recollection of the case. (It was so long ago.) But the record reflected that he never went into court and raised this vital and handy fact: El Burro and the Shahanis were total strangers.

I pulled into the driveway of Judge Blumenfeld. The man to whom I wrote as a child, whose chambers I visited as an adult, was now retired. He'd told me to keep in touch. I wanted to see if I was finally ready to talk to him, real talk.

"You made it!" the judge shouted from his doorstep. He was in blue jeans and a polo shirt.

"You look so casual. Where are your robes?" I like to tease my sources before an interview, loosen them (and me) up.

Blumenfeld lived in the nice part of Queens—not far from where I grew up, where many of my teachers in elementary school lived, the part with houses and front lawns. His entryway led to a living room with a big white carpet. It was sexy—not what I would've expected from a retiree.

"Should I take my shoes off?" I asked.

"No need."

His wife came up to me. "It's so lovely to finally meet you."

Finally? I'd become a topic of discussion at the Blumenfeld dinner table. His daughter would be arriving soon, to observe our interview. Although tragic health problems had disrupted her career, she had gone to journalism school and was an NPR listener. She wanted to say hello.

We passed a hallway covered in pictures of his granddaughter. The doorframe had pencil marks—taking tally as she grew taller.

"Some Thursdays I'd take her with me to court," the judge said. He wanted her to see what the system was like—a crash course in human folly and suffering. "You're never too young to learn." Public urination cases were her favorite. "She tells me, 'Pop-pop, you can go to jail for peeing?'"

We sat in his den. Mrs. Blumenfeld walked in to offer me tea or wine. I wanted a drink so badly but didn't want to seem like a lush.

"What are you having?" I asked the judge.

"I don't drink wine," he said. "But please go ahead."

No need to tell me twice.

His wife came back with a glass of Pinot Noir just as their daughter arrived. The den was starting to feel a little crowded, like a talk show set, not a quiet corner for a quick interview.

Blumenfeld seemed delighted. He was chatty. Without any prompting, he sat back in his armchair and shared his love story.

"I ended up getting a car that was unsafe at any speed," he began. It was a 1966 Chevy Corvair. None of his friends had cars. "So I became very popular for double dates." He wasn't looking to get involved with anyone (he'd just had a breakup). Then a buddy strong-armed him into going out one Saturday night for a movie and dinner. "I figured, what the hell, I'm going to have to eat anyway. May as well get this over with."

He glanced over at his wife, who giggled. She knew and liked the part that was coming next. "I don't think we could hear the movie because my stomach was growling." He was hungry. Instead of a restaurant, they all headed to his home, where she made omelets. "I'd had scrambled eggs before," he said, "but never an omelet. We've been together ever since and—"

A thunderclap interrupted him. It started pouring so hard outside, the raindrops sounded like stones about to shatter the windows. It happened to be the day after Father's Day.

I looked over to the Blumenfeld women, hoping they'd take this as a cue to clear out. No one moved.

"Um, usually when I interview people, um, I don't have others in the room," I tried to explain. That wasn't completely the case. I regularly interview sources on stage, at live events, in front of large audiences. But this was personal. "So, um, do you want your family here?"

"If this is the first time, you'll always remember your first time." The judge laughed. "Ask me what you want to ask me."

His wife stepped away while his daughter slipped into a corner seat, and I into reporter mode.

Blumenfeld spoke with authority, like an expert with no dog in the fight. He laid out a strategy that, he believes, would've gotten rid of the case pretty painlessly. It's called a severance.

Of the seven men charged, there were four Colombians who were allegedly members of the Cali cartel and three Indians who worked for Roopa Enterprises, Inc. Our counsel told us not to gamble on a trial because prosecutors would flash pictures of decapitated heads—the cartel's handiwork—and jurors wouldn't keep straight who did it. The drug traffickers and shopkeepers would just bleed into each other, so to speak.

Well, the obvious fix for that is to ask the court to hold two separate trials—one for the drug people, the other for Roopa. The judge would have granted it in a heartbeat, at which point the attorney general's office wouldn't have wanted to spend the money to call witnesses.

"You catch that part in the sentencing minutes, when the assistant attorney general said he's very rarely in this part of Queens?" the judge asked me.

No, I didn't catch that part.

"That meant, he doesn't try cases here. He would've gone along."

"Gone along with what?"

"A much sweeter deal." In court they'd insisted on jail time because, the judge said, we didn't push. We led with our fear. If we'd threatened to go to trial—this is his educated guess—prosecutors would have offered Dad and Uncle Ratan a little community service, maybe a fine.

I took a sip, or maybe it was a gulp of my wine. Everything he was saying was so obvious, it hurt. It didn't take a fancy legal maneuver to avoid ruin. It took a simple poker face.

The judge was not arguing that my dad, my uncle, and their accountant were innocent. Because they'd never threatened to go to trial, there was no discovery—the process in which prosecutors lay out all the evidence, not just the evidence they give a grand jury to indict a case. He'd heard that select evidence and—as he made clear in court even as the case was happening—he did not find it especially damning.

The judge's point was this: innocent or guilty is beside the point in the justice system. He was no longer in the theater he facilitated for decades, so he could be blunt. Our lawyers, whom he watched and winced at from the bench, could have done a whole lot more to make the case go away.

Though he did not go so far as to say our lawyers were incompetent. To rise to the level of ineffective counsel, the attorney would have to do something egregious like withhold information about a plea offer or snort coke off a stripper. By the justice system's chronically low standards, our lawyers did their job just fine. So did the prosecutor. It's a glaring double standard: the state can make a mistake (as they did with my uncle) and is forgiven. We normal people make mistakes and get banished.

"Where'd you get that guy Alan Kaufman?" Blumenfeld was referring to Dad's attorney. "All my years on the bench, I'd never seen him in court before."

I explained the funny backstory: private school leading to a jerk boss leading to his buddy.

The judge guessed it was a barter. "When you throw business to a friend, the friend throws you back some money," he said. "And knowing your boss's work history, you thought he's a good guy?"

"No, I didn't think he was a good guy," I said. "I just didn't know where else to turn." Everyone told us we had to hire a private attorney because Legal Aid lawyers are free, which must mean they can't be any good.

The judge strongly disagreed with that. He thought Legal Aid would have slaughtered the prosecution, and would have had fun doing it. "It's very rare they get people with no prior record." The judge chuckled.

He didn't believe Indians would be Cali foot soldiers. It's too risky for the cartel. "What if your dad and uncle got nervous and called the police?" There were plenty of Colombian businesses in the city, so the judge figured that's where the cartel would turn for real help. "My sense was that your uncle and your dad had no idea where the money came from nor did they want to lose the business. They were between a rock and a hard place: the people getting played, not the players."

For about an hour, I was on: erect posture, listening attentively, being playful, trying to get him off script so his real thoughts and not his rehearsed talking points would come out.

Just as I was getting ready to hit the road, Judge Blumenfeld made it clear we were not done. It was his turn to ask the questions.

"So you cover tech, huh. Ya like that?"

Oh! He wanted to know a little bit about my beat in Silicon Valley. New York is full of artists, lawyers, bankers—not math and science nerds. They're kind of exotic creatures, very different from us. And, of course, very powerful.

I began to give him a crash course: a handful of internet giants, based in the United States and China, are fighting over data like it's oil; they program algorithms that mine, shovel, and sculpt the data into new forms, not knowing what will come out the other end. That uncertainty—let the computers lead us, not vice versa—is the point of the experiment. It's the Wild West.

Only minutes into my fascinating overview, I saw his eyes glaze over. He didn't care. He wasn't asking about tech. He was asking about me, about my life choices.

"I remember calling you my most frequent pen pal," he said.

The pen pal thing again. *Jesus. Why does he always bring that up?*

"It was remarkable getting a letter from a kid who was so articulate," he said. "I mean, you were my daughter's age when you first wrote to me. I thought to myself, 'How would I feel if she had to go through what you're going through—if she had to do that for me?'"

We both looked over at his daughter, who was still sitting in the corner. Only now, the mood changed, like it was about to get personal. She was polite enough to get up and say good-bye.

As soon as the door closed, the judge charged ahead. "My prediction was you'd go into some form of advocacy work because you really got an inside insight into the criminal justice system, and you'd have a few kids, a husband."

Silence. I didn't want to explain myself. And, to be frank, he was saying what I worried about myself. *Aarti, you've strayed too far from home and lost your way.*

"Life moved on. And then you surfaced. And I'm thinking, God has a sense of humor. He gives you this gift, a skill—and a love of family. Such a love of family. And you're not living a life about what you were really born to do."

What you were really born to do. Did he mean, tear down the system that paid for this nice house in Queens and his comfortable retirement? Maybe I was meant to have nice things, too.

"Listen, it hurts me to see," he kept going. "You're off, all by yourself. You're covering tech, of all things. I mean, I know it's your life. You can do what you want. But c'mon."

This was one of those classic moments when a person who barely knows you and has the best intentions assumes a deep intimacy and tells you the truth about yourself (or, at least, their version of it), which you hear intently because it speaks to your own fears, uncertainties, inner dilemmas. And, of course, my moment had a twist, for dramatic effect: the stranger trying to play dad was the man who locked up my dad.

I chose tech journalism because it was a dream job, and yet maybe I was living someone else's dream.

The judge would not stop talking. "I'm saying to you," he continued, "as an old fart: why don't you get in touch with who you are and what you really care about?"

"Because people don't win." I blurted it out, a tinge of rage rising. At him. Yes, it was kind of this retired judge to take the time to talk with me. He didn't owe me anything. But he also didn't know a thing about me.

Our conversation could have gone in one of two ways. He could have asked me anything—any detail at all—about my life after he hit that gavel: the things I tried to do, for years, to make it better.

Or I could have turned the tables and put him on defense, not let him get away with playing the expert. It's such a safe role. Only, he was not just a man on the sidelines. I wish I'd said, "You were the man with the gavel, the one who locked Dad up—even though you saw, clear as day, it wasn't fair. If it was so obvious to you, why didn't you do something— besides pass the buck?"

He didn't go there. Neither did I.

We sat quietly. I noticed his saggy old-man cheeks, like Dad's. The judge gave a little smile and our eyes locked. "Look," he said, "I'm talking to you like a father, ya know." Yes, I'd noticed. "You were a spectacular daughter, and my concern is that you run away from the things that matter to you."

I wanted to feel more anger. But I collapsed, and the tears bottled up inside came pouring out. He wasn't all right, but partly right was enough.

"I'm sorry. Sorry. Sorry." He patted my knee. "This is good therapy. Good therapy. Get it all out."

"Thank God it's free." I tried to crack a joke.

At that moment Mrs. Blumenfeld walked in. "Dinner is ready," she announced amiably, as though she didn't just step into a cavern of despair.

It was perfect timing. I had two bowls of soup and another glass of wine.

ACT 4

Stranger Things

IT USED TO BE that Dad was my biggest problem—the impregnable wall between me and freedom, the dating and dancing police, the enforcer of skirt lengths. While he wasn't as blunt as his kid brother, Dad absolutely treated girls and boys differently. He expected me to be in the kitchen.

But once Dad's biggest problem became the threat of life exile, my core feeling about him changed: from adversarial to protective, from enemy to ally. Even if his own poor judgment got him into this mess, it didn't seem fair to keep punishing him—and with a punishment that punished us all.

He paid a high price for his sins. His first and only grandchild was taken away, and he, our patriarch, was helpless to get the baby back. Dad's store—the crowning achievement of his life—collapsed. After the arrest, suppliers and buyers stopped returning his calls. They didn't want trouble to follow them. And they knew they could get away with stiffing Dad on payment. With Uncle Ratan gone, Dad couldn't hand off the work of rebuilding a good name. He shut down Roopa Enterprises.

I had decided to stop going to college. I'd just finished junior year. The official reason for leaving was that I wanted to take some time to help liquidate my family's business. The real reason: I wanted to be as close to Dad as possible. I was afraid he'd die without dignity.

The time had arrived for Dad to serve his sentence. Instead of going upstate like Uncle Ratan did, Dad, we agreed, would stay local, at Rikers

Island—the spit of hell on earth by the airport. It was rougher but closer to us. We could visit three times a week instead of one.

Dad was supposed to serve eight months. But I knew it would be a life sentence or a death sentence. "A life sentence" because the immigration police would swoop Dad up and kick him out after he'd done his time. What was a surprise with my uncle was a certainty with Dad. We were aware of this fact.

That said, I didn't assume Dad would make it that far. His health took a nosedive.

"We need to extract all of his teeth," the dentist told me as Dad sat in the chair, his mouth wide open. His teeth had been loosening. Each wiggled and bled when he bit into food. Root canals and crowns would cost more than ten thousand dollars. We didn't have that kind of money. Extractions and dentures were a lot cheaper.

"That sounds kind of extreme," I said.

"Your grandfather will still be able to eat," she assured me.

"He's my dad, not my granddad."

The dentist wasn't the first person to get it wrong. It was happening a lot lately. While he was only fifty-nine years old, he'd aged a decade or two in a few months, dropping from 180 pounds to 140, and steadily down from there. I could easily imagine him having a heart attack inside or getting stabbed by a fellow inmate. It wasn't a stretch. Stabbings were a routine part of life on Rikers.

Mom and I had both come with Dad to the dentist's office. The dentist left us for a few minutes to talk amongst ourselves. We both looked at Dad for guidance. It was his mouth, after all.

"Daddy?"

"Dahling?" Mom said.

He just sat there, silent—not the silence we were used to, of a person who is observant but reserved. This silence was new.

"Dahling, you heard what the lady doctor said." Mom spoke louder. Maybe he didn't hear us. "What do you want to do?"

"It's fine," he said.

"What's fine?"

He didn't elaborate.

The dentist said if we did nothing, the pain would only get worse. She didn't know that the aging man before her was about to go to jail. I told Mom we needed to tell her, because we were under a strict deadline. We couldn't get an extension to finish dental work.

"Aarti, we can't tell her," Mom said. "You don't know how these people are." By that she meant our people, Indians. The dentist was one of us.

"Mom." I rolled my eyes. Nearly one in three American adults has a criminal record. It's as common as a college degree. "We're not unique. And we don't have any room to play with timelines."

Mom gave in. She wished she hadn't because she was right. As soon as we told the truth, the dentist turned ice cold. The patient in her chair was not an elderly man but a convict. And we had to pay in full before the work was done—not bit by bit, on a monthly schedule, as she'd first proposed.

We couldn't afford the fancy lawyer anymore. We switched to a cheaper one for the last leg of the case—the day of sentencing. He told me to assemble letters of support—testimonials from friends and family about the kind of person Dad was. We had to show he had "community ties"— jail-industry jargon meaning he wasn't without any friends or family (like so many prisoners). That would make him a stronger candidate for early release.

Letters came pouring in from our neighbors at 401. They still remembered us. Auntie Ione wrote about how her son called my father "daddy" as a toddler and continued doing so over the years. She added, "Namdev has not stopped being a father and role model to Kevin. Kevin is now proudly serving in the U.S. Armed Forces."

Members of the Christian cult that brought us groceries on Thanksgiving in 401 wrote about how hard Dad worked over the years to feed his family. They remembered. And they were kind enough not to mention the church by name. It would raise red flags. They printed their letters on personal letterhead.

My cousin Mala's letter nearly knocked me off my seat. She was raised in West Africa. Her father (another one of Dad's little brothers) let Mala come to the United States because we promised to take care of her. She wrote:

I really feel I owe a lot to [Uncle Namdev] . . . I come from a rather conservative family where girls are brought up to do only household chores and not get too much of an education. However, my Uncle Namdev helped me in breaking these conventions. He influenced my father's decision to support my academic and professional goals and I would not have been where I am today if it was not for his help. Uncle Namdev has two daughters and a son but I absolutely love the way he treats all of them with the same amount of educational opportunities and freedom. He has always been a good example to our family.

She made Dad sound like a feminist. I was so used to seeing how far he had to go, I hadn't noticed how far he'd come. The girls in our large extended family did. They admired him and envied us. He was parenting two self-confident American daughters, and, on top of that, discreetly (he was the epitome of discreet) he was setting an example for his Third World brothers to follow. After college, my cousin went on to start her own business.

We were peaceful the morning of Dad's sentencing. Deepak didn't throw a tantrum about how disrespectful Ang and I were. (Truth be told, he'd mostly stopped expressing any emotion since he lost Akshay.) He shaved Dad's head bald—the way we do for births and deaths. I didn't leave my hair in the shower drain.

Mom didn't oversalt the omelets, which all of us ate, except Dad, who could not chew. The wounds in his gums were still open after the extraction of all twenty-one teeth in his mouth. His dentures didn't fit.

"Kids, *Jai baba*." Mom called us together. Wrinkle, too. She did a Hindu prayer and then turned to me. "Aarti, say some words now." My siblings had stopped praying. I still talked to God, though I don't remember what I said.

We piled into the car. Deepak drove and no one backseat drove.

"All rise."

Dad was already separated from us in court. We sat behind the partition, and he alone on the stand. His defense attorney recited his medical condition like a nurse.

"[Mr. Shahani] underwent an extraction of a number of teeth," he told the judge, asking if there was emergency dental care at Rikers. He asked if Dad could be handcuffed with his hands in front, not behind. "He has had some type of arm problem." His shoulder was frozen and his arms couldn't bend. Then the lawyer slipped in an unexpected request: house arrest. "[Mr. Shahani] is certainly not a risk of violence to the community." Locking Dad up would cost the state a lot of money. An ankle bracelet was much cheaper.

Was avoiding jail possible? I thought it was too late to even ask. My ears perked up.

The judge, my pen pal Joel Blumenfeld, seemed warm to the idea. He began to walk down memory lane. "When this case was sent to me," he recalled, "after spending countless hours listening to all the tapes that existed in this case—and going over them and reading all the voluminous grand jury material involved . . . I asked the attorney general to look into the possibility of whether or not [a] non-incarceratory sentence was possible in this case with a substantial number of hours of community service. That is probably a just result of this case."

A "non-incarceratory sentence"—for a case involving a drug cartel? The judge made this request *after* reviewing the evidence? This was news to me. I guess he said it back when I was mad at Dad and not paying attention to the case.

I searched Dad's face for any reaction at all. I saw none—just cheeks that sagged because there were no teeth to perk them up.

But Judge Blumenfeld grew more and more animated. He pushed our lawyer aside and started negotiating with the prosecutor directly: What if Mr. Shahani got house arrest? No. OK. What if he got a six-month split? The defendant would do six months inside and then probation—five years continuous surveillance. That's better for you, Mr. Prosecutor; you keep leverage. "Leverage," he repeated, a leash to pull even when the defendant is done with jail. Doesn't that sound nice?

The prosecutor looked disheveled—shirt tucked in sloppily, hair out of place. Did he work too hard or have a drinking problem? He didn't make eye contact with Dad—not a single time. ("You should always be able to look a man in the eye," Dad would say.)

The prosecutor locked eyes with the judge when he explained why he would not budge: "I feel it would be unfair to his co-defendant"—by whom, the prosecutor meant, Uncle Ratan, the man he'd accidentally sent to prison for too long. How perverse! The guardian of justice was saying, Because one brother suffered, it's only fair the other does, too.

My mind jumped to the months before they accepted the guilty pleas, when Uncle Ratan asked if he could serve Dad's time for him. If the prosecutor was so concerned with the now-deported co-defendant's feelings, why not call and ask him what *he* wanted?

The problem with this exchange was that we had no leverage. "I believe he should be out," the judge commented from the bench. But he knew Dad had already accepted the guilty plea. Neither the judge nor our lawyer could get it back—unless Dad wanted to withdraw that plea and mount a fresh defense. He didn't have it in him.

The judge had read the medical reports I'd mailed to him. He could see Dad with his own eyes. "It is not my intent for this to be a death sentence or a life sentence."

An electrical current went through me. He said it: death sentence, life sentence. He named exactly what every one of us in that courtroom feared—except Dad, who was blank. He showed no reaction to any part of this debate about him.

The judge searched the room, past the partition, and found me in the audience. "I have no doubt if [Mr. Shahani] is not getting the appropriate medical care," he said, "my pen-pal relationship with his daughter will continue."

I wanted to be grateful. I knew I should be grateful. I felt pure rage. When powerful words elicit emotion but not real, tangible change, they are empty words. What good would it do for me to write to this judge if my father had died in a jail cell?

"[Mr. Shahani] and his brother have paid an exorbitant price in the infinite scheme of things for a nonviolent crime committed by men in their late fifties or early sixties as their first offense," the judge said, entering his concluding remarks. "It is clear he has otherwise lived a very law-abiding life. Maybe the law of too much money got to him . . . God knows what motivated him and his brother to do this stupid thing. I don't believe this one act of stupidity should draw a life sentence."

The guards carted Dad off in handcuffs that were in front, not behind his back.

A passport from one country, an identity from another. I knew lots of people like me in that way. Only now, American law wouldn't tolerate the mismatch.

My language makes me American. I don't mean English. I mean the certainty with which I say things I do not know, the inclination to lead in groups, the visceral joy in crass humor. Also my bright-eyed assumption that the world is supposed to be fair. In so many other cultures, people are resolved to exploitation and their crummy lot in life. No shortage of Indian aunties and uncles have said, "You are one hundred percent Americanized," as if that were a deep insight.

On paper, however, I was a citizen of India—a country I had visited only one time, and in which my parents were not born. A passport from India was my postcolonial inheritance. A passport from America was my ticket to protection that, as I was learning through family crises, I needed.

The more I read about the new immigration laws in the United States, the more I realized how easily people like me could be tossed out. I wondered if America was making a big mistake. Vietnamese kids who came here the legal way—as refugees, not overstaying visas like my family—were getting sent back because they fell in with the bad kids at school and took drugs. One woman got deported for shoplifting. While I'd never shoplifted, I did think about pulling off that trick I heard about at Brearley: buy a dress from a high-end store like Saks Fifth Avenue—the type of store that, unlike Bang Bang, would take back clothes when the tags were not attached—wear the dress, and return it for a full refund when done. If I did it, could that get me deported? With a zealous prosecutor, the answer was yes.

I didn't want to lose the only home I knew. It was time to become an American on paper.

"Eighty-eight!" a voice called from the loudspeaker. I was sitting in a waiting room in a Newark federal building, and it was my turn for the citizenship test.

"Have a seat right here, honey." My examiner pointed to a chair across her desk. She looked like a mall rat: tight pastel top, big bangs, a wad of bubble gum in her mouth. (I didn't know people our age still chewed bubble gum.)

"So how da ya say your name?" she asked.

"R—AHR-thee." I attempted the correct pronunciation. "AHR-thee." I had been practicing lately.

"Oh, I never heard that one before. It's pretty." She flattered me. I liked her.

"It's a really common Indian name."

She blew large pink bubbles, which she sucked in and popped between the questions in my oral exam.

What is the capital of the United States?
Washington, D.C.
POP!
Who was president during the Great Depression and World War II?
Franklin Delano Roosevelt
POP!
What river divides the country, running from north to south?
The Mississippi
POP!

"You got 'em all right." She smiled. I smiled back. But then she furrowed her brow ever so slightly. There was a "small" problem.

"OK, so like, um, I don't wanna, um, tell you what to do. But, um, like, if you're gonna say you won't bear arms, I mean—I get it! But, like, you should just change your answer." POP.

This was fascinating. The citizenship application is a land mine for gotchas. One question is, have you ever committed a crime for which you were not arrested? That means if you smoked marijuana on a Caribbean beach, you're supposed to admit it. If you don't and the U.S. government found a picture on the internet, they could come after you with denaturalization.

Question 48 asks if you'll bear arms for the United States. I had checked the box for no—though I really meant maybe. The Vietnam War class I took at Brearley with Ms. Leonard left a strong impression on me: 58,220 Americans died. The Vietnamese body count—which was hotly debated—could be more than 3 million. I felt it was my duty to honor life when possible, as a citizen and as a Buddhist. (The temple Mom joined in Flushing became my spiritual home.) Because maybe wasn't an option, I erred on the side of caution.

The mall rat was looking out for me when she advised otherwise. "Listen. You're not, like, the first one to check no. I've, like, seen other people do it. But, um, like, it's just gonna slow everything down. So, like, if ya want my advice, let's just change that answer."

I was baffled at how casual this process was. She scratched out my original response and put a checkmark that was bigger than her bangs in the box marked yes, I will bear arms.

"OK. That OK with you?!"

I shrugged.

"Good." Her bangs approved. "Congratulations! You're, like, an American." Pop.

When I close my eyes and say "American dream," no one image jumps to mind. Not the house with the white picket fence or the Mega Millions jackpot. (Those were Dad's dreams.) There is a dream I recall having, though, after my swearing in.

My father, brother, sister, and I were fleeing from danger. A tsunami was on its way to wipe out our town. Our only hope was to get to the upper floors of the tallest building and pray. I wasn't scared. Just anxious to get there already.

We walked together—slower than I would like, but I didn't want to leave anyone else behind. The tall building looked like a sacred phallus, the kind that villagers adorn with garlands and sit around to worship.

Everyone began to walk upstairs except Dad and me. He needed a break. I called Mom on the cell phone, so we could say good-bye. She wasn't with us. I cracked jokes, pretending it was just another conversation. But all I could think about was her life without us. She was about to lose us. I would rather die than live without my family.

Dad wouldn't get on the phone. I gave him the same stern look he used to give when I was little. He took the phone and then scolded Mom, "Go away!" He was picking a fight so she'd miss him less. His voice was cold, but his eyes were wet.

139

We said nothing as we walked upstairs. The room where everyone was preparing to die looked like a Latina girl's *quinceañera*—white lace table-cloth, balloons, pink rose petals dotting the path to the dance floor where a DJ played 1990s hip hop. Each table seated a family—grouped by the region of the United States they were from or headed to (I couldn't tell which). When we got to our table, miraculously, Mom was seated right there. She'd found us.

As the tsunami wave raced toward the glass windows, it grew taller. I could see the foam on its white crest. I took my parents' hands in mine and asked if we could dance together one last time. If we had to go out—it was a dream, not a nightmare—we would go out dancing.

"Shake your bra," the security guard told me.

"Huh?"

"I said: Shake. Your. BRA."

"I'm not wearing a bra."

"Say what?"

"I mean, just a sports bra."

She reached under and pulled the elastic band. It stung when she let go. I hadn't had my bra snapped since junior high.

This was Rikers Island. I was heading to visit Dad. And she was making sure I wasn't hiding a razor blade between my breasts.

I was trying to hide my breasts. I came in wearing my big brother's sweatshirt and sweatpants, my hair in a ponytail. I remembered my first visit, just after Dad was arrested. When we got up to say good-bye, another inmate catcalled me: "Yo, Pocahontas. Can I touch your hair?" He didn't give a damn that my father was right there, humiliated. Dad knew he couldn't say anything back to defend his daughter's honor. We pretended not to hear it. I didn't want a repeat of that.

"Hi, Daddy!" I sounded upbeat.

"Hi, doll." He looked like he hadn't slept. "Mumah didn't come with you?"

"No. I asked her to stay home. I wanted to talk to you. Alone." I'd never needed alone time with him.

Mom had started vomiting pretty much every meal. I think she felt guilty: like, she's the one who insisted on staying in America, and now

Dad was paying the price for it. Also, she was terrified of going back to his family. If he left, she would leave, too. I told her we could figure out how to live in two countries at once. She said we kids have that option but she, as a wife, did not. I understood. As much as the two of them fought, she would never forgive herself for not staying by his side.

In the lead-up to jail, we were so busy yanking teeth, I didn't have time to level with Dad about the game plan after jail (assuming there was an after).

"Dad, *when* you leave here, it's almost certain immigration will take you." (I didn't say *if* he left Rikers.)

"*Hah*, doll."

"And I'd like to know, how long are you willing to fight?"

"Fight? What do you mean fight?"

"*Fight your case* . . . to stay in this country. If they take you and put you in detention—that's another jail. How long are you willing to stay inside and *fight?*"

He shrugged. He didn't have an answer. While I didn't come prepared with a proposal, one leapt out of my mouth.

"I think it should be six months. From the day you're done here, you should be prepared to stay in detention six more months. And either we get you out or we agree to leave." (I said "we," not "you," without giving it a second thought.)

Dad said nothing.

"OK. We agree?"

He shrugged. I took it as a yes—and promptly jumped to the next topic. Feeling I would lose him, I wanted every moment to matter, to be full. (I hadn't yet learned that quiet can be full.) I spit out a question from my stockpile. "When did you go to Beirut exactly?"

The details of his past life were a blur to me. The question sparked something in him.

"I went to Lebanon 1960—I should say 1959. I was in the navy, in India, for a year and a half. In Beirut, I wanted to have my future better."

He had told me before he'd gotten doctored papers to make him a couple years older. I didn't realize it was to serve in the Indian navy first.

"How would it be better in Beirut?" I asked.

"In India, the salary was limited. I did good in Beirut. I was working in a jewelry store—or you can say arts and crafts store. We also had the jewelry." He went to Lebanon as a migrant worker. He didn't know how long he'd stay. "My customers were satisfied with me. My bosses, too. You can say I was admired. I made a good name for myself."

Good name. There he went again.

When Dad first moved to Beirut, he made, in U.S. dollars, ten dollars a month. He got room and board. All his expenses were covered. So that's money he could send back, in its entirety, to his family. After a year, he got quite a raise, to twenty-five dollars a month. In India, it would take months to make that kind of money.

Back then, Beirut was the "Paris of the Middle East." Cafés, poets, designers from the European runways. Dad didn't dabble in any of that. He was still too green, converting each Lebanese pound into Indian rupees, stashing until it was time to wire. The beaches were free, though. He'd walk on the sand, watch men surfing and women in bikinis. Such boldness in their lack of modesty. He was among the few Indians in the city. The others were students from rich families, studying at the American University of Beirut. Dad did not try to strike up conversation with them. They came from the same place, and yet they didn't.

"So what were your bosses like?" I asked.

I wanted a better sense of how a migrant worker was treated. I recalled back when I complained about Mr. Sagor, Dad was not sympathetic—but he was empathetic. He'd lived through his share of jerk bosses. I figured it was because New York schooled him. In fact, it was Beirut.

"I was happy to have the job. But, you can say, the bosses were not nice."

"How do you mean? Like, what's an example?"

He hesitated for a moment and then lowered his voice. "My father, he passed when I was working. They would not let me go for his funeral."

"You mean in India? They wouldn't let you fly back?"

"My boss said, 'Go if you want. Don't come back.' How can I do that?" His hands were tied. They were always tied—then and now. Even for the most simple things—to mourn with his blood and carry his father's ashes—he was not allowed. I could picture Dad sitting in a dark shop after closing time, by himself, sobbing against a wall because there was no one to lean on.

I know parents want to give to kids. But in that moment, there was so much I wanted to give to him. Though maybe, soon enough, I'd find myself in his position—destined to not be there when my father died.

While Dad was in jail and I was not in Chicago at school (in order to stay nearby), my big brother became my buddy. Or, rather, my personal trainer. I started going with Deepak to his gym in New Jersey, using the membership he'd gotten his now estranged wife. It had been sitting there since she'd left. We sometimes went six nights a week.

"OK, keep your back straight. Stupid, I said straight," Deepak told me.

He was balancing a bar on my shoulders, teaching me to do a squat with weights.

"Inhale when you go down. Don't let your knees go past your ankles. Exhale on the way up for power . . . I said straight, stupid."

"I think it's too much weight."

"It's not," he hissed.

Deepak didn't drop the pet name "stupid." But it didn't bug me the way it used to. And I liked what was happening to my body—the flesh of my inner thighs tightening around the muscle, lines forming a tic-tac-toe grid on my belly, biceps that told the world: get out of my way.

The only downside to all this "definition"—Deepak kept repeating that was my goal—was that my breasts evaporated. The same bench-pressing that made my brother's chest bigger made mine smaller. My prized possession—which I'd wrapped and presented in Lycra for so many years—was gone.

Our workouts would go on for two, sometimes three hours. We'd run on treadmills alongside each other, Deepak reaching over to increase my pace. In the weight room, we'd grunt, letting out the anger we didn't want to talk about.

My big brother was turning me into the shape of a little brother. And one day, when a buddy of his from Queens joined us at the gym, Deepak showed off. He had me lie on a bench—back flat, abs engaged, feet planted firmly on the ground—and do ten reps with ninety-five pounds of weight. My forearms twitched, but a big grunt got me through.

Stevie from Queens was next.

"Man, you wanna put some more weight on?" he asked, a little in-sulted at the insinuation that he and I were equally strong.

"Nah—it's fine like it is." Deepak smirked.

Stevie was too polite to insist. He began his reps. Only, he trembled at the midpoint. His arms couldn't make it to ten. Deepak had to grab the bar before it crashed into Stevie's prominent Adam's apple.

Deepak burst out laughing. "Yo, my little sister can bench more than you!"

"Shut up, man. Shut up." Stevie kept his voice low. "It ain't like that."

One evening Deepak came to give me moral support for another kind of heavy lift. I had to give a speech to a roomful of lawyers at the New York City Bar Association.

It sounds out of left field. It happened because of our five-foot TV. I noticed a program—on one of the Indian channels—with an immigration attorney. He was answering callers' questions, mostly about H1B visas and how to get green cards—not about what to do when you already have a green card and are about to lose it. We were part of a new trend.

The lawyer's email address flashed on the screen. I wrote him with a summary of Dad's criminal history, immigration status, and "equities"—more court jargon for things like having a family or doing volunteer work. He responded right away—not with legal advice, with an invitation to speak at an event.

Heavy wooden doors guarded the entrance to the New York City Bar Association. Deepak and I walked in, following a sea of suits past the marble columns, up the marble staircase, into a meeting hall that was standing room only.

"Crap, there's a whole lotta people here." I thought it would be much smaller, like a Tenants' Association meeting. Who knew so many people were interested in the niche issue of deportation for people with criminal records?

Deepak stayed in the back. I wormed my way up to the front and spotted the lawyer from TV.

"Hi, I'm AHR-thee," I introduced myself. The muscles in my mouth had gotten a handle on my name.

"So glad you could make it," he said with crisp enunciation. I assumed he played the violin in his spare time. "Please have a seat in the chairs we reserved. You'll come up to speak after the other remarks."

There was a panel, and on it were a U.S. congressman and the immigration agency's general counsel. Suddenly, the stakes were high. I'd come here thinking I'd find help for Dad. Now, I was learning, I would speak publicly about my father, for the first time, in front of the country's top deportation prosecutor. I wasn't sure if what I'd say could become part of a record that got Dad in trouble. It was too late to back out.

My research till now had focused on the letter of the law. I'd learned that Democrat Bill Clinton had signed two laws in 1996 that, together, created the hellhole my family was in. With the stroke of his pen, he turned deportation and detention into mandatory minimums. Judges couldn't judge. Families like mine would get tossed out in a rubber-stamp hearing. I felt betrayed by Clinton because, when he was campaigning to be president, my whole family cheered him on—especially after he went on *The Arsenio Hall Show* and played his saxophone.

In this room, I would begin to learn the politics behind the policies. Of all people, it was the immigration prosecutor who took the words right out of my mouth. He said, "It seems clear that the 1996 laws, in many ways, went too far and have created a number of situations in which there are apparent excesses, where enforcing them in the way that they are written would bring about results that seem to be unjust."

If this were church, I'd have shouted, "Amen!" He—not just the advocates—agreed that politicians went too far.

The congressman agreed, too—and pounced on the audience. "It's a lousy law, and the problem that we have confronted, frankly, is that we've had too much lawyering and not enough politics in trying to get rid of it," he said. "It is very easy to talk about how stupid this law is (because it is a really stupid law) and writing articles about how stupid a stupid law is [is] satisfying, but it does not advance the political cause."

Amen! I thought again. Let's get this army of lawyer suits marching from Times Square to the immigrant jail at 201 Varick.

But the talking went on. The congressman, a Democrat, was angry at how the law passed. It didn't go through any debate on the floor. The Republicans broke the rules, he said, by tacking the deportation laws onto a bigger bill. President Clinton was so committed to passing the bigger bill, to fund the government, he wouldn't veto it.

The congressman scolded the immigration prosecutor for enforcing the laws. "No law-enforcement body in the history of the world has ever enforced every law against everybody. But in the early stages," he charged, "[your agency] was terrified and they did go and scoop up some people whom no rational person would have scooped up because they were afraid of Congress yelling at them."

In other words, he was saying, the prosecutors were cowards.

When it was my turn to speak, I wasn't scared. I felt something more like relief—like I could finally get something off my chest, could say to these strangers things I couldn't talk about at home because doing so hurt.

"When we first came to this country, Dad and Mom skipped meals." I started with this fact. I remembered hiding it at Brearley. "My brother, who is sitting right over there, was then twelve years old, and he contributed to the family income by delivering newspapers every morning before school." Deepak and I never talked about how it was for him to be our second father. He, Ang, and I didn't admit to one another we'd noticed Dad's mind going. "Every so often, Dad will say something unintelligible or forget something like our zip code. We cannot help but wonder whether these slips are signs of something more severe than stress."

I was among the "regular immigrants" invited to speak. Because of the format—Important People first, we second—I came to understand my role in the room was to be the sob story, the tragic figure that emotes on humanity's behalf. That grated at me. I knew I had more to share than that. So I departed from the script and lectured the Important People.

During their talks, they seemed preoccupied with how the 1996 laws were being applied to people whose crimes happened before that date. "Retroactivity" was the big shocker. I begged to differ. "Nineteen ninety-six is not a magical date," I said. My dad pleaded guilty after the laws passed. The fact that he would face automatic exile was unjust, no matter the year of the conviction.

"A day in court is not a pardon for criminals." I concluded with a lesson I'd learned the first and only time I'd visited the Supreme Court. "It is a basic right. I hope that our nation of immigrants will one day restore this right for families."

My brother clapped for me. Had Mom been there, she would have shouted "Amen." Many people said thanks. Though—this was a life lesson in how political theater works—the vast majority did not go any further.

Only one lawyer in the roomful of lawyers asked me how I was doing. Nancy Morawetz tapped my shoulder and said, "I wanted to say hi before you left. Your dad is going to need a really good lawyer. I might be able to help with that." She handed me her business card.

When Ang and I were little, we didn't have cable, so we couldn't watch music videos. But we did have a radio. We played Z100 and Hot 97, and turned 401 into our stage. "Girls Just Wanna Have Fun" was one of our favorite songs. And even with Dad in jail, it seemed to remain Ang's theme song.

"Let's go together," my big sister told me one night.

I frowned. It was more efficient to rotate visits. Going one at a time, we could go more times and spread out the work of keeping Dad company. Doubling up was not a smart allocation of limited resources.

"It'll be more fun together," she insisted.

Fun! This wasn't meant to be fun. We had a duty, pure and simple. But I didn't fight her on it. Maybe going together was logical, because Dad usually had nothing to say. Our banter with each other could make him laugh, providing much-needed entertainment. I conceded.

We set off together on a Sunday morning. Ang is not a morning person. I insisted we leave first thing, to get to Rikers Island before anyone else. As the day drags on, the wait lines get longer.

"I think I want to get my nose pierced," Ang said on the train.

"For real?"

My sister had the perfect nose. Mine was *ethnic*, too wide for my narrow face, downward sloping like a hawk's beak. When I talked, the tip of my nose took on a life of its own—moving up and down as if it too were having its own conversation. Ang had the nose of a porcelain doll—narrow nostrils, a tip that stood still.

"But your nose is your prized possession," I told her. "It could fall off if you get an infection." I was joking. She didn't laugh. I felt bad. "No, no. I mean, it would look great. A nose ring would bring more attention to your perfect nose."

"Yeah, that's what I was thinking." She reengaged.

"Cool. So, when you wanna do it?"

"When?! I mean, I'd have to research—"

"You don't need to research," I said. "There are a million shops in the West Village. We can go today after Dad."

"Today?"

"Yeah. Unless . . ."

"No," Ang said. "Let's do it. I'm ready."

When we exited the subway at Queensboro Plaza, it was eerily quiet. The Chinese-Mexican fast-food restaurant was closed. So was the donut stand. We were the only passengers on the Q100 bus.

"Where is everyone?" I wondered.

"I guess sleeping in," Ang said. "They don't love their families the way we do." She was mocking—saying out loud what she knew her sanctimonious kid sister was thinking.

As we crossed the waters to enter the island, the sun was still rising—specks of gold on the gray sludge. I wondered what it was like for Dad to be in a place without windows, where he could not see the sun.

The visitor compound was empty.

"Attention, everyone," the corrections officer shouted, as if the line extended for miles. "No cell phones, no pagers." He rattled off the list of contraband. "We 'bout to start letting you in at seven A.M."

"Huh? It's not seven yet?" one of us asked.

"Nah, daylight savings. Check your watch."

Mystery solved. Again, this was before the smartphone era. People had to remember to twist a dial or press a button to turn time back.

The officer waved his wand over Ang, and it beeped. "What you got in there?" he asked her.

"Nothing." She was certain.

"This don't go off for nothing. I'm gonna ask you one more time: What. You. GOT?"

His voice boomed. He was dropping an atomic bomb on a kitten. *Pathetic*, I thought. *The power's gotten to his head*. Ang unzipped her coat and felt inside. Turns out, she had Deepak's tweezers in her pocket. He taught us each how to pluck our unibrow.

"That's contraband," the guard said. "Goes in the box." He pointed to an iron receptacle that looked like a trash bin. Visitors could toss items—drugs, guns, needles—no questions asked.

Angelly pleaded. "Officer. Please. These are really good tweezers. They're made in France. I really need them."

"Look at her eyebrows," I chimed in. "You can see she needs them."

He wasn't amused. "Y'all can toss them right here. Or you can get on that bus and go back to where you came from." *Did he mean Queensboro Plaza or Casablanca or Karachi?*

Ang and I stepped aside to huddle. We wanted to see Dad. We didn't want to lose the tweezers.

Ang had a napkin on her. "Oh! What if I wrap them up and hide them in the bushes?"

"Worth a try," I said.

She tiptoed behind an evergreen shrub, losing her balance (she wasn't one for nature or gravity), then grabbing onto a branch, which she broke. Mission accomplished.

"We're ready to go in," she came back and triumphantly told the officer.

He rolled his eyes and waved the wand one last time.

The checkpoints that can take four hours to get through were today a joyful sprint—and also I wasn't doing it alone.

"Dad, it was so easy to get here!" I delivered our productivity report.

"Hah." He nodded, not sharing my enthusiasm.

Ang and I gave anecdotes about our weeks and asked Dad for any detail at all about his time inside.

"One Puerto Rican came to me"—he mimicked the young man in his dorm—*"Papi, why you here, papi? Lemme get a cigarette from you, papi."* Dad didn't say no. He handed one over.

"You're giving out cigarettes?" Ang and I were surprised.

"Hah. One, two. I feel the pity for them. So many young boys here. Your ages—no one visiting them or giving them the money."

To get Marlboros, you had to buy them in the jail for five times the regular market price. Dad was one of the lucky few with family and cash.

I told him the big news. "Guess what! Ang is gonna pierce her nose!"

"Hah?" Dad turned and smiled at her.

"Yeah," she said tentatively. "What do you think?"

149

"It'll be very nice," he said.

What I took to be an act of rebellion by my sister, Dad took to be a return to the roots. Indian women pierce their noses. His elder daughter who could easily pronounce her own name (UHN-jah-lee) chose to butcher it ("it's ANN-jolly, like Angelina Jolie"). Now she was embracing tradition, being a good Indian instead of a failed Indian.

"What kind of ring will you put?" Dad asked.

"Just a small stud. Nothing too big. I don't want it to overshadow my nose."

"*Hah.*" Dad approved.

When the visit was over, the French tweezers were in the bush where Ang left them—a sign that luck was on her side. We rode the Q100 bus back to the subway station and took the Manhattan-bound E train to West 4th Street.

The moment of truth had arrived. I led Ang to a piercing and tattoo parlor a few doors down from a chess shop whose manager I had a crush on.

"They need to sterilize," Ang said as we walked in. "Do they sterilize their needles?"

"This isn't the corner butcher." I laughed. I thought she was being neurotic. "I'm sure they sterilize."

When it was her turn, Ang slipped into the chair and asked for my hand. (It was so unlike her. She was anti-affection with me.) She squeezed tight and let out a little yelp. The technician put the tiniest of cubic zirconia studs in the hole.

Ang's walk on the wild side—toward tradition or rebellion (who knows)—was short-lived. For a few days, she stared at the new puncture incessantly, fiddled with it, and wiped it with rubbing alcohol too often. The hole didn't heal as fast as she wanted—which is to say, overnight. She removed the stud in a panic.

"You're such a scaredy-cat." I laughed at her.

"Aarti, we don't all need to live on an adrenaline rush."

I wanted a fight we could win. That's why I encouraged my brother to lure his estranged wife into a family reunion, this time in London.

A year had passed since Anisha took Akshay. "International parental kidnapping"—as it's known in legal parlance (I was studying that area of

150

law, too)—is a federal felony, punishable by up to three years in prison, if she were ever convicted. Her parents, who aided and abetted, could be charged, too.

Our New Jersey lawyer said that he tended to see the man taking the child back to his home country—often India—where the courts favor fathers over mothers. He hadn't seen as many moms do it, he told us, because the United States is more supportive of mothers' rights relative to other legal systems.

He connected us to a barrister in London. Like America and unlike India, the United Kingdom signed the Hague Convention on child abduction. If Deepak could get Anisha on U.K. soil, then an international apparatus could go to work for us. A legal team, provided free of charge, would coordinate with INTERPOL (the international criminal police force) and U.K. courts to bring Akshay back to America, as the New Jersey court had already ordered.

This approach was a distinct possibility because—I was floored by this fact—Anisha was eager to get back together with Deepak.

She and my brother had been exchanging emails and had a few phone calls. In one of them, on September 20, 2000, she said eleven minutes and four seconds into the conversation that she'd taken "rash steps." (Deepak recorded each call without telling her.) At twenty-one minutes and thirty-four seconds, she said, without offering an apology, "Do you want me and Akshay to be in your life?" (According to her, they could only ever be a package deal.)

In two other calls, she told Deepak, "I couldn't ask God for a better husband" and "You were wonderful . . . I had nothing to complain about you." (So he was not an abuser after all.) In yet another, she admitted she'd alleged torture because she didn't know what else to do when she got the court order. While in writing she'd claimed she hadn't received any order, on the phone she copped to ignoring it.

Deepak and Anisha had a remarkable rift in opinion. She saw her departure as a blip on the map of their life together and told Deepak to focus on the future, not the past. He felt their trust was irrevocably broken, but he didn't file for divorce because he knew her fantasy of mending their marriage was the only leverage he had to get his son back.

And so it went on. Anisha asked repeatedly that Deepak meet her in

India to talk. Deepak played it cool, making it sound like he was in no rush. But then, once he sensed she was no longer overconfident, perhaps more pliable, he suggested a neutral location.

"I'm going to London on business." He told Anisha a white lie. "I can send you and Akshay tickets to join me. We can keep talking in person."

She agreed.

Ang and I decided to go with Deepak. I was the legal point person, and she the moral support. We knew this trip would be brutal. Another time on the phone, Anisha put Akshay on. He was learning to speak and said "Papa." Deepak started weeping. His son knew this word but had not felt its meaning.

When we landed in London, we made our way to Russell Square—a neighborhood where cabdrivers went on break and cheap motels dotted the streets. The exchange rate between the British pound and the dollar was not great, so everything cost us more. To stay on budget, we shared a room that smelled like smoke and sweat. (This was before the days of Airbnb.)

Our free-of-charge barrister instructed us to rent a place for Anisha, too, in a different motel. It was Deepak's responsibility to fund her house arrest. That was our mission: to get her placed under house arrest. It was step one in the international procedure.

It was midday when Anisha walked into the narrow hallway of her motel, a toddler in her arms. We were waiting for her. I had worried she'd bring someone else's kid, just in case. But the second I saw the baby, there was no mistaking him: big, black melancholic eyes; thick, long lashes that curled to touch his brow. *My brother's eyes*, I thought to myself. I instantly felt close to him.

Deepak didn't stretch out his arms for his child. He didn't smile or say a word. He just stood there, frozen, as if his heart knew there was no point coming out.

"Why are you just standing there, silly?" Anisha said. Her tone was light, whimsical. She didn't expect to see Ang and me in the hallway. But she didn't fixate on us. "This is your son, Deepak. Come say hello." She said it as if all Deepak lacked was basic training. She—with her mother's touch—could help.

As Deepak stepped closer, the baby pulled into his mom. "He thinks I'm a stranger," Deepak said.

Omar, the Puerto Rican motel manager watching this scene unfold, was trying to make out what was happening. It was hard to put the moment in a box.

That's when INTERPOL arrived. (Our barrister coordinated with them.) Men in uniform filed into the narrow hallway. *Thank God they're here,* I thought. *Let's get on with it, already.*

Omar the manager got nervous. "Is anyone here dealing drugs? No drug dealers allowed in here," he said. (I found that hard to believe.)

It took a few seconds for Anisha to get what was happening. Her husband brought her to a cheap motel where she did not belong, where officers had come in search of a criminal. When they headed to her instead, the pieces started to come together.

"Anisha Shahani, we are here to serve you under orders of Her Majesty the queen . . . You must turn over your passport . . . You have the right to an attorney, which will be provided if you request one . . ."

She would not go to jail, they explained. She would not be separated from her child. She and Akshay would stay here, at Deepak's expense. Or she could move to other accommodations, at her own expense.

Anisha flew into a rage. "Deepak, how dare you do this to me? How dare you? I am the mother of your child!"

I yanked my brother's arm. He didn't need to hear this. None of us did. She was still screaming as we left the motel and the door shut behind us.

That night, we ate quietly and took in the weight of a lose-lose situation. If we won the case, Anisha and the baby would be extradited to the United States. There, again in all likelihood, a court would not grant Deepak full custody; he would get joint custody. Deepak would not stay married, as Anisha assumed. They'd be a miserable, divorced couple, spending their lives fighting over how to raise their son, a problem further complicated by the international twist.

"I don't know if I can go through with it," Deepak said.

"Now is not the time to get emotional," I snapped at him. "Hold it together." I didn't want to hear it. *Man up.*

Anisha's defense was a continuation of the same sob story that she'd recanted in her calls with my brother. Only now, the plot thickened: we were drug traffickers. Turns out that in addition to stealing money and jewels, she'd taken a complete copy of Dad's criminal case file, mangled the facts, and painted a bleak picture of an innocent young bride fallen into a narco ring. She claimed we had a cousin arrested in our house for drug possession. She said she was not allowed to visit a doctor and was under constant supervision. Also, Deepak allegedly threw her against a wall and beat her.

This time, she made no mention of the abusive, wicked sisters-in-law (who were living under the same roof, working during summer break). Also omitted was any explanation of how my family could plunge her into "isolation" while her family stayed with us for four months.

The single word in her novella that jumped out at me most was "teacher." She told the court she was a teacher. She provided no proof of this career. We had a copy of her Social Security statement, showing she earned $548 total at the preschool—two weeks of work during her nearly two-year stay in America. It intrigued me that she attempted to portray herself as a hardworking professional.

Anisha was nowhere close to committing the perfect crime. She left a copious paper trail.

The letters she and her mom wrote us from India—about her dad Ashok's business gone kaput and his alcohol-induced temper flaring—demonstrated that life in India was not idyllic, as she'd suggested.

It was also evident she was neither denied medical care nor restricted in activities. Her doctor appointments and Lamaze classes (which Deepak attended with her) were easy to verify. She failed to wipe the hard drive on the home computer. Deepak submitted a pile of emails she'd sent to friends back home, gloating: her husband took her to the gym, restaurants, and nightclubs; they'd go on his business trips together (she'd get a spa treatment or shop while he worked); she was excited to pass her driver's test and was taking the car out on her own. The sheer volume of the emails indicated she was not locked up in a tower. She was free, with too much time on her hands.

We put these details in our Hague filing. We mentioned Mom was a home health aide, out of the house from 7:30 A.M. to 6 P.M. for a few of the months in question. We explained Dad's criminal case and included the transcript from the day of his sentencing, when the judge pleaded on our behalf. And, Deepak pointed out, he had two educated, modern sisters, who would not tolerate domestic violence.

"Wrinkle should sue her ass," Ang or I said.

Of all the allegations Anisha made, her continued slander of our dog bothered us most. Or, it was the easiest to laugh at. Anisha insisted that Wrinkle clawed her pregnant belly and repeatedly attacked her at our beckoning.

Our legal team marveled at the story. Helen, the earnest one, asked my brother if he was doing OK. Character assassination can be hard to take.

The other, who went by the nickname Dizzy, was gasping for air. The defense was so ludicrous, she was certain we'd win. She'd won much harder fights. "I'm Kashmiri and Afghani"—she gave a devilish smile—"I was born with warrior blood." It was all but certain that the court would rule in Deepak's favor.

Our last night in London, Angelly, Deepak, and I went to a traditional pub—not for the cuisine. We (and it seemed all of London) preferred Indian food, which is why our people had so many restaurants in that city. But we wanted to eavesdrop on Old London—make out what the bartenders were saying in their heavily accented English, which sounded like another language to us.

When we settled our bill and got ready to walk back to the motel, Angelly told us to go ahead without her.

"I need to make a quick stop," she said. "I'll meet you there."

"Where are you going?" Deepak asked, sounding bossy again.

"Nowhere. Just—I'll be there soon."

I figured she needed tampons. My brother and I walked on.

An hour later, Ang still wasn't back. "Where the hell is she?" we wondered aloud. And then the thought flashed like a lightning bolt: *Oh no. Anisha got her.* In our high-stakes, transnational mission, we let down our guard for a split second, and the opposition sent a thug to attack. There were plenty of Indians in London. There must be Indian thugs for hire.

Deepak and I hit the streets in search of our sister, retracing our

155

steps—from the pub to the grocery store to the restaurant strip to the unlit streets where her brutalized body could be lying.

Maybe Anisha didn't even need to hire an Indian. Maybe she got the motel keeper to lure Ang into a room. Maybe he was raping her.

"Let's go to Anisha's motel," one of us said.

It was not an establishment with twenty-four-hour service. The front door was locked, and no one opened when we knocked, over and over again. Ang could be captive in there. Deepak banged louder. I kicked the door. When still no one answered, he took out his credit card, jammed it between the frame and the door, just above where the bolt inside would be, and then he rammed the card down hard and fast to pop the bolt in. The door opened.

"I learned that in Flushing," he said.

"Show me how." I wanted to learn.

"Later, stupid."

The entryway was dark. The lights were off. Deepak found the switch and flipped them on. As we approached the staircase, the motel keeper reappeared.

"WHAT are you doing here?" he said accusingly, his eyes red, no sign of blood on his hands.

"Have you seen our sister?" one of us asked.

"No, why would I see her? I've had enough of your family." He wasn't happy about the INTERPOL visit. And he seemed too confident in his own anger to be hiding something. Deepak and I slunk away.

Back at our motel room, Angelly was laid out, and very drunk. "Hey guys," she giggled, "I was hanging out with the foreign exchange students at the pub."

Turns out, she was dying to ditch us. We were massive downers. The other tables at the pub were more fun. We tore into her for being so careless.

"We were worried sick. We broke into Anisha's motel to find you," we each recounted.

Instead of apologize, Ang got indignant: "Oh, you figured poor, sweet, slow Ang. If anyone's gonna be hit, it would be her. She's the weakest link."

When we three Shahani musketeers or stooges left London, it was with the promise of an extradition (the courts would take a while, but Anisha would be compelled to bring back the baby) and the discovery that Ang, the middle child, would no longer put up with being underestimated.

I had had enough sibling time. Back in New York, I made a solo trip to visit Dad.

It took three hours to get to the last checkpoint—the open-air gym with the tiny tables. There was one woman standing in line in front of me, and she had enormous breasts. I could see a third of them heaving from her V-neck.

"Oh my goodness, I hope I recognize him," she turned back and told me.

"Huh?" I didn't understand.

"My girlfriend set me up. I can't tell which one he is."

"You haven't met before?"

"Nah, but he's gonna be out soon."

This woman was at Rikers Island on a first date. A blind first date. I wanted to shake her. *Girl, I love a captive audience too, but this is taking it too far. Wait till he's out!*

"Good luck" were the words I managed to mouth. A corrections officer pointed to the tiny table where she'd meet her man (no guesswork required) and then pointed me to Dad.

"You look tired, my doll," he said as we sat down.

"No, I'm good."

"Are you eating enough?"

"Yeah, Dad. I'm eating plenty."

That question got on my nerves. Mom—who was still vomiting multiple times a day—would ask me it too. And, sensing my irritation, she'd latch on—persisting either as martyr mom (*Aarti, I ask because I'm your mother!*) or as infomercial mom (*I have homeopathic pills; try them*). Dad had the sense to back off.

I gave him the London debrief, ending with how Ang went missing. He laughed a deep laugh. That daughter of his could brighten any day. She was so different from him and me that way, a constant reminder of how good it could be if you just let loose sometimes.

A few tables over, an inmate sprung from his steel chair and threw it against the wall. Guards raced over and pinned his face and shoulders down. I thought they were about to call off visitation for everyone. They didn't. They just dragged him away.

"You're not where you thought you'd be, huh?" I said to Dad.

He shook his head. *No, not at all,* he said without saying.

The silence lingered for a moment. Conversation didn't come naturally. Inside jail, outside—it always took effort with us.

"How'd you learn Arabic?" I decided to try the interview approach. "Did you have books, tapes?"

"No, I learned by attending the customers," he said. "Each day, I listened for the important words. Slowly, slowly, I picked up very good Arabic."

"Important words like what?"

"*Kayf halikum . . . barak allah fik . . . arak lahiqaan . . . ana uhebuk habibti . . .* How are you? God bless you. See you . . . You are my love."

That last one stood out. "Who taught you *that*?" I asked. There's no way Dad's boss taught it to him.

"It's a funny thing. You make me go back so many years." He smiled and hesitated for a moment. "It was an Armenian girl. She asked me for a date. She said in Arabic as well as in Armenian, "*Ana uhibbuka.* I love you."

"Did you say it back to her?"

"I was nervous. I was shocked. I never had a girlfriend. I never went out with anybody. It was strange for me to hear someone say that. But we did go to see a movie. It was *In the Heat of the Night.*"

That was the Sidney Poitier film where an African American detective goes to the Deep South and gets wrongfully arrested for the murder of a white businessman. Dad was a twenty-five-year-old migrant worker out with an Armenian flight attendant, watching a movie about American race relations. My first date was *Boyz n the Hood*. I was in seventh grade, out with a Chinese American boy who won my heart because he could name every highway that crossed through Queens. Neither Dad nor I were allowed to date. I didn't mention these parallels.

He continued. "In the theater, I came to know she spoke English too. I didn't know that before. We came out of the theater, we spoke English, French, Arabic. It was nice."

I began to imagine what she looked like in the dark, if Dad turned to see her profile or just stared straight ahead the whole time, if their fingers or forearms brushed as they strolled the beach after the movie, if they listened to the waves lap, or if she found conversation with him more easily than I did.

They met when she came to the tourist trap where he worked. She bought leather sandals and brass vases, little trinkets for family and friends. She came back, again and again. Then one day she asked him if he had time to go for coffee.

"At that time I didn't have permission. The bosses were strict. On some Sundays, I was allowed to leave. So we went for coffee a few times. But the cinema was just once."

"Why not more?" I asked him. "You love movies."

"Because I couldn't afford it. She was spending money all the time—I didn't like that. I had limited pocket expenses. I had to think of my family first. When I went back to India, she wrote me a letter. She said, 'I'm waiting for you' and she sent me a photo. She told me, 'Show to your family.'"

"Did you?" I asked.

"Yes, I showed them. My mother, brothers, sisters. They said, 'Who's that girl? Are you taking up the foreign way—having a girlfriend?'" Dad shrugged. "I didn't much bother about it—because I knew I wouldn't be able to and also take care of my family."

"I see," I began to paraphrase. "Because you knew if you were going to pursue a relationship, you couldn't send as much money back home. So you either could have a girlfriend or be a good son?"

"Yes, that's true."

I felt sorry for young Dad and this Armenian romantic who thought love could transcend distance.

Dad hadn't answered my question, which I repeated. "OK, so then did you ever tell her 'I love you' back?"

"No! I didn't say anything." He laughed at himself. "I was nervous and just smiling and putting my head down like a girl. I'm sorry to say. But a fact is a fact."

"Time's up," a guard called out to us. Time never flies with Dad. This was a first.

159

As I boarded the white bus that went back to the visitors' center, the woman who'd had her blind date slipped onto the bench beside me.

"How'd it go?" I felt obligated to ask her.

"Really well!" She smiled ear to ear. "We're gonna see each other again."

"That's great." I feigned approval.

Yes, I was judging her. Though the uncanny resemblance was not lost on me. She was at Rikers, getting to know a stranger. So was I.

We were about to meet the lawyer who might fight Dad's deportation, and I gave Mom crystal clear instructions. "Whatever happens, leave the talking to me."

"Did I say anything?" she snapped back.

"I don't mean here in the elevator. I mean when we're in his office."

"I won't talk—not even one word!" she said.

I had a flashback to Brearley—my admissions interview, when I was twelve years old. I wanted to go alone, but the school required a guardian. Mom came, and I worried she sabotaged it. The interviewer asked me about where I grew up. I was about to describe all the religions that coexist peacefully in Flushing. Mom jumped in and dominated the conversation with details about the slumlord and her work to clean up the building. I felt robbed of my time to shine and mortified that Mom would tell these fancy people how we really lived.

I did not want a repeat of that moment in a meeting that would cost $250 an hour—money out of my pocket. A legal consultation is billed in fifteen-minute increments. I wanted to talk as fast as possible and make sure every minute—which cost $4.17—was well used.

"We're here for Mr. Moseley," I told the receptionist on the twenty-sixth floor. Mom stayed mute.

Thomas Moseley used to be a federal prosecutor—the man who would have tried to nail us. But he switched sides and started a private practice in Newark. He came highly recommended by the one lawyer at the Bar Association who asked me if I needed help. She was a law professor at New York University. I wanted her to take the case. I trusted her. But she didn't offer that, and I felt too self-conscious to ask. She told me this man was one of the sharpest legal minds on the East Coast. This time, I had a feeling she was not an adult passing the buck but someone looking out for my best interests.

Moseley's law firm looked legit. A woman walked us to the conference room overlooking downtown Newark. Mom and I sat in swivel chairs that smelled like real leather.

"Such a pleasure to meet you." Moseley walked in with a fat book under his arm. It could be a weapon—and it was, in the form of case law. Thousands of decisions that had passed through the courts, recapped in tiny font; fact patterns, judgments about other people's lives that could help or hurt us.

"How are you holding up, Mrs. Shahani?" he asked Mom. His voice was gentle. *Is he kind? Or hustling?* We hadn't hired him yet. So it could have been his sales-pitch voice.

Mom nodded and dropped her eyes to the floor. He and I both paused   an awkward moment of silence—waiting for a word to leave her mouth. None did.

"It's been really hard." I filled the void. "I brought the documents you requested, Mr. Moseley."

Laid out like brochures at a job fair were Dad's green card, indictment, plea agreement, and the sentencing minutes from the day he went to jail. This was the hard skeleton of our story, no support letters or family photos or artifacts that made the flesh and blood of our life in this country.

"Oh, very good." Moseley had a formality to him. "Let me have a look."

Moseley had polio as a child, which left him with a hunchback. It was the first thing I noticed when he walked in—the contour of his shoulders forming a diagonal, one sharply above the other. *Don't look, Aarti.* I mostly did not look. Mom, however, could not stop staring. I wanted to kick her under the table.

"This is clearly not an aggravated felony," Moseley said.

"Huh?" That's the last sentence I'd expected out of his mouth.

Every lawyer I'd consulted on the case said Dad's conviction would fall into that sprawling, catchall category that leads to automatic deportation. It was a financial crime involving more than ten thousand dollars. Even if Dad never spent a day in jail, lawyers told me, it would still be an aggravated felony.

"It's really just a simple matter of law," Moseley explained. He slid a few stapled sheets of paper across the conference table toward me. It was another case decision—one not in the fat book. "The Board of Immigration Appeals ruled that for a money-laundering conviction to qualify as an aggravated felony, it must have the interstate commerce element of the federal statute."

A month earlier, that sentence would have sounded like gibberish to me. But I'd read so much law and talked with so many lawyers, I immediately got the gist of the argument.

Dad was convicted in New York State. Never—not in the indictment or on the day he pleaded—never did the prosecution say or establish that money was laundered across state lines. It may have gone between Queens and Manhattan, but not down to Miami or Cali.

Deportation is a federal process based on the federal definitions of crimes. The federal definition of money laundering says that the dirty money has to pass state lines.

In that discrepancy—the interstate element, which was in the federal law but not the state law—Dad had a nearly airtight defense.

"It's called the categorical approach," Moseley continued.

My heart leapt. How could such an obvious argument have escaped so many others I'd consulted? Then I noticed the date on the stapled pages: December 1, 2000. The case and court decision had just happened.

It hit me how clever this lawyer was—not solely in finding the precedent, a needle that only recently fell in the haystack. He was clever in the voice he used to talk about it. I would have been a breathless mess: *OMG, you won't believe what just happened!* He was subdued, certain. *Of course Mr. Shahani is not an aggravated felon, like we knew all along.* Moseley was the guy you wanted on your poker team.

And he was the first lawyer to present me with an argument based purely on legal technicalities. Plenty of others told me we could make an ethical case for justice. *Your dad's deportation would cause exceptional hardship to four American citizens.* I already knew that wouldn't work. Justice is morally bankrupt, the legal practice a hunt for loopholes or ambiguities that can be exploited.

We agreed on a retainer plan to pay Moseley. The day before Dad was

scheduled to leave Rikers Island—and go into immigration custody—
this immigration lawyer would go into federal court in Brooklyn and say,
"Hey, Judge: The feds don't know how to read the law. This man isn't
even deportable. Let him out."

I glanced at my watch. The meeting lasted twenty-five minutes—
which rounds to half an hour. It felt like money well spent. Mom and I
got up to leave.

"I hope you're holding up OK, Mrs. Shahani," Moseley said on our
way out.

Mom unmuted herself to say, "Thank you. Please help us."

"I'll do everything I can."

At the elevator bank, when we were out of earshot, Mom asked what
happened in there. "You both were talking too fast."

I put my arm around her and squeezed. "A miracle. A total miracle."
By which I meant, an esoteric technical argument.

I didn't let myself get excited. In high-stakes situations, it's best to pro-
ceed with mechanical precision, not feelings. Ang said I was becoming an
apathetic person. It was a rare instance when my big sister got it totally
wrong. The emotions were just too strong; I needed to lock them up.

"What percentage guarantee did the attorney give?" Dad asked me.

"It doesn't work that way," I tried to explain.

"How can it not work that way?" he pressed. "You should have made
him tell you."

Dad could not comprehend a service that you pay for without a clearly
stated return on investment. When a customer paid him for two thousand Casio watches, that's exactly what they got. But in law, the retainer
was an act of faith, alms to God.

Just as with Uncle Ratan, it was months into Dad's sentence, and
no one from the immigration agency called to let us know they were
taking him. This time, we knew to look for the signs. I kept checking his
status on a city website that locates where an inmate is. One day "hold"
appeared by Dad's name. It made him sound like a library book, and
it meant immigration hold. It's the only place the government spelled
out its intention to deport him. Dad was moved from a cell block with

military veterans who'd been locked up for marijuana over to "general population"—the place where beatings (by inmates and guards) are part and parcel.

As we anticipated, the immigration prosecutors filed the biggest charges they could—asserting Dad was an "aggravated felon." According to them, we had no right to go before a judge and seek a pardon. And, according to them, Dad could not pay a bond to be outside while fighting his case. This aging father of three American citizens—who'd by now lived in the U.S. longer than he'd lived in any other country—was too great a threat to society and a flight risk. He could march off in his Velcro sneakers and go into hiding in the Palisades.

We all knew that having taxpayers (myself included) pay 159 dollars a day to keep Dad caged up wasn't a way to protect the public. It was a way to break him down so he wouldn't want to fight. It's a very smart strategy.

On the final day of Dad's eight-month stay at Rikers Island, he was loaded onto a big white bus with grates over the windows. If the driver went down the FDR Drive instead of over the Williamsburg Bridge, they would have passed the UN headquarters and then Union Square, turned right to cross the NYU campus, and finally stopped at the post office-cum-jail to unload the human cargo.

Dad called after he'd been "processed"—measured, weighed, surveyed for disease. He was no longer an "inmate." He was a "detainee"—under civil, not criminal, hold. It's a legal fiction. The immigrant prisoner is still locked up, sometimes even in the same jail or prison—just with a different-color jumpsuit. And—this is counterintuitive—there are fewer rights: no right to a public defender or bond while fighting the case, no constitutional protection from cruel and unusual punishment.

"Remember what we talked about," I reminded Dad on the phone.

"*Hah.* Six months," he said.

I didn't expect him to remember. I felt grateful the words came out of his mouth. He was agreeing.

Our lawyer bypassed the kangaroo court that is an immigration hearing and jumped right into the major leagues—the federal court where judges were allowed to read the law and use their judgment. They didn't have to rubber-stamp the prosecutor's memo. It was time to take that needle we'd found and poke.

It worked. And how long it took is the real shocker: four days. In the same amount of time that my uncle went missing in a system we didn't know existed, we managed to secure Dad's freedom from that same system. What a difference the tiniest bit of knowledge makes.

The calls from Moseley and Dad came at roughly the same time. The federal court bought our argument. Immigration authorities were releasing Dad without requiring a single dollar for bail. It wasn't over. But it was a strong start.

"Aarti doll, they told me I'm leaving today," Dad said on the phone.

"What?!"

"Come before they change their mind."

If you were experiencing the single happiest moment of your life, would you know it? I did. I grabbed Ang. We both happened to be at home.

"What?!" she gasped.

"Let's go get him."

"Should we take Mom?"

"No," I said. "Let's make sure this is for real."

When we got to Varick Street and turned the corner, I could make out a familiar figure halfway down the block: a lean man with a bit of a belly, thinning gray hair, clean shaven, a cigarette in his mouth.

"Dad, you're already smoking!" I screamed.

"No, doll!" he assured me. The cigarette was between his lips solely out of habit. "I won't light it until we do the *pooja* at home first."

The three of us hugged in one big, funny embrace—more of a huddle than a hug. Then he took each of us in his arms, one at a time. When I was little, I wanted him to squeeze tighter. Now he squeezed tight. He felt so thin.

"They asked me if I wanted to keep the jumpsuit. I said NO WAY. You can burn it."

"Why didn't you take it, Dad?" I got upset. I wanted to keep it, as a vestige of our victory. Only, I couldn't say that. "I could have worn it as pajamas," I told him, awkwardly.

His eyes were red. "When I left, they were fighting over who would get my bed." He smiled. "They think it's a lucky bed."

We took the 1 train uptown and then New Jersey Transit. My sister and I were quiet with the weight of the moment—or was it the weight finally lifting? Dad was arrested when we were kids. The problem that was supposed to go away kept getting bigger. We grew up in its shadow. And, finally, it might leave us.

"It's a miracle." Dad broke the silence. "It's a miracle. Aarti doll, you got me out of jail. You brought me back. And Angelly, my doll, you've reduced a lot. You're looking GREAT."

We burst into laughter. Shedding pounds, beating the feds—these were equal feats.

When our train pulled into the station, Mom was waiting. I'd called her to say Ang and I had a heavy package. We needed the car to bring it home. She paced the parking lot when her eyes fell on Dad. Her knees gave a little.

Dad beamed. He'd made it out, back to her. She stood still and, as he approached, both arms extended, he pulled her into him.

"*Kaisse?* How?" she asked, her head buried in his chest, not sure this moment was real.

"God's will," he said.

That night, she put the wedding ring back on his finger.

It was Sunday morning, Father's Day. I didn't think we'd have Dad back. I had assumed he'd be inside when I drafted this press advisory:

> This Father's Day, families personally affected by the 1996 immigration laws will rally against the inhumane and unconstitutional deportation of our loved ones.
>
> We will share our stories and read statements from the people held at the Detention Center at Varick Street. Please join us.
> HELP KEEP OUR FAMILIES TOGETHER!!!

Three exclamation points. I was determined to make it matter.

I had observed at that New York City Bar event that it's easy to get experts to drone on about their expertise. It's much harder to get real people, living through real problems, to talk. We feel we can't afford to be vulnerable. Our words can be twisted and turned against us. Yet it's through speaking that I found concrete help (like the lawyer) and a little catharsis. I was a new recruit to the church of public witness. And if I brought others, we could get journalists to pay attention.

The NYU law professor who'd introduced me to our attorney also introduced me to an activist group. They were the white soccer moms of the immigrant rights movement: women whose own families were under attack, whose husbands were in deportation like Dad. The group's founder was based in Texas, in a suburb of Dallas. I was their brown New York node, and the Father's Day vigil their event.

The day Dad went into detention, I'd asked him to get me the names and phone numbers of other detainees' families. He didn't want to. He could get in trouble for it. And, as a rule, he liked to keep to himself. When I insisted, he obliged.

I also recruited from the visitation line. I am perfectly capable of not talking to people. I hate small talk. I'll take silence over small talk any day. But when I visited Uncle Ratan and then Dad, I needed to know who else was there with me. And there was no such thing as small talk. No one said "great weather" or "How 'bout those Knicks?" The icebreakers were more like "What's he in for?" or "What country's he being shipped to?" or "You moving back with him?" I put my arm around a woman who was sobbing before I knew her name.

It felt surreal and yet devastatingly real. Every story was like salt on an open wound. I could see the pain etched all over people's faces. I'd swear I saw a little girl, maybe ten, with premature crow's-feet.

I remember meeting Wilma Sanchez, Angie Hamilton, Agatha Joseph, Maria Muentes—all black and brown women, Latina, West Indian, Asian. We were the United Nations without Europe.

I was not going to cancel the rally because Dad was out. We would go as the Shahanis, to let the detainees who were fighting over his bed know we'd not forgotten them. I told everyone at home that attendance was mandatory. I didn't need to say that. Everyone wanted to be there— aunties and uncles and cousins, including Mala (who'd described Dad as a freedom fighter for girls' education). She brought her college sweet- heart, who'd become her groom.

It was pouring that day, Indian monsoon rains. Water filled the potholes, spraying us when a car drove by. Our posters got so soggy, the ink dripping, they looked like they'd had a good cry.

I was dating a man who'd helped me make the posters. We were at his place in the East Village the night before. I didn't know what to put on them. I was new to activism. He was not. He teased me about how wonky I was being.

"What do we want?" he mock shouted the call and response of a rally leader and followers. "Repeal of the 1996 immigration laws that result in the mandatory deportation of aggravated felons. When do we want it? In the current congressional session before recess!!!"

"Ha, ha." I fake laughed. "You're so funny." He was.

The two anti-immigrant laws from 1996 are the Antiterrorism and Effective Death Penalty Act (passed on the anniversary of a white American terrorist bombing a building in Oklahoma) and the Illegal Immigration Reform and Immigrant Responsibility Act. People are not typically for terrorism or against responsibility. So those didn't lend themselves to signage.

I settled on the slogans: "Don't Tear Families Apart" (which got to the heart of the matter) and "Fix '96" (which cited policy).

As he and I made the posters, I harbored a fantasy: if I poured my heart into this campaign without holding back, if I let my entire being want it and dedicated my entire mind and body to getting it—I would. Light candles, lead chants, set off a shock wave that ripples from here to D.C. and wipes the 1996 laws off the books. Father's Day at 201 Varick would get us one-tenth of the way there. By the end of the year, we'd sprint to a home run in legal reform, just like we sprinted to Dad's freedom.

Noon was the start time. The journalists were superpunctual and ready to get started. Sunday is a slow news day (another reason I planned for that day). We were guaranteed coverage. Only, fellow protesters were trickling in ever so slowly, on Colored People Time. That's slightly better than Indian Standard Time, though not by much.

To protect ourselves from the pouring rain, we took shelter under the scaffolding. (The building was under construction.) The NYU law professor showed up. She brought her whole family and her own homemade sign. This wasn't just a day job. It was in her bones.

A reporter leaned in and whispered to me, "Give speeches. Start giving speeches now."

"Now?" I asked her. "More people are on the way."

"Yeah, but it's late," she tutored. "The press release says noon. You should get started before you start losing the reporters. We're not patient people."

I didn't have a speech prepared. I wasn't sure who did. I did a shout out, "Anyone want to tell their story? Come, tell your story!" One by one, several people gave testimony, speaking through the bullhorn I'd borrowed.

Then, out of nowhere, the nephew of Al Sharpton came by. He didn't know anyone being deported. I asked him. But he wanted to get on TV. He wrenched the bullhorn from my hand. And he made some kind of nebulous, generalized shout-out for justice. I don't think he knew what the rally was for. He was rally hopping.

My family hadn't spoken yet. I was wondering which one of us would go. I thought maybe Mom or Deepak. But my big brother nudged me.

Dad stood by my side as I explained, again saying to the world what I could not say at home, *Dad is out, but I know his case isn't over; he could be taken from us at any moment; I don't want to lose him.*

There was lightning and there was thunder. Only, it wasn't thunder. It was the prisoners above. A woman pointed to the upper floors of the building: "It's coming from upstairs. Listen!" Visitors must have told detainees. "They're banging! They're telling us they hear us!" It grew louder and louder, drowning out the rain itself.

The final straggler to the rally was another Indian American, about my age. He was my height, too. He'd grown a long beard, which he braided and tied in small rubber bands. It was not a good look.

"Great job." He came over to congratulate me. "I was just talking with your folks. They told me you organized this thing. I'm Subhash."

I was strangely tongue-tied. Maybe it was his statement beard, or the sensation that we'd met before, in a past life.

Republicans and Democrats wanted to meet families like mine—who'd lived in the United States for decades, who now faced possible exile because a relative with a green card had broken the law. Our niche area didn't fit neatly into a box. We were getting bipartisan interest, even support.

Dad, Mom, and Ang joined me on a trip to Washington, D.C. The Texas-based group had organized it. Thirty or forty people from around the country joined.

"How thoughtful of you to get us a room!" Ang snickered as she dropped her bag. I'd booked a Holiday Inn standard room with two queen beds. "I thought you'd have us sleep in other families' bathtubs."

She was making a joke about my thrift (which she called "cheap"). I threw down my bag and jumped on top of her. She was lying on one of the beds.

"Take it back!" I screamed as I tickled her.

"No!"

"Aarti, STOP THIS." Dad raised his voice. *Hee bewakoof chaa hai.* Stop this stupidity.

I didn't listen. It was too much fun. Until, with a force from nowhere, Ang pushed out her arms and legs and threw me off. "I've been working out, too," she said. I had no idea.

It was time to get to work. I gave my sister and parents a crash course in how to do congressional visits. I'd recently learned myself. "Talk about where we've gone to college . . . Don't argue about the criminal case or criticize the criminal justice system. They won't understand . . . Talk about Wrinkle, *a lot*. People working on the Hill love to hear about dogs."

Mom and Dad listened. Ang took notes. It was bizarre. One moment I was kid sister; the next, I was coach.

We went downstairs to have dinner with the other families, and sat at a table with Kenny.

"I been in Texas my whole life," he said in a charming drawl. "I love my guns. I love my barbecue. Call me a redneck, tha's right. My neck so red you could slap the back and color won't change." He had a mullet, too. I hadn't seen a mullet since childhood. I thought they'd gone out of style. Seeing one after all these years, I could not understand how they were ever in style.

Kenny was the first man from the South we'd met. He wasn't completely unfamiliar. Like Uncle Ratan, he was politically incorrect. "Houston's a real nice town," Kenny explained. "But 'cha know, i's been changin' lately. We got those—what'chu call 'em?—Chinamen." Chinamen. Was that a word people in the twenty-first century still used? Then there were the Mexicans, or "wetbacks," as he called them. His filter wasn't just broken when it came to race. He called children with Down syndrome "Mongoloid lookin'."

There's a famous line attributed to Martin Luther King Jr.: "If you are comfortable in your coalition, your coalition is too small." With Kenny, I was certain my coalition was not too small.

Like me, he spent his whole life assuming he was American. Only, his explanation for why was astounding. It was his skin color. I wouldn't point to my caramel complexion and say, "C'mon, with skin like this." But that is exactly what Kenny did. "Them immigration agents come on by, tell me, You're Canadian. Get outta here!" he said, and then pointed to his forearms. "You gotta be kiddin'. I mean, look at me." It was white privilege, distilled to its purest form.

I wished the other men in our dinner meeting could have his sense of entitlement. They looked foreign—by which I mean, not white. They felt they needed to cower in the face of authority, hide any indignation, because now was the time to lower one's head and seek pity. That's what Dad felt he had to do. Not Kenny, though. Kenny held his mullet high.

The next morning, we headed to the Rayburn Building—one of three office buildings for members of the House of Representatives. Ang and Mom were on one team, Dad and I on another. We'd spread out to visit more offices. Even if we weren't from a district, the staff agreed to meet us, curious about our stories.

"We'll talk to the congressman himself?" Dad asked as we stepped into our first appointment.

"No. To his staffer—the person who reports to him. But it'll be a senior staffer. Not a kid."

So many of the people in these offices looked my age, even went to my school. I could have been seated on their side of the table. Destiny put me on Dad's side.

We visited Democratic and Republican offices. I felt like I was roleplaying what an American is supposed to sound like. For the first time ever, I embraced New Jersey. "We live in a house in New Jersey!" I said with pride. "Our dog's name is Wrinkle." I showed pictures of her at

Ang's graduation from Mount Holyoke. I talked about how Wrinkle and Dad pray together, omitting the prayers were Hindu and not Christian. I downplayed our extensive family connections abroad.

"He hasn't lived in India since the 1950s," I told the aide, not mentioning Dad's stops in Lebanon, Algeria, and Morocco before we came to Queens. Dad and I exchanged knowing looks. He saw what I was doing. "Dad, do you want to add anything?" I asked when I was done. He shook his head no, self-conscious of his accent.

Ang told Uncle Ratan's story in detention—how he had to open his mouth wide so that another inmate could reach in and extract his tooth. "I don't understand: if he did his sentence, more than his sentence, why put him in prison again? The law says it's a 'civil' proceeding. What other civil proceeding locks someone up like that?"

The staffer—Ang was in a Republican office—squirmed, expressing her condolences for what our uncle went through.

My world felt stable again—well, stable enough to go back and finish college. The year off from UChicago was the most productive of my entire life.

It wasn't exotic. I didn't backpack across Europe or erect solar panels in a developing country. I fought injustice (which happened to include a trip to Europe). The abduction of the youngest Shahani, the deportation of the eldest—these were matters not yet settled. Home was still missing Akshay and at risk of losing Dad. But everything we could do to make things right had been done. And—because I'd learned justice is never swift—it was time to practice patience. (I needed a lot of practice.)

The time I spent focused on my family didn't set me back. It gave me purpose. I joined my first political campaign; I became a U.S. citizen; and, for the first time in my life, I felt I knew my father. He wasn't a stranger or an enemy. He had become a friend—a three-dimensional man I admired for the responsibilities he shouldered at my age and whose ups and downs taught me how the world really works.

Before heading back to the University of Chicago, I needed to swing by Washington, D.C., one last time. The Texas group had a breakthrough. A much larger organization wanted to adopt our cause as theirs. The American Civil Liberties Union had a new executive director, thirty-six years old, openly gay and Latino. He wanted to make Fix '96 a priority. Like any good leader, he knew he had to convince his followers. He'd invited us to speak at his first board meeting, to help earn their support.

The only problem was the timing. I was supposed to take Dad for his "check-in." It wasn't like the prep school check-ins, when someone wanted to know how you were feeling. It was the immigration-prosecutor type, when an agent wanted to make sure you knew you were a dog on a very short leash. Dad had to go to another office building, 26 Federal Plaza in Lower Manhattan, once every two weeks.

It was a meeting where he could be suddenly redetained, without notice. I'd been going with him because I didn't want him going alone. Only now, I really wanted to go to the ACLU meeting. We were on the verge of historic change. I could feel it. I was going to help make history.

"Dad, do you mind if Deepak goes with you?" I asked. My big brother offered.

"Is it necessary, doll?" Dad meant the D.C. meeting. Even though I got involved because of him, he reacted sometimes just as he did to Mom's tenant meetings in Flushing. He wanted us to be home, not fighting the good fight but eating a good dinner together.

"Yes, Dad." I got annoyed. "It's necessary."

"OK, my doll. Be wise." That's how Dad said good-bye. Be wise.

He didn't want to upset me. Our relationship had come a long way. He was raised believing he was supposed to be the master of his home. While he still tried to be with Mom, he stopped trying with me.

I boarded Amtrak before 7 A.M. It was a full train, the rush-hour commute from New York to D.C. The train would arrive around 10 A.M., which gave me thirty minutes to speed-walk to the board meeting.

Minutes before pulling into the final stop, the train stalled.

"What the—" more than one passenger grumbled.

"I hate Amtrak . . . This is why we need to defund Amtrak," some guy across the aisle said, loud enough to get a lot of chuckles.

"Ladies and gentlemen," the conductor came on the loudspeaker, "trains have been ordered to stop." Yes, Sherlock, we got that. Only, he didn't sound robotic. He paused, needing to take in what he'd just heard. "We've been told the Pentagon has been hit."

173

Gasps down the corridor. "Oh my god . . . that can't be."

Moments later, someone shouted: "The World Trade Center has been hit. The Twin Towers."

"What?" I found myself shouting. "My brother works there!" That's where Deepak went every single morning. I started to panic. Did Deepak finish Dad's immigration check-in? Did Deepak go back to work?

A passenger reached over to lend me his BlackBerry. "Call. See if you can get anyone."

The call didn't go through. The lines were jammed. More news streamed in, from the conductor, from the people with phones: 8:46 A.M., American Airlines Flight 11 crashed into the North Tower; 9:03 A.M., United Flight 175 into South Tower; 9:59 A.M., South Tower collapses; 10:28 A.M., North Tower collapses.

The train sat still. I had one hour to imagine the worst. My brother was under rubble. My brother was burning alive. My brother jumped out of a window, to his death, to escape death by fire.

The man with the BlackBerry passed me his phone again. "Keep trying."

I finally got a hold of Deepak. "You're OK?!"

"We're OK. We're OK." He told me to stay calm.

Dad and Deepak were at Federal Plaza when it happened. The officers working behind the glass broke the news and told everyone to evacuate the building. They were swept into a procession, tens of thousands of New Yorkers flooding the streets and heading north. Deepak turned back to see a gaping hole in the North Tower, where he worked. Dad had a hard time keeping up. His foot was going numb lately. He held Deepak's arm for support.

"Is Dad with you?" I asked. "Lemme talk to Dad."

He passed the phone.

"My *pichikery*. I never in my life thought I'd see such a thing. The buildings fell down. BOOM. One after the other. So terrible. *Arre baap re!*" Dear Lord.

As they marched, he kept turning back, seeing smoke billow from the ashes. They passed Canal Street; then Varick Street, where Dad had been detained; then 28th Street, where our store used to be. They paused so Dad could catch his breath. One pizza place was charging ten dollars for a bottle of water—price gouging in a moment of crisis. Another gave water out for free. The totality of human nature came out.

I told Dad I was on Amtrak and that the Pentagon was hit, too. He didn't know that yet.

"Come home, doll. Come home." He didn't want me out there alone.

"I can't, Dad. I need to go to the meeting."

My train pulled into the station. My meeting wasn't canceled. The ACLU powerhouse wasn't jumping ship. While we didn't know who was behind the attacks, we knew the campaign we were working on—for immigrant families like mine—had nothing to do with it. We had to push on.

ACT 5

Stretch Goal

HISTORY IS FULL OF screwups. Adolf Hitler's would-be assassin nudged the briefcase bomb under the conference table, thereby blowing up four others but not his target. NASA launched the nearly $1 billion *Mars Observer* into space and then, somehow, lost it.

Immigration history is no different. U.S. authorities confirmed with a flight school in Florida that, yes, two of the 9/11 hijackers were approved for student visas to learn aviation—six months *after* they'd perpetrated the attacks.

It should have come as no surprise, then, that India made its own unremarkable gaffe. It issued a replacement passport to Anisha—*after* she lost the international case and was ordered to return to the United States with the baby. That is, India gave her an escape hatch.

London's highest court ruled in our favor. We had a decisive victory, on paper. Anisha was to bring Akshay back and pursue whatever claims she might have in U.S. courts. But with her new travel documents, she slipped out of the United Kingdom and into India, beyond our reach.

To lose Akshay not once but twice was devastating. We couldn't go to India, where, Anisha made clear, she would use the courts against us as we'd done with her. We'd orchestrated such a meticulous campaign—with legal teams on two continents and stockpiles of data proving, by the most objective measures, the Shahanis were not abusers. And yet we failed.

I could see the frost set in my brother's heart. In the most formative years of life, Akshay would believe his father didn't care and that his mother was the victim of domestic violence. What other irreparable harm would happen to Akshay in a home of liars and leeches? All Deepak could do was finalize his divorce from Anisha. I told my brother it was a stalemate. Really, it was decisive defeat.

The fight I knew how to keep fighting was in my country.

Everything changed that day. That's what we Americans say about the terrorist attacks. But how do you know it's the truth and not a cliché? What clue in everyday life makes it clear the world is "post-9/11"?

Dad and I could answer that in a split second: a door. It comes down to a simple, mundane door.

One evening, I got home and knocked on the door. When Dad opened, he looked beside himself, weary, stiff.

"You thought I was immigration?" I said.

"Hah," he replied. "Sorry, my doll."

I was making a joke. It was supposed to be funny. It wasn't.

My father—who sat in his recliner, as he'd done ever since I could remember—was now sitting differently, not at ease but on alert, in a kind of forever lookout, contracting at the mere knock of a door. I didn't stop to let this fact sink in. I was too busy becoming a door knocker.

If September 11th had never happened, I would have spent my last year at the University of Chicago campaigning for Fix '96. Republicans and Democrats were on board. It felt "winnable"—a new word in my vocabulary. I decided post-9/11, it was still winnable. We, the immigrant families, had nothing to do with the terrorist attacks. I stayed the course.

Senior year held strong. Even though my friends were no longer there (they'd graduated during my year off), I had no time to feel anxious about college things—like if someone invited me to a party or if a professor was going to give me an A (OK, maybe that got me a little anxious).

I was mostly too busy keeping in touch with fellow activists, becoming the ghostwriter of profiles and fact sheets we continued to deliver to Congress. Also, I was making a new best friend: Subhash Kateel, the young man with the tragic facial hair who showed up late to the Father's Day rally.

Subhash was my first desi friend. "Desi" is slang for a person of South Asian descent—could be from India, Pakistan, Guyana, Trinidad, Zimbabwe, wherever. As a kid, I did what Mom did—avoided our own. At Brearley, the only other Indian in my class was a soft-spoken wealthy girl with superb manners who'd once told me her education was grooming for an arranged marriage. In other words, my opposite. In college, the Desi Table was a collection of J.Crew T-shirts who lived off their daddies' credit cards and breathlessly gossiped about who got into McKinsey and who didn't. Not my cup of chai.

Subhash was different. I could relate to him. Growing up, his family didn't have a lot of money, like mine. His parents fought, like mine. I told Subhash about a time in my childhood when Mom and I slept at our Buddhist temple because she was angry at Dad for smoking. Subhash and his mom left home together too, staying at a shelter.

He was the first desi man I met who talked about the double standards in our families like they were a real problem—not empty complaints from women who liked to complain. If I had to put a label on it (I often did), I would say Subhash was a feminist. Only, he wouldn't use that word.

"Men who call themselves feminist are just trying to get ass," he'd told me.

I did a quick tally in my head. "Damn. I think you're right."

It was easy to be honest with him. In activism, when I'd visit Congress or speak at rallies (these were becoming regular parts of my life), I had to paint the picture of a perfect family. It was theater of the absurd. No family is perfect. With Subhash, I didn't have to pretend.

He'd recently graduated from Columbia University, where he got his masters in social work. He had to muster up the confidence to apply. He once told me, "When I got in, I was like, Yo. For realz? You fools accepting me."

He grew up in Saginaw, Michigan—"it's close to Flint," he always needed to add. While I went to the Midwest to finish college, he stayed in my hometown. Over the phone—we could talk for hours—he became my lifeline to New York City.

Only, the New York he described to me was different from the one I remembered. He was working two jobs: one for a desi community group in Queens, the other for a Jesuit refugee group in New Jersey. His entire world was becoming the immigrant roundups.

"They're going into folks' homes," he told me. I'd been trying to get ahold of Subhash for days. He finally called back. "Cops are literally busting down doors in Jackson Heights. I ain't seen nothing like this." He became the person wives and daughters called after Ahmed or Mohammed or Khan got taken away. Subhash was trying to get lawyers for the "suspected terrorists" whose faces (they looked so much like Dad) flashed on the nightly news.

Subhash told me about the steady stream of predictable backstabbing. Just like Dad's childhood friend preyed on us when we had no papers, other immigrants saw an opportunity to make a buck—calling the Terrorism Tips hotline to report on a business rival or selling legal services without being a lawyer.

And then there were the uncles (as we called them)—the desi men who got on TV after a Hindu or Sikh had been attacked in a hate crime to explain how our turbans or uncut facial hair were different from that of a Muslim.

"What are they even trying to say?" we each asked. "You got the wrong brown man? Go after the Muslims?"

Subhash wasn't afraid. He was angry, and also optimistic. These raids can't last that long. America is better than that. Rage in the moment and hope in the long term were the heart of our relationship.

Punctuality was not. I was waiting for Subhash, again. This time at a West Village café.

The school year came and went. My parents and siblings attended graduation. So did my godfather from the Moonies (our Christian cult in Queens). Ang bought me the outfit I wore under my cap and gown: a long linen skirt, the lightest of baby blues, and a ribbed black tank top from Banana Republic. We'd never shopped there, and the items were not on sale. "Live a little," she told me.

I felt like I finally was. After college, I didn't have to go back to the soul-sucking law firm. A strange by-product of 9/11 was that philanthropists were interested in deportation. The same system I learned about before the attacks—because of my uncle and Dad—was a cause célèbre among the liberal elite.

I got a fellowship—a salary of $35,000 a year—from a nonprofit supported by the Ford Foundation. Subhash got a similar one from billionaire George Soros's Open Society Institute. We had each proposed to work directly with immigrant families—getting them to speak to journalists, using media to shame the government into ending the raids locally, and organizing trips to Washington, D.C., to school the lawmakers.

My timeline for change had stretched. My original one year had come and gone. The 9/11 attacks were an unexpected event, but not, in my opinion, a total game changer. I felt that if we really focused, we could accomplish our goals in eighteen months. Subhash just needed to be on time.

I sat in Caffe Dell'Artista, in a vintage velvet armchair I could never land during rush hour. The room was so empty, I could see the flecks of dust that are always suspended in air, in the thousands, backlit by the midafternoon sun. Glass bottles with long candles melted onto their mouths lined the walls. Outside, the NYU crowd walked by—girls in booty shorts and platforms, dressed like I used to before I started hanging out with immigrants who preferred to repress their sexuality and prisoners who were forced into repression.

"Yo, sorry I'm late." Subhash gave me his standard greeting.

"I got myself a tea. You want anything?"

"Yeah, lemme take a look."

His finger ran across each line of the beverage list as if it were scripture. When the waiter came, he had a litany of questions about dark and light roasts, the cortado, if they might happen to have Turkish coffee—"I know it's not on the menu, but it's my favorite"—though he also liked Bustelo because, of course, "Dominicans don't play." I would not have taken Subhash for a coffee snob, probably because of his do-rag.

Our task at hand—which I thought would take thirty minutes—was to draft the agenda for our first "family meeting." He and I each had built a small network of people being deported. We wanted to merge them into one group—"the base," he called it. Our base was open to anyone caught up in the system, not just select groups.

This really mattered to me. Back when I had to find help for my family, I got a list of nonprofits at the detention center—large, reputable agencies, protecting immigrants for decades. Yet each one I called said some version of, "We don't help criminals." As soon as there was a record, no other record about who we were mattered.

Meanwhile, after 9/11 I felt disappointed in the Texas-based group. Too many members repeated "we're the legal ones." Even if they didn't mean to imply the roundups were OK for the "illegals," that's how it sounded to me. During one of our D.C. trips, the self-professed redneck Kenny rode the hate wave, calling Arabs "sand niggers." His political incorrectness, which I used to laugh off (laughing at him, not with him), was now unbearably offensive. I didn't want to hear it.

The world had changed. And I was looking for my tribe.

"So how do we wanna start the meeting?" Subhash asked.

"Um, I guess . . . well, we wanna get to the point quickly."

For me, the point was to pump a steady stream of families into the halls of Congress. Whether people were picked up before the attacks or after, the same set of unjust laws were being used to hurt our chances of staying here. Only now, more officers were sent out to get us.

For Subhash, it wasn't that clear-cut. He began what sounded like a tangent. "So have you ever heard of this guy called Paulo Freire? He wrote *Pedagogy of the Oppressed*."

"No." I hated to admit when I didn't know something.

Apparently, there was a man in Brazil who worked with peasants. He made the case that you can't just give directives to people whose lives are being ruined—be it by a greedy landlord or a deportation agent. You have to stop and ask them what they want and be open to hearing things you didn't expect. Otherwise, you're just repeating the oppression—turning them into pawns instead of owners of their own destiny.

That struck me as mildly profound. But I was stuck on the title of the book. "If this guy—Fray?—cares so much about communicating with the masses, why didn't he name his book something easier to understand? 'Pedagogy' is ivory tower." With this astute point, I felt smart again.

Subhash turned our half-hour meeting into a three-hour deep dive into "process"—the steps we needed to take to know that "we" wasn't just one person speaking for a group that didn't exist. He suggested that instead of assuming trips to D.C. were the priority, we should ask. It could be that bigger priorities were getting lawyers for people detained (the fact that no public defender was appointed for deportation cases came as a shock to most families) or stopping the abuse in detention (guards were siccing attack dogs on detainees and denying medications).

"I don't feel D.C. is negotiable," I pushed back. I didn't want to ask questions when I knew the answers. The people who hate us were flooding Congress. I wanted to as well.

Subhash often turned his suggestions into questions. "Maybe we wanna start the meeting asking folks to go around and share their story? A lot of folks haven't been able to talk shit out."

With that, I agreed. Deportation was like AIDS—a crisis no one talked about in public. It had been a couple years since I stopped feeling ashamed. I'd almost forgotten how paralyzing it was. Maybe because Subhash was going to jail to visit prisoners so often, drinking it in through a fire hose, he hadn't. (Though, like it or not, I would insist on the D.C. trips. Much like exercise and eating greens, they were nonnegotiables.)

Subhash fascinated me. "You know, Jesus was the best radical who ever lived," he threw in at some point in our long afternoon, which didn't feel long. "He hung out with prostitutes and poor people." Subhash was highly opinionated yet open-minded. He was highly sensitive, a feelings guy, yet not seeking others' approval. He called himself a "radical." I did not—at least not yet. So many of the words coming out of his mouth ("movement," "building," the compound "movement-building") I heard in air quotes—until I started saying them, too.

We were both young and passionate and felt there should not be lines between professional and personal life. "That's some bougie bullshit," he'd say. I couldn't agree more—though, fresh out of college, I had a hard time not thinking, *you mean bourgeois.*

"Doll, you want hummus, tabouli, and *keema* kebab?" Dad asked.

"I think *keema* is too expensive." I didn't know the price of ground lamb. While my family ate meat, I'd become vegetarian many years back. "Skip it."

"No, doll," he insisted. "Not everyone is veg. Let them enjoy."

This was an unexpected turn of events. My father—the man who insisted Mom make his breakfast back in 401, even when she had a job and he didn't—had become the chef for family meetings. Turns out, individual founders really do set the culture of a collective body. We didn't know how to have meetings shorter than three hours. At that length, there had to be food.

"I can't believe the things Papa will do for you," Mom told me. "He's so different with you." She said it with a tinge of jealousy. It made me wonder if it's hard or rewarding for a woman to see her husband be a better man to their daughter.

Where Mom had to hide her activism as president of the Tenants' Association, I could declare mine and enlist Dad to cook, to call people on our growing "member list," and to translate on the fly when people who spoke Arabic, Urdu, or French (not English) called the office.

We had an office. It was the basement of a West Village town house, owned by the NYU professor. She and her husband were both lawyers focused on the surging deportations.

Subhash and I were working so much together, he ended up making it his office, too. It happened gradually, not explicitly—until the husband-wife team brought it up: "So, um, we notice Subhash comes around here a lot." They said he could stay. I felt they saw in us a little bit of themselves.

Dad was happy his daughter finally made a desi friend but wondered why it had to be this one—not a clean-cut doctor but a social worker who tied his beard in little rubber bands. Dad gave Subhash a tentative handshake, not an embrace, when he came over—which was often. Because Dad and I hadn't gotten our driver's licenses, Subhash chauffeured the trays of food Dad prepared from New Jersey to the town house. Dad hated the way he drove.

The people who came to family meetings reminded me of our old 401 neighbors. Carol MacDonald was a U.S. citizen and a nutritionist at a hospital. She came from Guyana, as did her husband, Linden. He was a Rastafarian. "He likes the herb," she said in our opening go-around. "He used it to meditate. That's his religion. One day, NYPD—they stopped him. He told them what he had was for personal use." They arrested him and he spent a couple of weeks at Rikers. Then, New York City handed him off to immigration agents, who shipped him to an immigration prison in Louisiana. He'd been held there for nearly a year, not allowed to post bond.

Lefty Lee was from China, and he got the name Lefty because he played handball with his left hand. His wife was Puerto Rican, and they had three kids. He was being deported for fraud, and, representing himself, he clawed his way out of detention—though his case had not ended.

At the family meeting, Lefty pulled out a necklace made of Doritos wrappers intricately folded and interlinked. "I made this inside. I bought chips from the commissary and kept the bags for art." Lefty's accent bewitched me, Chinese meets Bushwick in a low, even baritone. He could read a phone book and I'd listen. He passed the origami necklace around the room. "Be careful. It cost a lot of money!" We all laughed at the inside joke, each remembering the prison commissary, where items are sold at markups as high as 500 percent.

Jean Montrevil, who came from Haiti with a green card, got arrested at the height of the drug wars. Police stopped him while he was driving and found an ounce of crack hidden under his car. Had he been taken to federal court, he could have gotten five years. But, caught in the state of Virginia, he got twenty-seven years.

Jean was a glass-half-full kind of guy. "Prison saved my life," he said. After serving eleven years, he got released early and returned to Brooklyn. He opened a religious goods store and married Janay, an African American woman from Brooklyn. They started a family.

"The government's trying to rob my children of their father. Don't make me a single mother," she said and the room nodded.

Mariana Gonzalez was another American citizen, from a tight-knit Dominican family. She said her cousin Juan, who lived with her and was like a brother, was detained when he went into Federal Plaza for his citizenship application. (That was the same place Dad went for his check-ins.) Juan's interview was a setup—a premeditated effort to kick out the nineteen-year-old so quickly, there was not even time for a lawyer's visit. He got shackled at 4 P.M. and was on a plane by the next sunrise.

"He was enlisting in the army. He wanted to serve our country." Mariana wept. While Juan thought he had a valid green card, he was likely ordered deported as a child—and just didn't know it.

I didn't know that could happen. I'd take notes, reminding myself to ask the lawyers I'd been meeting about a fact pattern that was new to me. Sometimes, things didn't add up—either because people didn't know key details or didn't want to admit what was really going on. I began asking to see people's paperwork. So did Subhash. We learned, and then explained what we learned to the family affected. If they had any fighting chance, we tried to connect them to counsel. While I'd worked at a law firm as a secretary, I hadn't worked directly with the people in trouble, like I did now.

It didn't feel clinical. I identified strongly with quite a few people at the family meetings, like Navila—a sassy, fast-talking teenager who worked hard at school. Her dad was taken away in a new post-9/11 program called Special Registration. The attorney general called on men and boys from mostly Muslim countries to "register" themselves by showing up to Federal Plaza.

Navila begged her dad to not go. She was afraid he was being duped. He insisted, "This is America. They would never trick us here." He was wrong. She was right. Of the roughly 84,000 who showed up, trusting the government, nearly 14,000 were put into deportation proceedings. Navila's dad was one of them. He was taken on the spot from Federal Plaza to a jail in New Jersey. Navila found herself the head of a household—the main breadwinner for her mom and her two siblings, both born in the Bronx.

She and I had so much in common. Two brown girls with long, thick black hair, intense eyes, and opinions. Like me, her parents brought her as a child and overstayed their visas. Unlike me, she still did not have papers. She couldn't find a way to get a green card.

In policy debates, Navila and I were assigned to separate groups. I was legal and she "illegal." My family "criminal alien," and hers not criminal. But in the real world, we were both native New Yorkers trying to keep our families together.

If I had to shrink the feeling in our support group down to a single word, it wouldn't be "fear" or "pain." It was "disbelief." America is a "nation of immigrants." That wasn't a throwaway line. It was supposed to be true, in good times and in bad. When, in response to the Civil War draft, thousands of newly arrived Irish rioted and lynched blacks—a clear-cut case of a foreign mob attacking innocent Americans—New York City didn't hand them off for deportation. The political establishment punished crime, but not by way of immigration status.

America was the first country on earth to put birthright citizenship in the Constitution. Former slaves pushed for it because former masters were trying to deport them to Africa, even though they were born in Mississippi, Alabama, Georgia. Their win became our collective legacy.

The feeling of belonging within a single generation—that if your kids are born here, they are of here—is American. My cousins who are second- and third-generation in Dubai—which has become another global city—don't think of themselves as citizens. They are not, by law or in spirit. They are constantly reminded, and they have internalized: they will only ever be guests.

If the go-around in the family meeting got to Dad before me, he'd deflect, "I am Namdev Shahani, father of Aarti," which was my cue to pick up.

"Go ahead, Dad," I'd nudge.

A few times he did. "I am in the deportation. I am a businessman. I had a shop on Twenty-eighth Street and Broadway." He didn't say the reason he was being deported—that he'd been convicted of a felony. He didn't like when I said it. Though I felt I had to. We needed to be role models for others grappling with their shame.

These meetings were life coming full circle. After all the years I'd spent denying where I came from, now I was right back, by choice. I didn't feel trapped. I felt at home. Mom attended, too. She called people "brother" and "sister"—a habit she'd picked up in 401, because she was terrible at remembering names. I began doing the same. It felt intimate, not forced. Many "members"—is that what they were becoming?—referred to each other that way.

After an hour or two, talking fatigue would set in. The smell of the food was distracting. Dad, itching to get up from the second it began (he did not like sharing circles), went over to heat the trays. As people lined up, Dad hovered, watching what went and what was left untouched.

"Is the salt OK?" he'd ask. "Any suggestions you have?" Lots of people skipped the tabouli. "Do not be afraid to try." He'd try to coax them. "It is a grain and parsley, very popular in Middle East, where I lived. Delicious."

"I thought your family was from India," someone or other would say.

"Yes," he'd nod and end it right there, an awkward pause, not inter-ested in giving the postcolonial lecture needed to understand his winding path to the Manhattan basement.

One other person in the room was from Dad's birthplace, Karachi.

Ali was much younger, in his twenties. He came to America as a teenager and got picked up when police came knocking down his door. He grew up hustling and looked like Ali G (the Sacha Baron Cohen character): FUBU jacket, diagonals shaved into his fade and his eyebrows, gold caps on his teeth, heavy chains. Come to think of it, he may have inspired Ali G.

Dad once looked our Ali up and down and said, mischievously, "What's up, my niggah?"

Ali and I both did a double take. *Did Dad learn that word at Rikers?*

"Yo, you funny Uncle," Ali said. And then, turning to me, he repeated, "Your pop's real funny."

Subhash and I didn't kiss the night of our first sleepover. That would have been awkward. We were with three little kids and a newly single mom.

Razia lived by the Jackson Heights subway stop. Her husband was taken in one of the home raids. The family couldn't visit him in jail because, although the kids were born in Queens, Razia had no papers. She'd get detained if she went.

"Why doesn't she come to family meetings?" I asked Subhash on our way to her home.

"I don't think she went out a lot without her husband," he said. "And he's the one who worked. She probably can't buy a MetroCard right now."

On the second point, I felt bad for her. On the first, I felt judgment. This is America. Women can't lock themselves up until the man comes home.

Then I met her. She was a sassy young mom whom I liked more because she had a sassy daughter. At age five, Zara served as translator, helping her mom, who spoke Urdu, explain the raid and their legal history. Zara saw the men in uniform, with guns, and followed their orders when they screamed, "Hands in the air."

I wondered if Zara would get to stay here and be a rebellious teenager before going off to college or if she'd go back to Pakistan—though "back" is incorrect, since she'd never been there—and follow in her mom's footsteps.

"Mutton! Mutton!" Razia offered Subhash and me goat curry. While she couldn't buy a MetroCard, she would find the money to feed her guests. That's her (our) culture.

"Oh, I'm veg," I tried to explain.

She scavenged carrots and onions from the meat broth and offered it to me in a bowl.

Subhash laughed. "That's the Pakistani version of vegetarian."

"Husband?" Razia pointed to him and asked me. I was clearly of childbearing age. Was I married to this man who traveled around the city with me?

"No, no!" I said.

Though, for the tiniest, most minuscule, nanosecond of a split second, I thought about it. Subhash was whip smart, and his funny features were fading into the background as I started to notice his striking shy-guy smile and his luminous eyes—determined, like the Lord Shiva.

He got up to clear the plates and do the dishes when we were done eating. I didn't know there was an Indian man on earth who did that. Definitely none of the men in my family. And he was so good with kids. Zara had a crush on him. As soon as she was done being the translator, she turned back into a little girl, bringing out her toys for Subhash to play.

"Stay, stay here." Razia insisted we spend the night. We'd arrived late and talked, with body language or words, for hours. The family liked having the company. We were living out of our backpacks. Why not?

Not long after that night—where I took the couch and Subhash a blanket on the floor—he and I went clubbing. Familiar turf for the both of us, a much easier place to have our first kiss.

"As-salaam alaikum." Irfan opened the door to his office.

"Wa alaikum salaam." I touched my hand to my heart, the greeting Muslim members taught me.

Irfan looked young, my age, but I suspected he was older because he was in a powerful position: a chief at the Consulate General of Pakistan.

Subhash and I had made a "power map" with every point of contact an immigrant in deportation has with a government agency. We were looking for pressure points, anything we could push, prod, smother, or woo in our favor—like the New York office of a foreign country.

I came in to talk with Irfan about one of his citizens—an elderly man in the Bronx who was being deported because he trusted the U.S. government and showed up for Special Registration.

"Malik Uncle couldn't come with me today because he has a high fever," I said, explaining why I came alone. He was not my uncle, but I was being respectful—and demonstrating that there was at least one custom I knew from "back home."

"Where is your family from?" Irfan asked. He reminded me of a university professor.

"Queens," I said.

"No," he smirked, a flash of pity, as if long-lost foreigners like me had Stockholm syndrome at the hands of the American continent. "Aarti, I mean before Queens."

"Oh, like where are we *from* from?"

"Precisely."

"My mom was born in Hyderabad (the one in Pakistan, not India). Dad in Karachi. My siblings and I in Morocco."

"Ah, so your parents left during Partition." I didn't have to explain 1947 to him. He knew.

Around the world, it's said, Americans don't know geography; we only know where a country is when we go to war with it. Irfan didn't think we knew even that. "I am Pashtun," he began to explain his origins, "ethnic Afghans . . . you know, the country America started attacking in 2001. In the fifteenth and sixteenth centuries, my ancestors crossed the mountains into Pakistan. We are Aryans." Irfan had olive skin and little specks of gold in his irises, like a cat. He was strikingly handsome, if too skinny.

His family story ended where mine began. "My father is from the same city as your father."

"And now globalization has brought us together," I said, "in a small office by Central Park." I wanted to get back to Malik Uncle.

"It's not small!" He was flirting. "If you'd like, I shall recommend a book that is an excellent history of Pakistan." He reached for a piece of paper to begin writing. "Once you've read it, we can meet again to discuss it, perhaps in a more . . . festive environment."

I did not want to be rude because I was here to get help for a member. It was hard to know Irfan's intentions. Maybe he was aching to share his intellectual passions. Or maybe he was trying to recruit for a political cause back home, and the history book was a test. Or maybe he just wanted to go out on a date.

"Thank you, Irfan." I took the note with the book title and surprised myself when I addressed him by his first name. "About Malik Uncle—he was told he'll be put on a plane at the end of this week. He's dealing with a ton of health issues." I listed them out: coronary artery disease, renal failure, anemia, diabetes, shortness of breath, hypertension. One of his children sponsored him for a green card. Unlike most immigrants who have no path to citizenship, he had one. So he just needed time to let the application run its course.

I did not know what the Pakistani consulate could do. But they were in our power map. If ever there were a case for humanitarian relief, it was Malik Uncle. The consulate could help us make it.

"What did you say his name was?" Irfan asked. He did not have questions about the medical or legal issues.

"His name is Malik Khan."

Irfan riffled through a pile on his desk. "Khan." He pulled out what looked like an index card. "Here he is." The yellow specks of Irfan's eyes widened. He set the card aside, at the far corner of the table, away from the others. "These are all the requests for travel documents the American government has sent for me to approve," he said, pointing to the main pile. "If I don't approve a request to put a Pakistani on a plane, it cannot happen." He snapped his fingers. "Problem solved."

With deportation, it takes two to tango—a sending country and a receiving country. The Pakistani consulate didn't need to mount an overt humanitarian campaign. They could be a quiet bureaucratic nuisance, drag their feet. Sometimes, that's all it takes. I marveled at this profound lesson. *Don't make every ask sound so overwhelming, Aarti,* I told myself on the way home. When it feels easy to do, people are more likely to do it.

Irfan's move set the stage for one of our first great victories. Malik Uncle stayed in the United States long enough to get his papers and see his family grow in the Bronx. When his son married a lovely young woman, Dad and I attended the wedding. Subhash teased me, "Yo, Malik Uncle stayed cuz some dude had a crush on you. That's gangsta."

I found myself going to Federal Plaza with men besides Dad. It started because we asked the families—like Subhash wanted to—and that's what they needed: accompaniment, plain and simple.

It wasn't superstition. We had a theory, based on anecdote, that if the person checking in went with a plus one, the immigration agent would be less likely to redetain. That's why I wouldn't let Dad go alone, though it was too expensive to pay a lawyer to do it.

Jorge Emilio Cabrera and I met in front of Federal Plaza. He gave me a bear hug. He knew no other. He was a big man with a big bounce in his step and his belly. He dreamed big, too. Before this morning, I'd only ever met him in family meetings.

"Ju all—lemme explain ju how we gonna let all them people know what's goin' on with the deportation," he'd say in the sharing circle and then pause, as if waiting for a drumroll or snaps. "Ju wanna to hear it?"

"Shout it out, papi," someone prodded.

"OK." He didn't take much prodding. "We get el numero fo' Oprah. Tha's right. *La dueña* Oprah Winfrey. And she gonna do a show about us. *Us!* The Freedom Families."

He didn't always get our name right. We were in fact called Families for Freedom—a name the members voted on, and proof that titles should not be decided democratically.

His suggestion—to aim high, be bold—woke up the room. And then Cabrera walked out.

"Where you going?" I'd shout. "The meeting's not over. Don't you wanna talk about how we'll reach Oprah?"

"I gotta take a call, mami."

"Is it Oprah?"

"Ha. Ju wish." He'd wink on his way to the door.

The morning of Cabrera's check-in, I saw a different side to him: the aggressive effervescence gone; in its place, pure, abject fear. This building was the reminder that life exile was right around the corner— coming as soon as noon today. Cabrera was a father who wanted to not be absent. He wanted to raise his kids in Washington Heights, their lifelong home.

"Hacemos una oración." He stopped me to do a prayer just before we entered the room.

We mostly spoke Spanish together. I'd learned the language by hearing Mom talk to her friends when I was a kid. As an activist, I was picking up a lot of words related to God and prisons.

"Señor, por favor envía a tus ángeles esta mañana para protegernos e iluminar el camino en la oscuridad." We asked for God's angels to guide us into the light. *"Por favor, no me pongas esposas . . . Amén."* The Spanish word for "hand-cuffs" is *"esposas,"* which is also the word for "wife."

I opened my eyes and held his round cheeks in my hands. *"Dios le bendiga."* God bless you. Praying with people came naturally to me because I saw Mom do it when we were little.

The wait in the immigration office could be five minutes or four hours. I wasn't sure why. Cabrera had a theory. "If the officer—he call ju right away, then we good," he said. "But if ju wait till afternoon, tha's cuz they wanna make sure i's too late to call ju law-jer." The closer it got to 5 P.M., the harder it would be for a lawyer to run into federal court with an emergency suit.

He wasn't called right away. I made use of the time by handing out the brochures in my backpack. Each of the two dozen or so other people checking in could become a member.

"Hi, sir, could I trouble you for a moment?" I would walk up to a stranger who was as anxious as Cabrera. "I'm part of a human rights organization, helping families—like yours—who are facing this unjust deportation system. You can read the stories of our members here." I'd point to the inner flap of the brochure, where we'd written profiles and included our hotline number.

The only other people doing this kind of outreach were lawyers looking for clients. Plenty of people assumed that's what I was doing and gave me a perfunctory thank-you. I kept one eye on the door, where deportation agents were walking in and out. I didn't want to get caught recruiting. While it was not illegal, it could get Cabrera roughed up.

"Cabrera," an agent called for him. We both got up and walked over. "Who's she?" The agent looked at me and asked him. "That your lawyer?"

"No, I'm an advocate with a nonprofit organization." I handed him my card and did not use the term "human rights." That might sound radical, not professional—and we needed to get a specific job done. "Mr. Cabrera has an appeal pending, and so we thought it best for me to accompany him today, to make sure there are no issues."

"Just a moment." The officer took Cabrera's check-in paper and told us to wait. That put Cabrera at ease, because he hated going into the guarded back room, where he could no longer see the outside world and vice versa.

"We good, Aah-tee. We good." He was back to being the man who'd lead us to Oprah.

Not yet, I thought to myself. Cabrera had an appeal in court, but he did not have a stay of deportation—an initial decision by a judge that would prohibit him from being put on a plane. Without this stay, the appeal didn't mean a thing.

Whether Cabrera got detained this time came down to a choice by an officer. There were factors we had no way to see, like if the jail cells were empty or full, but also if the officer's morning cereal gave him in-digestion or if his wife just filed for divorce. The decision to incarcerate or grant liberty can come down to the whim of the low-level bureaucrat who happens to be in charge.

"We checked with the federal circuit court, and you do not have a stay." The officer was back with us, stating the fact I'd hoped would escape him.

"What ju mean, not a stay? I got my appeals right here." Cabrera pushed papers in his hand, as if to say, *You want papers, I got papers! If that's no good, I'll get you some other papers.*

I was about to weigh in—give a rundown of the political offices we'd informed about Cabrera, the letters of support (more papers) we could get. Many people want to see him receive his day in court. But I didn't need to.

"Here's what we're gonna do," the officer said. "It's almost lunchtime. I'm not going to take you in today. But you gotta get a stay for next time."

"Ju got it, bro. Ju got it." Cabrera gripped his shoulder with the strength of his gratitude.

"Have a good day," the officer said.

On our way out, Cabrera was a fountain of sweet nothings. *"Mi pre-ciosa, mi milagro, mi ángel."*

I was too shaken to eke out warmth or snark. This man who made us all laugh at meetings was far closer to being put on a plane than I had realized.

I hadn't stepped inside the Supreme Court since the humiliating high school trip. I still had the copy of the Constitution that Ruth Bader Ginsburg handed me. Now I was back, leading a rally to defend one of its amendments.

"Rally" may be too generous a term. It conjures up images of hundreds if not thousands of people, arms interlocked, free-styling pithy chants between civil rights hymns. That's how I saw it in my fantasy life. In real life, it was Dad, Subhash, me, and a handful of other members, and we looked like we were loitering.

Most of the Freedom Families (aka Families for Freedom), including my siblings, had day jobs and couldn't make it. Mom's vomiting had not stopped yet. She was years into it and didn't have healthcare, so her main treatment was herbal remedies and rest.

"Does smoking keep your mouth warm?" I asked Dad, genuinely wanting to know. It was the dead of winter. He glared, thinking I was being a smart-ass.

I assumed a tidal wave of New York protesters would come crashing in because the case being heard was exactly what they were looking for: the domestic face of the war on terror. Bombs had not yet dropped in Iraq. Preempting that was the antiwar movement's main goal. Leading activists made the point in more than one citywide meeting: to recruit more protesters, the movement needed to highlight issues playing out right here, not just in faraway places like the Middle East or Guantánamo Bay, Cuba.

We had the very thing they were looking for.

The government was on a crusade to win a case called *Demore v. Kim*. Their claim: the United States can lock up immigrants without any time limit, without any need to ask a judge for permission. It was an extremist position. In no other context, anywhere in this country, did prosecutors have that power. The outcome would directly impact tens of thousands of people—including Dad.

Unfortunately for us, courtroom battles are a lot like Hollywood movies. Casting matters. The immigrant in the case was the wrong race. To fit into the identity politics of the day—to appeal to journalists and the antiwar crowd—he needed to be from the Middle East or South Asia, to look like my father or the "suspected terrorists" as seen on TV. Instead, our leading man was Korean. Not even North Korean, but a South Korean. He was Mr. Kim, not Mr. Hussein.

Stereotypes about Koreans in the United States focus on kimchi and Kumon math camp. News junkies might recall stories of racial tensions between Koreans and blacks in Brooklyn groceries. But that's about it. The defendant didn't fit the national security narrative or the model minority one. He had stolen tools from someone else's toolshed. He was taken for deportation after he served his time. And, shocker (I'm being sarcastic), that catchall term "aggravated felon" was applied to him.

I'd tried to explain the case to an influential activist—a woman who could fill four buses with protesters easily. "I know it's confusing—because in the news it's just my people under attack—but the government is using 9/11 to target a lot of other people."

She asked for details. I researched—much like I did our members' cases—and prepared an informational packet for her. That was a pro move. But then, like a rookie, I failed to ask, You sending me protesters or not? I just crossed my fingers. It was a life lesson in how not to close a deal.

My fingers were freezer burned, trembling as they held a plain vanilla poster I'd quickly scribbled with the words "Don't take my daddy." I had a new appreciation for the paltry Falun Gong group I often passed in Manhattan. Their signs—with graphic pictures of torture—were at least memorable.

Buses full of schoolkids unloaded at the courthouse steps. "You think they would like to come help us?" Dad asked, unironically. I glared at him.

While I failed to get our side to care, the opposition did not. Men in suits from a cross-section of law enforcement agencies and Congress filed into the front rows. They knew how much was riding on this decision.

Even though we were in the nation's highest court—a model for rule of law the world over—it felt like that courtroom in Queens. The prosecution and the supporters of the prosecution were largely white; our side—call it the "defense"—was full of many more people of color. I was beginning to see racial division as *the* central feature of America's justice system.

The one person notably absent from court proceedings was the defendant, Hyung Joon Kim. "Is he testifying?" I asked Subhash, who sat next to me. He shrugged.

Mr. Kim, even if he had shown up, would not be allowed to speak.

196

I wondered if that made it easier for the government and one justice in particular to lie about the facts. Justice Antonin Scalia insisted that Mr. Kim was "illegal." That was not true. He came to the United States when he was six, and he had a green card.

"He's here illegally, has no right to be at large," Justice Scalia said. "It seems to me that even if none of them would flee, if they have no right to be here, if they've committed a crime, why cannot they [be] held [in] custody until they leave?"

Was the justice playing dumb? He spoke as if a green card—also known as lawful permanent residency—meant nothing; and there's no point to having deportation courts because if a prosecutor decides someone should be out, it must be true. Sitting in the audience, watching, blood boiling, I could easily list off a dozen major cases where that was not true—where overzealous prosecutors got it wrong. I would happily share my research with him.

The government did a superb job in casting their lead. To litigate the case, they chose a man who did not appear to be familiar with the facts, but who was a widower. His wife died in the 9/11 attacks. He did not correct the justice's misstatements. And he added another: he said detainees are held for just forty-seven days—a little over a month, on average. That's not very long. Nothing to make a fuss about.

Subhash and I looked cross-eyed. *That number can't be right.* We kept seeing people inside much longer. It sounded like the government was lying.

The lawyer for Mr. Kim tried her best to explain the huge stakes: not just the fate of one man, but of the Fifth Amendment, due process. Is America a country that's cavalier about incarceration—readily adopting the prosecutor's mind-set and stripping people of liberty? Or do we believe judges exist for a reason? To judge. In this case, to judge if the man fighting his deportation needs to be locked up the whole time or if he should be granted a bond. (It could be a very high bond.)

The oral arguments felt like trying to reason with a child having a temper tantrum. The anti-immigrant emotions were so inflamed, appeals to reason were utterly futile.

My old pal, who was in the minority, gave it a try. "Suppose," Justice Ginsburg told the government lawyer, "someone would not be able to get bail despite a good claim that [prosecutors] are counting a crime that

197

doesn't qualify as one of these serious offenses." Suppose a person was wrongly classified as an "aggravated felon." She was making the same point she made to me as a Brearley student: let each side argue; let judges judge. That's what due process looks like.

The court issued its decision three months later: the majority—five out of nine—ruled in favor of the government. Yes, prosecutors can lock up noncitizens. No time limit. No need to ask a judge's opinion. Because of this case and another, Dad too was under threat of being redetained.

The written opinion cited that stat that didn't sit right: that detainees typically are locked up for an average of forty-seven days. A decade later, the truth would come out: the government made "several significant errors" on its math, the Justice Department admitted. For the people like Mr. Kim, who are appealing, detention lasts 382 days on average—which is 813 percent more time. But just as prosecutors got away with their error against my uncle, they got away with this one. The correction was a forgotten footnote in history.

If you came of age after 9/11, it's easy to remember the frenzy. As soon as I got my own cell phone (another gift from my big sister), it rang at all hours. I lived in sweatpants and a sweatshirt, in case I needed to stop by a jail. Ang saw me in blue jeans one day and said, "My, my! What's the special occasion?"

What's harder to remember is what I actively ignored—namely, how my father was really doing.

One time, I heard Dad try to get work. He was on the phone, hurrying his words. It sounded like the person on the other end was about to hang up. "Please, if you need any help at all, keep me in mind," Dad said. "Thank you." The call may have ended before he was done speaking.

Dad went back to Broadway a few times, to see if he could collect money from the stores that took his merchandise on credit and hadn't paid. He also looked into whether anyone could make use of his language and math skills. He didn't have a good name, but he had those.

Dad ran out of places to go. He was approaching sixty-five—not yet retirement age. And he was the man who was supposed to work till he died, by choice. He didn't know what else to do with himself. Work is worship. That old keychain of his hung on a nail, collecting dust.

I began to talk to Dad like he was a problem to be solved—which is the single worst way to talk to a person with chronic depression. *Did you see if McDonald's or Walmart is hiring? Why don't you go to a senior center and make new friends?* Each question reinforced the thought he was trapped in: you are a failure.

"Doll, what do you think?" Dad said to me one time in the living room. "Should I sign out?"

"Why? What the hell are you talking about?" I was scalding hot. His case was at a peculiar standstill. While deportation agents could come cart him off, he at least didn't have to go to court or check in at 26 Federal Plaza anymore. He was in a quiet limbo. Our strategy—my strategy—was for Dad to keep laying low.

"Never mind." Dad let it go. The conversation ended before it began.

What if it hadn't? What if we had a family meeting—I mean, in my own family? If I stopped trying to be other people's caped crusader, could I hear the truth that was unfolding at home?

Maybe Dad would get things off his chest: *In America I'm a felon, an alien, a poor man. If I leave, maybe I can find my life's purpose again. I helped my brothers get out of India and get jobs. They're offering to give me a job. You can visit. And besides, I've been coming to the family meetings, to Congress, to the Supreme Court. We both see it's getting worse, not better.*

It was getting a lot worse. On a recent night I sat alone in the town house basement, convulsing with tears. The reason was not another terror attack or another member put on a plane. It was the creation of a new agency that, in three simple letters, spelled out a wildly new path for America.

The agency had the sole mission of deporting immigrants. America never had this before. At no point in U.S. history was a single, permanent, and well-funded bureaucracy charged with combing through the country in search of people who'd lived within the borders for years and decades and kicking them out. Kicking us out. There were raids before, absolutely. But they were more cyclical, not as constantly and unflappably churning. Earlier politicians knew that a rigid deportation machine would be incompatible with a nation of immigrants. Today's politicians had forgotten that fact. The new creation was called U.S. Immigration and Customs Enforcement, or simply ICE.

It felt so big. I didn't know how to put my arms around it. I emailed my college professor—the one who taught me and thousands of elite university students that migration isn't a random personal choice, that it's how people from below cope with a world that's changed from above. I wanted someone who saw more clearly than I to make plain what the rest of us are supposed to do. She didn't have an answer.

I couldn't see a world where Dad's and my paths diverged, where he signed out and I kept fighting for others here. He was a man of so few words that when he bothered to talk it's because he put real thought into it first. When he tried to talk to me, I didn't recognize the moment for what it was: his attempt to make a decision about his life.

There was no hiding the scorn I felt when I stomped out of the living room: *After all I've done for you, this is how you repay me?*

There's that cliché: there's no point having regrets in life. Well, I will always regret how I was too scared to stop and listen. Blinded by my own fears, I added to the sense of failure that weighed Dad down.

A lead actor from one of Hollywood's greatest films mailed us a check for ten thousand dollars. We didn't ask for it. And we were so busy answering calls and visiting jails, we didn't stop to find out how our names came on this generous soul's radar.

It was the best kind of money—not earmarked for a special project. We could use it as we saw fit. Subhash and I talked about what work it would fund. Our lawyer Benita Jain—we had a real lawyer—joined the conversation. She, too, threw professional and personal boundaries to the wind. Our brainstorm session was in her little sister's bedroom.

We could save the cash for overhead. Little things were adding up, like having food at the meetings. We could buy our own bullhorn for rallies (we were too big to keep borrowing from others).

Then another idea hit us: Why don't we use the money to take a bunch of members to Oakdale?

"We can use the trip to publicize New York transfers," Benita said. "Let's pack a court if anyone has a hearing coming up."

Oakdale Federal Detention Center was a prison in southern Louisiana. It was full of New Yorkers. We believed ICE shipped our immigrant relatives thousands of miles away to break them down. It's harder to fight when you can't see your loved ones. And when you got in front of a judge, you'd be all alone—no family in the room to show your ties to America. Down South, judges basically wouldn't let immigrants exercise their right to appeal.

"It'd just be good for folks to see their people again," Subhash said. "I mean, even if that's all we do."

Here was his magic on display. I was the group whip, pushing us to keep pushing. Subhash had plenty of fight in him (which showed up in his long rants on current events). But he kept sensing the basic needs of others—like human contact.

Several women in our group hadn't seen their husbands, brothers, or sons because it was too expensive. They had to choose between paying lawyers or saying good-bye in person. Our nonprofit could give them a weekend worth of memories.

And we could meet our "jailhouse lawyers" in person. A couple of detainees took on the role of organizing from the inside, compiling fellow prisoners' legal questions for Benita to respond to in bulk, which was more efficient than having them send individual letters. We couldn't keep up with the volume of questions coming in.

Benita called airlines to get group ticket rates. The total cost, with motel and ground transit, was roughly $350 a person. We asked members to contribute what they could, and we'd pick up the rest. It was hard to coordinate. A dozen of us ended up flying down to New Orleans.

What I witnessed on this trip haunted me for years—and I don't just mean what happened in the prison.

Subhash and Benita drove minivans from the airport to Allen Parish. Carol was one of the moms on board. She brought Natasha, who was seven years old. Linden used to lift their daughter on his shoulders and take her to school every morning. That was nearly two years ago. They hadn't seen each other since his marijuana arrest.

Carol told their little girl that "daddy's working" or "daddy's out with his friends." In other words, she did what my mom did when my father went away for a long time. She tried to hide it and then felt guilty about it.

Benita, who'd studied with the NYU law professor, was kind to a fault. When we first met, I thought she'd chosen the wrong profession. I couldn't picture her tearing down anyone in a cross-examination. Then her hawk eyes came out. She loved the hunt for loopholes and paid obsessive attention to detail.

"They didn't approve your visitation form," Benita told me once we got there. She'd just gotten off the phone with Oakdale.

"Why?" I got upset. "Did you and Subhash get in?"

"Yes," she said. "I'm really sorry." Every visitor went through a background check and was approved, except me. "I did my best to try to persuade them to let you in, but it was hard because you don't have a close family member inside or a legal relationship that I can push."

"It's OK." I tried to sound understanding.

I spent the first evening in the motel room, alone. I could have felt gloriously alone—gone for a run, binge-watched movies. Or just savored the quiet, sat with myself, let the beaten-down core inside me convalesce. Instead, it was bad alone—the sulking, anxious type of alone. I needed to feel busy, looking for urgency in my emails and on my phone.

When the group came back, they looked like they'd seen a ghost.

"How'd it go?" I asked.

"So we found out what they did to Richard," Benita said.

Richard Rust, a thirty-four-year-old man from Brooklyn, collapsed on the floor and died. It happened right before we boarded the flight for Louisiana. During the visit, one of the jailhouse lawyers slipped Benita a note, written hastily in pencil, detailing what he saw and listing fellow prisoners who could corroborate his account or add details.

According to them, guards (who are supposed to provide emergency care) did not perform CPR. Medical staff, a two-minute walk away, did not come over. The ambulance arrived about forty minutes later, when it was already too late.

Carol couldn't push down her tears: "They just left his body there. They didn't pick him up off the floor."

Natasha was sitting on the edge of a bed, quietly taking in what she'd learned that day. Her dad was not working. He was in prison. That's why he couldn't take her on his shoulders to school. And another man, who'd lived not far from them in Brooklyn, died a sudden death. "Why doesn't Daddy make like a roach and crawl out?" she asked. Her mom wished they'd never come.

If I said my response to this horrific news was only grief or outrage,

202

I'd be lying. And this is what frightens me, to this day. I couldn't feel the fact of such a grave loss. It didn't register inside anymore.

The thought that nagged at me when I was alone in the motel room kept on nagging: *Could Benita have worked harder to include me? Did she like leaving me out?* My sense of exclusion was heightened because I'd missed out on a real showstopper.

This reaction I am describing, which is revolting, is not unique—I've come to learn. A journalist who covers mass shootings once told me about how he gets a thrill from the numbers. He wants each shooting to be bigger than the last. "It needs to be bigger," he said, "to make it to the weekend news cycle." He knows it's wrong to think that. But sometimes it feels as if there's no point grieving and it's best to think practical thoughts. Plus, his identity has become rooted in mass shootings.

What can be so tricky about mission-driven work—in my case, activism—is that it starts off as wonderfully liberating. Break the shackles of shame; feel empowered to make change; be bigger than you ever knew was possible. Until, that is, you're shrunk down to a simplistic identity.

Empowerment became for me self-entrapment; from "I'm an activist fighting for this cause" to "this cause better not exist without me." I calcified from the inside out. Others' loss was starting to become instrumental, a thing to be used. As a kid, I learned "don't use people." Now, my mind raced to how a tragic death could get us a headline. While justice was far out of reach, the media was not.

"Should we call reporters?" I asked. "Let them know?"

"We should probably find his family first," Subhash said, "make sure they want that."

For a split second, I had forgotten the deceased had a family.

Dad worried I was working too much. "Mumah and I are going to Atlantic City," he told me one morning. "Do you want to come?" He must have just convinced her to do the drive.

"Should I invite Subhash?" I asked.

"No, no, no! Please. Let's go just us. Me, you, Mumah."

Subhash had become a fixture in the Shahani home. Mom loved him because he listened to her stories and washed his own dishes. Deepak liked calling Subhash my "midget boyfriend." My brother couldn't care less if we were dating; he just liked to laugh at our expense. Ang liked Subhash well enough, except for the time he answered his cell phone while we were at a movie. "He's so ghetto." She wrung my wrist. "Do you have to bring him everywhere?" Dad was terrified that Subhash and I would get married, raise revolutionary social worker kids, and be poor—having only our values to feast on.

"OK, OK," I said. "We can go, just us."

On the drive down I-95, Mom popped in her Wayne Dyer self-help CD. "He's my soul mate," she said of the life coach. "He can express his feelings."

I leaned in from the backseat. "Can you shut that off so we can talk?" Dad hit EJECT.

"Hhhhhhhh," Mom heaved, her thin cheeks expanding with hot air. "OK, so what do you want to talk about?"

"Dad." I turned to him. "Where were you on Independence Day? I mean, Indian independence."

Mom was an infant at the time, too young to remember. I'd never heard Dad's story.

He was a six-year-old boy holding his mom's hand. Although he was the second son, he was her favorite. His family boarded a ship. It went from their hometown of Karachi to Bombay. The trip would take about one day. "I prayed there would be no fight," he said. "I saw the *sardarjis* with long knives hanging in their belts." The boat had Hindus, Sikhs, and Muslims, who could begin butchering one another at the smallest provocation.

"At six you were aware of that possibility?"

"Of course. I saw it happen on land," he said.

A sensation went through me. For a split second I could see fresh blood washing over dusty streets, a little boy's eyes tracing the rivulet.

"And then you lived in Bombay?" I pushed on with the chronology.

For the next ten years, Dad and his growing family—they were seven brothers, four sisters, and two parents in total—lived in a single room. The bathroom was outside, a few meters away. The floor inside was made of cow dung, which wore out. "I had to spread the fresh dung on the floors." That was their version of mopping.

A local holy man became Dad's patron and gave him a scholarship for school.

"Really?" I said. "That's like me!" I wondered why Dad didn't tell me we had that in common back when I got into Brearley.

Dad graduated two years early. He'd hoped one day to become a lawyer, like his hero, Mahatma Gandhi.

"That's like me too," I said.

"Dahling, you've never told me these things," Mom piped in, accusingly. Just as Dad was getting going, she was complaining about how little he expresses.

"Well, he's telling us now," I said.

The conversation ended.

Mom and Dad had a coupon for one free night at the Tropicana. Casino offers were the only junk mail Dad got these days. He'd long stopped being courted by Visa or Mastercard. His credit score tanked.

"How much do you think I'll make?" he asked us. He wasn't kidding. That's why he wanted to come. The casino was the one place where he felt he could earn cash.

"Five hundred," Mom said.

She was ever the optimist. I just hoped he broke even. I gave him two hundred dollars to play for me. I didn't gamble. Mom and I wandered the boardwalk. If I squinted hard enough, the empty soda bottles blanketing the shore looked like seashells. Then we headed to our free room to read. A while later, the phone rang. Dad was calling.

"Aarti doll, why don't you join me?"

"I don't like those games, Dad."

"Doll, just have the experience. You should try everything once."

"OK, I'm coming."

Dad was at a five-dollar roulette table. He'd just finished blackjack and was up more than a hundred dollars. But it was too soon to gloat. He focused on the spinning wheel, his lips slightly parted. We looked the same when we concentrated.

Dad explained the rules of roulette. You put your chips on numbers or bet on odds or evens or bet on a color—red or white. Dad had twenty dollars riding on 10, 13, and 19. He was betting my birthday and his.

"Dad, we both know you're unlucky," I teased him. "You sure you want to play those numbers?"

"*Hah.*" He smiled and slammed his chips on the felt table.

I followed his lead, playing the same numbers as him, as well as a color. Maybe it was my beginner's luck. We kept winning.

Dad waved his hand at a waitress.

"Please, can I have scotch on the rocks?" he asked her, and then turned to me. "What do you want, doll?"

"*Dad!* I don't drink!" Except for my twentieth birthday party, I didn't touch alcohol. All my years of underage clubbing, I did sober.

"Have one," Dad pressed. "They're free." He turned to the waitress. "Can you make that two scotch? One for my daughter." When our scotch arrived, Dad tipped a five-dollar chip. ("Always tip," he taught us. "You must have class.")

By the end of the night, which had become morning, we were up more than six hundred dollars. Mom had underestimated. And I had become a gambler and a drinker to bond with my father.

A stretch goal is when you're so exceeding expectations, you up the ante, setting out to achieve even more. I was living the anti–stretch goal. My eighteen-month time line to change the laws (which itself was an extension) had come and gone.

The America we lived in was different from the one in which I'd started my activism. It was wounded—first by the loss of human life, then by the opportunists who are always waiting in the wings, ready to hijack a recovery.

I wanted to find that sand we could throw into the gears of the deportation system—to make it come to a grinding halt. I kept searching for that sand and, pressed up so close to the ground, I'd stopped looking up.

I lost touch with any part of life not directly connected to my nonprofit. When my old teacher Ms. Leonard had arranged for me to deliver a speech to a full assembly at Brearley, I could have gone in search of supporters. I knew from my days there that quite a few teenagers commanded influence over their very influential parents. Instead, I stood on stage feeling constricted. This sea of mostly white faces wouldn't understand, I told myself.

Though other times, all I wanted to do was explain, explain, explain. I suggested to some members and colleagues that we launch an educational workshop and call it Deportation for Dummies. Benita said that name could turn people off. We settled on Deportation 101, a course for lawyers, journalists, social workers, congressional staffers, city council members, and families in crisis. These were the constituents who called us nonstop.

We'd pack into a daylong intensive the points we'd found ourselves repeating over and over: how people got taken into custody (primarily after some contact with law enforcement), what kinds of crimes could trigger deportation (pretty much all of them, including misdemeanors), if it mattered that the immigrant had a citizen spouse or children (it usually did not), and the architecture of the new ICE apparatus. Its office in New York City at 26 Federal Plaza was a location any practitioner should know in case of emergencies.

The NYU law professor arranged for us to have a lecture hall at her school. I figured a couple dozen people would show up. It was more like a couple hundred. Our first Deportation 101 was standing room only. And it was packed with defense lawyers who were shocked by the same fact that shocked me years earlier: an immigrant who's been here for decades can be kicked out for just about anything.

Dad had long stopped coming to our events. I wished he could be at this one. Whenever a relative asked what I did for a living, he'd say, "She is a lawyer." It annoyed me to no end, but "community organizer" was not a phrase he'd repeat. Now, lawyers were getting official credit from the Bar Association for taking my class.

It was so popular, we repeated Deportation 101 and it turned into a small community institution. A film director heard of it and came by for research. He was making a movie about a young immigrant getting deported after 9/11 and a lonely, elderly white American man who, meeting the immigrant serendipitously, tries to help keep him here.

The Visitor was nominated for an Oscar, and the filmmaker told me that one of the characters was based on me. When I watched it, I looked for her. I was anticipating a fiery, tireless activist in sweatpants, holding her iconic bullhorn. That's not what the filmmaker saw. He turned me into a lawyer in a small, dusty office in Queens—hardworking and impatient, snapping at a client who was still coping with shock.

I winced. The filmmaker did what great fiction does: render us in our essence. Except for one detail he got profoundly wrong. He made me a man, a son. Being a daughter was always central to my character.

ACT 6

Leaving and Finding Home

IN ONE VERSION OF the story, the darkness passed and then there was light. Dad bounced back. He found a job. He started watching the weekend news shows again. We'd sip chai on Sunday afternoons and he'd debrief me on the latest from *Face the Nation* and Christiane Amanpour. I'd debrief him on the latest in local roundups and the humble victories we did manage to eke out. Drawing on his past—as a lifelong migrant and business owner—he'd coach me, helping me wrangle the twin demons of ego and cynicism. I would rediscover my faith in fighting the good fight and, with a clear conscience, forge ahead in my destiny: to become a lawyer who does God's work, be it putting away the real bad guys or securing the human rights of immigrants. This is the future Judge Blumenfeld optimistically envisioned for me.

But in the real world, people cannot make themselves what you think they should be. I couldn't make Dad or myself. The "lesson in should" continued.

I was sitting on the floor of my parents' new home. We had to sell the dream house and downsize. I had a basket of cotton pads and gauze.

"Does it hurt?" I asked Dad.

"No," he said. "No pain."

Part of Dad's right foot had been sawed off. The surgeon took the big toe and a chunk of the metatarsal bone, leaving the inner edge concave, as if a dog took a bite. Wrinkle was no longer with us. When she passed, we all wept, especially Dad. She'd become his best friend, and the first member of our family to go.

One morning, on the way to the kitchen, Mom accidentally stubbed Dad's toe. The wound didn't close on its own. He had diabetes. I was now changing his dressing, peeling the mesh that had glued to his flesh with dried blood.

"Careful, doll," he said. This was his least favorite part.

Next was my favorite: pouring the hydrogen peroxide, which fizzled on contact. "The color looks good, Dad." I felt cheerful. "I'm sure it'll heal soon."

I was wrong. Over the weeks, the palette of his wound went from pinks and reds to black and blue. Dad had developed gangrene. A lifetime of chain-smoking didn't help. There was so much nicotine inside, it had narrowed or clogged his arteries altogether. His heart couldn't pump enough blood to his foot. The whole thing had to go.

"No, no, no," Mom exclaimed in the hospital room.

"I'm sorry, Mrs. Shahani," the surgeon said. "I believe if we take this artery from the hip to the knee and reroute—stitch it to his ankle—that should get enough blood flowing to work."

Should. In other words, there was a chance the foot couldn't be saved. The surgeon would use other parts of Dad's leg to try. He had Medicare now. While he was not a citizen, he was a senior citizen, still under threat of deportation but with a green card, eligible for government-subsidized coverage. I joked with friends that what the government extracted in legal costs it would now repay in healthcare costs.

Mom had to sit down. Her lower lip was trembling. I could read her thoughts: *All these years of hard work, being poor, making it, losing it, I've never cared about having expensive things. I've just wanted my husband's companionship. All these years I kept going, thinking we could at least enjoy old age together. Now we won't even have that. When grandchildren come into our lives again, how will we hold them in our arms and feed pigeons in the park if my husband can't even walk? What kind of life is there with a man who can't carry his own weight?*

Dad's stare was blank, much like it was when the dentist said all his teeth had to go years back.

"Mrs. Shahani, I know it sounds scary. But we'll be able to get him a prosthetic and he'll regain ambulatory movement," the surgeon assured her.

I wondered how many years into medicine it took for doctors to replace "walk" with jargon like "ambulatory movement." Maybe it happened orientation week at med school.

"Dahling," Mom said to Dad. *"Tho kai chaa khhapai?"*

He did not reply with what he wanted to do. It was exactly like at the dentist's office.

The doctor proceeded with surgery and made one simple request to Dad: "Please do not smoke on the days we give you oxygen." They'd put Dad in a special tank, pumping his body with O_2 to help the wound finally heal.

Of course, Dad smoked. Angelly caught him. "What the hell are you doing?" she snapped, and cried. He didn't have a good answer. It's the only time I can remember Ang snapping at him. The rest of us were doing it regularly.

My big sister had been studying the science of Dad's condition, becoming his faux doctor, just as I'd been his faux lawyer. Mom was his nurse. We three found ourselves in and out of the hospital for a few years, visiting his revolving door of surgeries, follow-ups, progress reports, relapses, three heart attacks, and five amputations that ultimately removed his entire leg, up to the thigh.

Deepak, who'd moved out, made himself keep showing up, but he couldn't keep down the resentment he'd held in over the years. After Dad's open heart surgery—he had that, too—he didn't put in the effort to do physical therapy. "We try so hard," my brother said. "Can't he do the most basic things?"

That familiar old feeling that lay in wait rose up in me, too: Dad holds me back. It was different this time because I couldn't say exactly what he was holding me back from. I no longer knew what I wanted to be when I wasn't busy being an immigrant daughter.

I'd left Families for Freedom. I couldn't do it anymore. My pragmatism wouldn't let me keep fighting the good fight. We never (or barely ever) won.

Subhash left, too, around the same time, in fact, and not long after we'd broken up. It was inevitable. We did fall in love. The same chemistry that brought us together for family meetings brought us together. He was my first true love: the man who made me laugh till my stomach hurt and think till my brain hurt; who made promises he always kept; who was there for Dad, not just me, time and time again.

We built a robust community, who kept attending our spate of "surprise" birthday parties. Subhash and I had gotten into a funny habit. Each year, we'd attempt to surprise each other with an intimate party of a hundred or so "movement friends." It was pretty much always at a lounge playing hip hop. We'd dance until 2 or 3 A.M. and cut cake. By year three, we'd each feign surprise. But by year four, the parties stopped.

While Subhash and I adored the fire in each other, we burned at both ends. Our relationship born from tragedy was stuck there. Too many conversations were about what was wrong in the world. As soon as the room emptied and we were left to ourselves, we were a caricature of grief, not a model of how to share a life with someone. We looked for ways out of this trap together. When no door opened, we called a cease-fire and walked away separately.

My inner romantic is still shaking her head. To meet a soul mate once in this lifetime is so rare. How could I let it go? My inner skeptic says, *Of course you didn't last.* Building a campaign with no end in sight is hard enough. To add dating to that is a recipe for disaster. Twenty-four/seven contact is a sure way to kill love.

As Dad sat there decaying, I picked up odd jobs and sulked. For more than a year, I curled up on the couch, watching sitcoms, just as I did when I was a child, only now with a pint of Häagen-Dazs, eating until I fell asleep, waking up with remnants of butter pecan in my mouth.

As much as I didn't want to, I kept turning my attention back to Dad—like a driver rubbernecking after an accident.

"Dad, do you want to apply for citizenship?" I found myself asking him one day.

"You think it's wise?" he punted back to me.

Citizenship was the ultimate gamble. Eight years had passed since Dad was first tagged for deportation, and we were in a highly unusual situation: we'd never gotten a judgment by the immigration authorities. We likely benefited from the post-9/11 chaos. Shortly after the terrorist attacks, an officer at 26 Federal Plaza told Dad to stop coming for his check-ins. "We'll call you back," he said.

Only, he never called us back. Our lawyer figured ICE was so overcommitted—rounding up people without competent representation, who were far easier targets than Dad—that the agency decided to push his case to the back of the line. When the years kept passing and ICE didn't reach out, we figured they'd lost his file.

It would have felt like a huge relief—except that ICE had no statute of limitations. If they wanted to pick up the case in a day or a decade, they could. I needed finality.

If we submitted an application for Dad to become a U.S. citizen, he would jump back on ICE's radar. Anyone who wants citizenship gets a deportation screening first. There was only a minuscule chance Dad would get a swearing-in ceremony and a far greater chance he'd be diverted to court and ordered exiled.

"Let's do it," I said. "You're not happy here."

"Hah," he agreed.

If Dad became an American, legally, he'd have the freedom to come and go. He could visit his family abroad and return safely; he could hear the door knock without worrying who was on the other side. And if it didn't work—well, we didn't talk about what that would mean.

My father was so deep into depression, finding a therapist or family counselor would have been a sensible step before knocking on ICE's door. I just couldn't see that step. Again, I needed finality.

The same clever lawyer who got Dad out of detention prepared the memo we'd include in his citizenship application. The case we'd relied on years ago, to argue that Dad was not an "aggravated felon," had been overturned. That happened right after 9/11. Our lawyer would make the same argument again, from scratch. While precedent was not on our side, we had a different layer of padding: a thick stack of more than a hundred letters of support I'd collected, on letterhead, from friends I'd made at prestigious universities and companies and even from a Republican member of Congress. The legal memo was the polite offering—a simple out for immigration authorities to use to get rid of the Shahani nuisance without setting a precedent that would help other families. The support stack was the threat. *Let Mr. Shahani go, or his daughter will make the TV rounds.*

"Are you certain you want to submit this?" Moseley asked me. "I'm positive I can defend your father, but I am obligated to warn you there is potential for litigation." It was more than potential. It was near certainty.

"Yes, I'm certain." I took the liberty of speaking on behalf of Dad.

When a school is going to admit you, they mail an oversize envelope with a congratulatory message and piles of paperwork to sign. When they've rejected you, they send a regular envelope with a form letter. That's why I was terrified when the response from the authorities arrived.

"Doll, I have received a mail from the Citizenship and Immigration Services," Dad told me on the phone.

"What size is it?"

"*Kya?*" He didn't understand the question.

"Is it a big envelope or a normal one?"

"A normal one."

My heart dropped into my stomach. *Here we go again. Why do I always respond to problems by rocking the boat?*

"What does it say?" I asked him.

He hadn't opened it yet. He put me on speakerphone. Mom was standing by him. "Dear Mr. Shahani: Thank you for submitting your application for U.S. citizenship. Your naturalization interview is on Tuesday, August fifth, at eight A.M. in Newark . . ."

"WHAT?" my voice boomed. "They said you have a naturalization interview?"

"*Hah*, doll."

"I can't believe it."

It worked. ICE wasn't knocking on our door to lock up the man they'd forgotten. They were letting him in. Dad would become an American citizen.

All he had to do was pass the history exam. We studied together for a month. Ang and I printed out sample tests and drilled him. He read on his own when we were at work. He was getting every question right, almost.

"Who wrote the Declaration of Independence?" we asked.

"Thomas Jefferson," he said.

"When was the Constitution written?"

"1787."

"Name one of the longest rivers in the U.S."

"Misses Pee-pee," he said.

"Noooo!" Though that would be a great name for it. "It's Misses Sippy. Sip the water. Don't pee-pee in it. Misses Sippy."

The test date came—and went. Dad missed it. He'd landed back in the hospital. Our lawyer wrote to the government to ask for a new appointment. When that date arrived, I asked Moseley to join us. I wanted Homeland Security to see we were lawyered up, ready to rumble if that's what they wanted. He agreed to come and asked first that I "replenish" his retainer.

I emailed my siblings, "Hey Guys—We have a new natz interview date . . . Moseley wants more money. Can we split the bill?"

Ang responded a minute later: "Ask him how he would feel about reflexology in exchange for his presence and expertise. See what that gets you. Deepak and I will then discuss splitting the rest."

One of the odd jobs I'd picked up was masseuse. Massage felt like a more tangible good to me than law. I'd been massaging Mom since I was little, after she got hit by the car. I thought maybe physical therapy could be my next career.

Deepak chimed in with the right response. "Yes," he emailed. "We can split . . . of course."

"Deepak, you give in too easily," Ang darted back. "Aarti's nimble little fingers could work [her] magic and then instead of splitting 1,000, we split 50 dollars ;) . . . I'm afraid Aarti would have to use more than her fingers to get us that discount."

My sister was wasting my time. I wrote, "u have no idea how much i am NOT finding u funny."

She replied, "I don't believe you :) I think you are laughing really hard."

Crass, vulgar, insensitive. I could count on my family for that. Teamwork, too. We split the bill. Though not before Ang got in one last jab about her kid sister and the straitlaced lawyer.

"You'd be the most exotic dish Moseley ever had, minus the one time he ordered stir-fry from Wok Around the Clock," she wrote. And then, "hehehehe (Sorry, I'm convulsing in my chair)."

I pushed Dad's wheelchair into the same room I went for my citizenship test. Just as he'd told me to dress up for my big day, he dressed up for his. He wore his favorite navy blue suit and paisley tie.

The officer asked the civics questions. I held my breath before each answer. Dad had been through yet another emergency room visit. He was heavily medicated, his face swollen. Still, I saw something in it I hadn't seen in a very long time: pride. He held his head up. It didn't slump down. He was proud of himself for doing something right again. He scored 100 percent.

"Congratulations, Mr. Shahani," the officer said after the test. "You are going to be an American citizen." Our lawyer didn't have to pull anyone aside and explain away the felony conviction. It was over.

Over. This was how our immigrant family tragedy would finally end. Not with one of us tossed across the ocean but with all of us together. The constant legal threat that defined our lives in America—the lives of millions of immigrants—could have had a very different ending. Oxygen rushed into my lungs. It was not euphoria. It was nothing like euphoria. It was the end of a more than decadelong anxiety attack. The hand that kept tearing open a wound inside me would finally leave me alone and let the wound close. Life without an open wound. *I haven't had that before. Is it very different?* I didn't know.

I leaned down to wrap my arms around Dad. "You did great," I told him. "I'm so proud of you."

"Of course, my doll! What did you expect?"

I didn't expect to leave home as fast as possible. And I won't try to explain in any detail the psychological and professional jujitsu it takes to go from leftist activist to mainstream business journalist in two years flat. But my story, in broad brushstrokes, is this:

I peeled myself off the couch. It wasn't because of an aha! moment that came to me in the depths of solitude. It was a copycat move. A close friend who'd also been a community organizer was applying to graduate schools. I decided two weeks before the first deadline to follow her lead. The schools were the Harvard Kennedy School of Government and Harvard Business School.

Why I did it, honestly: I needed to get out of New York City, where I felt like the sludge that collects between the subway tracks. And everyone wants to go to Harvard. The written-essay reasons: I wanted to achieve "structural change" by creating "transformative institutions" that were built "to scale"—or something like that.

The choice not to pursue my childhood dream of law school was an easy one. The practice of law cultivates the reflex to distrust, to be argumentative, to see others as enemies. That is, it feeds on character flaws I'd proved I had in spades—and that made me miserable. I didn't want to poison myself any further.

The government school did not require an interview. I was certain that was why they admitted me—and gave me a full two-year scholarship. I would get my master's degree, at Harvard University, debt-free. The business school did require an interview—which meant a human could see me contort my face and body as I strained to pretend I knew what I wanted. No applicant has a clue. But rising business leaders are much better at hiding this fact. I got rejected.

No matter. Harvard in any shape or form would get the job done. I just needed the H-bomb to obliterate my identity and start afresh.

Dad's swearing-in ceremony happened to coincide with my first month in grad school (if you believe in coincidence). I came back for it. As Dad raised his right hand, Mom, Deepak, Ang, and I flanked him. He was the first of us to land in America, and the last to cross the finish line.

It felt strangely intimate. I was not sharing this moment with the activist community I'd made along the way. I'd mostly cut them off, feeling I needed to build a wall between me and them so I could keep going. I didn't organize a party of one or two hundred people, as I would have back in the day.

Though, in a quieter way, we *were* celebrating with a hundred or two. The people in the room. I did a double take. The swearing-in looked like our old building, our 401 neighbors: black, brown, and Asian faces, a few white sprinkled in between. My upbringing in Queens was America's future. What some did not want this country to be, it is destined to be— that home with an unrivaled capacity to absorb and contain difference. Maybe my eighteen-month extended timeline was too short, and we were winning after all.

America's first black president—the first of many, we hoped—came on the TV to congratulate the newest citizens. "This is now officially your country," he said. "You've traveled a long path to get here."

A cardboard cutout of him and his wife was set up for photo ops. My family gathered around them. And then the country music played. "I'm proud to be an American, where at least I know I'm free. And I won't forget the men who died, who gave that life to me."

Patriotic songs make me choke up because the sentiment is so seductive. Yes! We must be united. And yet the history of America's freedom is far messier, darker, bloodstained. We Shahanis turned to each other with a knowing look. Dad had said more than once that this country is full of "confused" people. Here we saw, in the sacred ceremony, the comedy of contradictions.

The move to become a technology journalist right out of Harvard was not another return to the womb—the beat ordained to the child of an electronics shopkeeper on Broadway. Our old store had nothing to do with it. It was a cold, hard calculation—the first in my life, which I made at age thirty-one.

My guesses about what I wanted to do were wrong. While at Harvard, I'd thought about the State Department, the agency that manages America's relationships with other countries. I'd worked with many countries (in the form of their consulates). Then I met classmates who'd held State Department jobs. I didn't fit in with them.

I thought about "social enterprise"—a trendy term for companies that want to save the world and make money. A criticism of nonprofits (like the one I'd started) is that they can't grow quickly enough to meet the needs that their big, bold visions entail. Only for-profits, with "market discipline," can grow fast enough for that—or so the thinking goes. But there was no company I wanted to start or join.

The first time I thought about journalism as a career was, oddly enough, when my body was pressed up against a police barricade. It was a post-9/11 protest. No one was allowed to cross the line—except for men and women with press credentials. Fascinating. Reporters could walk freely where I was not welcome. They had access. I wanted that.

At school, I got to meet many journalists. They came as visiting fellows or to give talks. The best of them were smart without trying to sound smart. I admired them.

Harvard got me into a program where I reported a story for *The Washington Post*—and it landed on the front page. The first person to call and congratulate me was an NPR reporter—the one who investigated the death of the young detainee from Brooklyn who'd collapsed in the

Louisiana prison. The reporter could reach me because, after all these years, my cell phone number hadn't changed.

"What the heck are you doing reporting?" he asked me.

"I'm trying to be you."

He introduced me to his bosses at NPR and encouraged me to apply for a much-vaunted fellowship, bankrolled with money from the McDonald's empire. In journalism—an industry full of underpaid, dead-end jobs—the fellowship was the rare fast track to a real job. I told myself I would either get it and become a journalist or I'd move on (to what, I didn't know). I got it.

Now here's where the calculation comes in. NPR had sent me to California, to work at a local member station. This was a "rotation," where I would prove my worth.

"I know you'll make it, my doll," Mom said one day when I was visiting home. "You always do. God's angels protect you."

As she spoke, I wondered if immigrant parents live in a fiction where, because they did the hard work of nation jumping, they believe all the hard work has been done.

"God's angels?" I lashed out. "No, Mom! It's not angels. It's work. I make it because I work my ass off. Because I worry. Because I do things for myself and don't count on anyone else doing it for me."

I explained to her that in California, I would focus on technology stories because there was less competition on that beat. If I wanted to be the premier prison or immigration reporter of our time, I'd get quashed. Senior reporters claimed that turf. But tech was easier to step into. The year was 2012. While America was beginning to run on smartphones and apps, while there was curiosity about the "creepy" data scientists, the hard-hitting questions about whether tech titans were harming democracy and our health had not yet come to the fore.

Mom found it strange that I would have such an extraordinary megaphone—the NPR audience is 37.7 million people—and I was using it to talk about subjects that were important, sure, but not close to my heart. Oprah wouldn't do that.

"Always let this come first." Mom touched her hand to my chest. "Your heart above your head."

"Are you kidding me?" I pushed her hand away. "I tried that for, like, all of my twenties. Because of you people. And see where that got me."

You people. By that I meant my parents.

My new strategy was to lock my heart in a box. That way, I wouldn't have to keep losing people I cared about to deportation. I could see what I was made of when I led with my brains.

I finally got my driver's license. I found a twin-size bed I could afford in San Francisco. It was tucked away in a makeshift bedroom under a staircase. And my big break came when I set out to drive from my new home to Las Vegas for a story.

I didn't know what story. I'd assigned myself the task of going to the Consumer Electronics Show—the biggest, splashiest tech expo in the United States, possibly the world. I wanted to show NPR editors that I could parachute into any place and file fast. I needed to file two stories to cover the cost of the rental car, gas, and my motel room. A third story, if I got one, would be my keep.

The Las Vegas Convention Center was lined with thousands of booths. I sat in concept cars that would fly one day and met CEOs of the largest companies. The power differential between their lives and mine was ludicrous. I tried to not be intimidated (it was hard).

I looked for quirky uses of the smartphone. That was the trend of the moment. I found a company that synced an electric toothbrush with an iPhone app, to quantify your brushing regimen and tell you where to brush longer. A Chinese company showed me their smartphone with a camera that rivaled the iPhone's, and for one-third the price. A fashion designer put a blazer on me. The shoulder pads, connected to Google Maps, would vibrate left or right, telling me when to turn.

It was a far cry from investigative reporting. I wanted to hashtag my vibrating-blazer selfie: #FallenFreedomFighter. I was in my thirties, a grown woman, starting all over.

Dad happened to call that day. He called me every day. He worried I was so far away. I forgot to tell him I'd gone to Vegas.

"Oh my god, you are at the CES!?" He was beyond excited. "I always wanted to attend that show."

"You know about it?"

"*Hah.* Of course. So many customers from around the world. But the booth was too expensive for us to go."

The pavilion looked different all of a sudden. The lines and lines of small business owners I'd passed—not interested in their stories because they weren't good for radio—and it didn't occur to me that my father, at the peak of his career, aspired to be one of them. I'd arrived so easily in the place Dad couldn't enter.

"How much do you have to pay to go?" Dad asked me.

"Nothing. I'm a journalist, so I get a free press pass."

"Wow!" He was so happy for me. "God bless you, my doll."

His excitement was infectious. I started to brag, "I can interview the director of the entire thing if I want to. Because I report for NPR, his people have been nagging me to meet. I guess he wants to be on air."

Not long after that road trip, NPR gave me a full-time job. The head of the business desk told me I'd impressed them with the speed of my work and my knack for finding sources—that is, talking to the right strangers. I almost said, I learned that from years of power mapping, when I was a community organizer. But I caught myself. Newsrooms are leery of activists.

NPR, like many media companies, was looking to hire in Silicon Valley. I put myself in the very place where demand for journalism was about to explode. Migration—across countries, inside countries—is a bet. I made the right bet.

When I got my press credentials, it was euphoria—not because I landed a dream job but because I landed a real job. Alongside my name, EMPLOYEE was in caps—not "contractor" or "subcontractor" or "freelancer." I entered that class of society where you can count on healthcare and retirement benefits. My parents never had a job with either.

Also, I had an identity outside of their crises.

It was 5:39 P.M. and I had a choice to make: hit SEND or DELETE.

I had just finished reading an essay that brought me to tears. A young man who'd won a Pulitzer Prize was now coming out as an undocumented immigrant. His account was easily one of the best I'd ever read. It ran in *The New York Times Magazine*.

"[Being undocumented] means keeping my family photos in a shoebox rather than displaying them on shelves in my home, so friends don't ask about them," he wrote.

For all the years I'd known families without papers and been part of one myself, I'd never thought of that. He did what great journalism does: excavate the lost details, to help the rest of us see clearly. And it was riveting: a member of the underclass—an "illegal"—is supposed to be hidden until translated by the professional class. This journalist was proving he could be the narrator of his own life, in the pages of the most elite publication on earth.

The email I'd written was to a new mentor of mine—a man who used to be the executive editor of *The Washington Post* and who'd shepherded that story of mine onto the front page.

"Dear Len," I began to write and delete. "Dear . . . Prof. Downie." We met through the Harvard network. I wasn't sure if we were on a first-name basis. I wanted to ask him for personal advice: Is there a way to make my career transition without choosing between my values and my ambitions? Could I be connected to where I come from while still moving forward?

That kind of raw vulnerability felt too risky. So, instead, I did what journalists do. Take an item that has deep personal meaning and turn it into an artifact. "You've undoubtedly seen this article," I began my succinct message. "I like it as an example of how a journalist with a strong personal story can tell it in a dignified way that balances personal voice with professional standards." I didn't ask if we could talk about it. I simply shared the link. Throw it at his in-box and see what sticks.

He responded fifty minutes later with one line: "Call me so I can explain why I disagree about your conclusion about [the author's] professional standards." He included his cell number.

"He lied to me," Len said on the phone. Those were his first words, as I recall them.

It turns out my mentor was also a mentor to the young man who'd written the essay. Small world.

This veteran editor felt the undocumented journalist was not trustworthy because, on the job, he had covered up a key aspect of his life: his immigration status. And, to take it a step further, that status made him unqualified to report on the topic.

"He covered immigration for us." Len sounded exasperated. "I let him cover immigration."

All I could think to myself was, *Everyone has an immigration status. U.S. citizen is a status. We all walk into the newsroom with our biases.* It seemed to me those biases were credentials—not conflicts of interest—when they were elite. CNN had given a show to a business journalist who'd worked for Goldman Sachs. ABC made a Democratic Party advisor a chief anchor and the chief political correspondent. But if you'd been a jailhouse lawyer, that would disqualify you from covering the prisons that locked you up because, although you'd built institutional expertise, you could not be "objective."

What I ended up saying was something like, "I'm sorry he lied to you, Len." We were on a first-name basis. I wanted to keep it that way.

The digital trial of the century was about to happen, a Goliath and Goliath fight. And it was mine to cover. The most powerful law enforcement agency and the single largest company on earth were butting heads. The Federal Bureau of Investigation wanted Apple to unlock the iPhone of a mass shooter. Apple said no; if they created an extra-special, all-purpose key for this iPhone, it could get stolen and used by criminals and warlords for others. A federal judge in Riverside, California, would rule on the matter.

I headed to the airport with my shotgun mic and sleeping bag. Seating at the hearing was on a first-come, first-serve basis. I'd planned to sleep on the courthouse steps to secure the NPR spot.

"Now boarding Flight 2043," the United attendant announced on the loudspeaker. As I stood on the long line, checking Twitter, news broke: the FBI said it might be able to break into the locked iPhone without Apple's help after all. The hearing might get canceled.

Minutes later, Apple sent an email inviting journalists to a telephonic briefing with their lawyer. It was such an agile move. We in the press corps were aching to understand. By moving so swiftly to meet that need of ours, and beating the FBI to the punch, Apple would have the upper hand in framing the rapidly unfolding debate.

I stepped off the United line to dial into the call. Passengers were moving like snails. There was time to make the call and the flight.

"Thanks for joining us so last minute," an Apple employee facilitated, "and now I'd like to turn it over to Ted Olson."

Ted Olson. Why does that name sound so familiar? I had just been assigned this story. It was growing so quickly, NPR put more reporters on it. As he spoke—he was so witty, confident, charming—I googled his name and saw: oh my god! He's the same guy who was at the Supreme Court years ago, after September 11th, arguing on behalf of the government to detain the Korean green-card holder.

Back then I was a silent voice, with Dad, in the audience—our family's fate hanging in the balance. Now I didn't have to be silent. Sure, I was on mute in the conference call. But when it came time for questions, I could unmute. I could have a reckoning.

"Next question from Aarti Shahani with NPR." I recall the facilitator pronounced my name correctly.

You were among those responsible for families like mine being destroyed because our dads and brothers and mothers and sisters couldn't claw their way out of mandatory detention. You were so clearly on the wrong side of history. Glad to see you landed on your feet. Do you fight for justice or the highest bidder?

Never had the gap between my inner and outer monologue been greater. I said something more like: "Thanks for taking my question. Mr. Olson, do you believe the FBI's announcement is coming now—on the eve of court—because they're afraid of losing and setting a harmful precedent?"

I'd spent so many years fighting for my convictions, it felt like it was time to live life on the sidelines, to quiet down and hear the perspectives I could not while shouting through a bullhorn. Sometimes a profound curiosity was my guide. Sometimes it was more like cowardice.

I recall a date I was on. I'd met a man at an event. He went to the best schools and was over six feet tall. Height suddenly mattered. While my first love was quite a few inches shorter than that, I'd now found myself only looking at men who were towering.

This new man was a terrible bore, except for when he made the most unexpected off-color jokes. He had political ambitions. He was running for office. I wasn't sure if it was some pie-in-the-sky dream or if he had a real chance. I also wasn't sure if he and I would have gotten along in my past life—when I was the grassroots protester, not the mainstream journalist.

The most fun I had with him was at a Bollywood theater in Fremont, the Little India of Silicon Valley. The movie was so bad, it was good. Our last time together was a dinner that cost well over a hundred dollars. He was chivalrous, picking up the check and then holding the door as I slid into his luxury car.

When we got in front of my place, he turned to me and peered. There was something serious on his mind.

"Aarti, I have a question to ask you," he said.

"Yes?"

"It's delicate."

"Delicate" is a peculiar word to use with a person you're getting to know.

"Go ahead," I told him. "It's OK."

"Well, um." He fumbled for a second. "How do you think your dad's whole story would affect my career?"

My dad's whole story. Did this man know my dad's whole story? I was just beginning to understand it myself. I'd recently had the fortune or misfortune, recounted earlier, of visiting the judge's chambers and having to sit through him telling me, "Your dad should never have taken that guilty plea. What a mistake." What was the whole story? It's not on Google.

What I wish I had said in that passenger seat was, "Screw you!" Instead, I stuttered, "I, I—I'm not sure I understand why you're asking."

My date planned to be a rising star in the Democratic Party. There was no consensus on families like mine. The lines were still being drawn. Dad could inspire sympathy or tarnish the would-be politician with "criminal alien" headlines. My family was a wild card.

The politician and I agreed to stop seeing each other.

"Thanks," he said. "You're really easy to talk to."

I'd taken my new mantra—be a good listener—quite far. I didn't know if there was any other way. When you climb into a fancy new world where you don't belong, there are lots of payoffs. Being your authentic self is not one of them. *Nothing in life comes free,* as Dad would say.

There was a fact in my family that was too painful to say out loud: one of us was missing. I'm talking about Akshay, my nephew, the first Shahani born in this country. The courtroom strategy had failed. Our extended family (people who "know the culture," as Dad's brothers would say) failed, too. For a brief moment, when Akshay was becoming a teenager, his mom expressed interest in sending him to the United States for his education. But then she walked back on that proposal. Life moved on.

Except that it didn't.

My siblings had gotten married—Ang to a man from Maryland, whom she met at a party for the satirical paper *The Onion*. Roy was handsome like a Viking, and the two of them could not stop laughing together. Deepak married a woman from the Czech Republic he'd met dancing in the city. Hana was tall like a supermodel—several inches taller than him—and so built, she could lift him with perfect form.

"Oh my god, how funny they look together!" Mom whined.

"Be nice," I said not nicely. "It takes a confident man to be with a taller woman."

What I liked most about my siblings' choice in partners was, while they were each distinct personalities, they were both diligent and honest. They were a fit for the Shahanis.

Neither couple had children. I couldn't ask why. It felt too sensitive. But I was certain they each wanted to. It just wasn't happening. The barrier was not medical. It was something else, I felt. A curse.

"Papi, why not go back to India?" I asked Dad during one of my business trips back east. While I'd left activism, I took with me the Dominican word for "dad." Without intending to, I'd gotten in the habit of calling mine "papi."

"Huh?" He got up from his nap.

Napping was his new default state—the background music I didn't mind speaking over.

"Do you want to go to India?" I asked him, louder this time. His hearing was going, too. "To meet Akshay."

My gut told me that Dad had to be the one to break the curse. By going, he'd hit the cosmic play button and we'd stop living life on pause. Our family could be whole and grow.

There was no barrier, no hard-and-fast excuse. Sure, his health was fragile. But he'd been stable, had not checked into a hospital for more than a year. And he had a U.S. passport.

"Do you think he'll receive us?" Dad asked.

It took more than an ounce of courage for him to ask his question. He was naming his fear, not pretending it wasn't there. When Akshay was first taken, we were the victims. After so many years passing, it felt more complicated, like we'd become guilty of something, too.

The right response would have been words along the lines of, "Even if Akshay doesn't show it at first, he'll be so happy to see you made the effort. You're his grandfather. It's not too late."

I had not yet gotten to the kindness section of my self-help library. So my actual response was more like, "Papi, what the hell does it matter: 'Will he receive us?!' You show up. You finally do the right thing. The rest is up to God."

Two months later, my parents were on a plane to India. It was not a straight shot from the airport to Akshay. Mom and Dad stopped to visit his kid sister. She lived in Bombay, which was now called Mumbai. I knew very little about my aunties and their children. They'd stayed in India and traveled little. One of my cousins married a *filmwalla*, like Dad in his youth. Only, this young man didn't carry Bollywood reels through the Arab world. He ran three movie theaters and did quite well.

"Aarti, doll, there's an elevator here." Dad called me from the modern house our relatives had recently built. "And you'll never guess where we went. Guess!"

"Um, was it Kailash Parbat?"

"Oh! How did you know?!"

Kailash Parbat was one of Dad's old haunts—a *chaat* restaurant around the corner from the storied Taj Mahal Hotel. Dad reminisced about the place more than once, especially the *pani puri*.

Pani puri is the snack of choice for locals, kind of like knishes used to be for native New Yorkers. Imagine a tiny tortilla—made of chickpea flour instead of corn—deep fried so that the top and bottom separate and pop up into a perfectly round, hollow, crunchy ball. You punch a little hole in the ball with your finger, pour in tangy pickled water (*pani*) and shove the whole thing into your mouth. You can't eat *pani puri* in bites like you could a potato chip. The water would come gushing out and spill all over your chin. It's an all-or-nothing food experience, one with which Dad was very experienced.

His family took him, maneuvering his wheelchair along the narrow, bumpy streets. They talked with Dad about getting a new prosthetic leg. They had a great doctor in mind.

"Aarti, doll, they are telling me to stay a little longer." He called again from the house with an elevator. "They will show me to their doctor. What do you think?"

The right response would have been, "How generous your sister and her family are! We've barely spoken to them all these years, and they really want to take care of you."

My actual response: "You haven't had a leg for so long. Why do you need one now? Get yourself to Pune. Meet your grandson."

Pune is three hours southeast of Bombay. It really is uncanny how history repeats itself. The grandchild born in America and brought back to the motherland was raised in the same town where Dad landed as a little boy.

Akshay's flat was a few minutes from the dung-floored hut that housed the Shahani refugees after Partition, and another few minutes from the current home of Dad's elder sister. My parents stayed with this other auntie I barely knew. And on a warm, sunny morning, in her narrow hallway, the universe bent. Parallel worlds came together. Akshay rang the doorbell.

"Oh my god, you're such a big boy!" Mom went to answer and pulled him in. "Come, come."

"It's nice to meet you, Dadi," he said in his calm voice. He spoke perfect English and Hindi.

She was his *dadi*. While my paternal grandmother wouldn't hold me because I was the wrong gender, Mom wouldn't let go of her grandchild. The last time she held him, he was about ten pounds. Now he was a young man, almost sixteen years old, with a lean, muscular frame. His mom once said we couldn't have a relationship with him unless we accepted her demands. Yet his drive to know us was so strong, he'd decided otherwise for himself.

"Where is *Dadu*?" he asked.

"Dadu" is "paternal grandfather." These are words my parents had been but not heard for many years. Akshay had had no reason to say them.

"Wow, you're so built up." Mom squeezed his biceps and gave a thumbs-up. "Very nice!"

He blushed. "No, no, Dadi. I'm just normal."

His eyes still looked exactly like his father's—large, black, slanting at the edges like a crescent moon. His unibrow had grown in, thickened in the middle, again like his father (before tweezing). Mom and Akshay both heard a scream.

"Oh, that's your *dadu*," Mom said. "He's having phantom pain."

"Uuuh, what's phantom pain?"

"Oh, it's when you feel someone is stabbing your leg."

"That's awful. Does his leg have a cut?"

"No, no. He doesn't have the leg anymore. That's why it's a phantom."

"I see."

Phantom pain is one of the more mysterious, cruel side effects of amputation. The brain believes the missing limb is still there and that it's writhing in pain. There is no way to treat it. Dad sometimes woke up in the middle of the night, punching the mattress where his leg would have been.

Akshay left his shoes at the doorstep, and Mom led him to the bedroom.

"Hello, my boy." Dad sat up and raised his arms, waiting for his grandson to step into the void that had been left years ago.

Akshay bent down first, to touch Dad's remaining foot. It's a tradition to show respect to one's elders called *pere-pow*. "No, no." Dad pulled Akshay's elbow up and feigned resistance. Though he was probably relieved his grandson was showing respect.

Mom and Dad gave Akshay gifts—a couple dollars in *kaarchi* (blessed money), Nike T-shirts Angelly had chosen, and a small statue of the elephant god, Ganesha. They were supposed to eat breakfast together, but Dad's phantom pain was the worst it had ever been. He was up all night.

"Maybe he's too excited right now," Mom told Akshay.

It was the type of frustrating situation she'd found herself in over and over again. She wanted to have a picture-perfect moment. She could see it, smell it, hear it. The morning should have been home-cooked parathas and hearing all about their grandson's interests, classes, friends. She wanted time to look for the little signs of who he'd become—if he makes eye contact, if his smile is wide or his frown deep.

But that wasn't this morning. Dad was trying, without success, not to howl in pain. And Akshay was in the middle of exams. They agreed to meet again the next day.

Still, my parents called that night, gushing: Akshay is so handsome. He lifts weights, just like Deepak. He's so respectful. He speaks so gently. Dad used that word, "gentle," which was his highest praise—the true mark of strength, what made a man a gentleman.

It sounded like a dream start to me. It could have gone so badly. Akshay could have walked in ready to litigate the past: How did you let so many years go by? Do you even care about me? Instead, the teenager was open and positive. I wished I'd been there to be part of it.

Careful what you wish for.

The next morning, a cousin called me to say Dad was in the hospital. He'd fallen in the bathroom. His blood sugar was jumping all over the place. They'd put him in the ICU, and he was hanging on by a thread. I should come immediately.

Then Mom called. "Aarti, you focus on your work. No need to come here. We are OK." She was trying to be strong. She knew I'd just gotten hired in a job I needed.

"Are you sure it's OK?" I asked. *"Kasam thhei."* It's one of the few phrases I know in our language. It means, "Swear upon me" or "tell me the truth."

She gave a little laugh. My pronunciation was awful. "He's stable," she insisted. "It was probably just all the excitement of being here."

The doctor got on the phone and said my relatives were overreacting. I breathed a sigh of relief. Until, a few hours later, he called back. "My dear, if you are going to come, do it now. I don't know how much longer your father has."

Of all the moments Dad could die, why was he doing it now? Of course he was doing it now. He'd survived all these years, far longer than any of us expected, because he needed to return home.

I booked a one-way ticket from San Francisco to Mumbai. My siblings and I had a conference call before I flew out.

"Should we come, too?" one of them asked.

"No," I said confidently. (The greater the fear, the higher the degree of confidence in my voice.) "I got us into this mess. Lemme figure out what's going on. I'll let you know if you need to come."

"Did you buy travel insurance for Dad?" Ang asked.

"No."

While I'd been very proud of myself for buying the plane tickets, I'd neglected to add the $130 medical protection for a man who was chronically ill. An airlift back to a U.S. hospital would cost $40,000. The victim of my thrift wasn't me. It was Dad.

My siblings didn't say a single critical word. We had a moment of silence. And then Ang read my mind.

"You know, it's funny," she said. "We've spent so many years fighting to be in this country. But it's like, no, Dad wasn't meant to stay here. He belonged there."

We could each see it clearly now and admit it. I pushed the most aggressively, for so many years, against his deportation. My fight for Dad missed the central fact of his life: America wasn't home.

I headed to the airport with my U.S. passport. Ever since I became a U.S. citizen, I needed a visa to visit India—which I did not have.

"I applied for an emergency visa over the internet," I told the young man at the airline counter. "It takes one business day. I'll get it before I land in Bombay."

"I cannot let you board," he told me firmly. "It is illegal to check in a passenger without a visa for the destination country."

"Well, I have a layover in Doha. Americans don't need a visa for Qatar. I can just wait there until the Indians email me my visa." I also pointed out I had just a backpack—nothing to check in that could get lost.

"Madam, I cannot let you board," he told me sternly.

I looked at him—a hard stare—and clarified my position: "My father is about to die. I am getting on that flight. I do not care what happens next."

Years of living had taught me this was not the way for a woman to convince a traditional man of anything. (His accent told me he grew up in the Old World.) But something must have touched him inside. He printed my boarding pass and gave me his blessings. "May Allah protect you."

The visa was in my Gmail when I got to my layover. When I got to Mumbai, a taxi was waiting to take me on the three-hour drive. The cousin with the elevator arranged it.

The city of more than eighteen million people had changed. When I was a child, my family visited here one time, for a cousin's wedding. Back then, in the airport bathroom, I saw a woman with a compressed torso and no legs, a stump for an arm, fingers seemingly extending from her shoulder. She was a leper, begging. Just outside the exit, standing beside a cow, there was a little girl (she'd looked younger than me), also begging. I begged my parents to feed her. Now, where she and the cow once stood, there was a Starbucks.

I arrived at my auntie's home at 2 A.M. Mom was in her kaftan, waiting up for me. "I'm sorry," she said, like a child who'd broken a vase.

Her tiny arms wrapped around my waist, my long arms around her shoulders. "Go to sleep," I told her. "I'm going to Dad. Meet us in the morning."

The hospital was a few kilometers away. It was pouring rain. No rickshaw could drive. I opened my Uber and Lyft apps. They were both young companies I reported on. Uber worked in this city. A young man named Sunil dropped me off at the hospital door. I gave him a five-star rating but no tip. (In the early days, the app didn't let you tip. The drivers had to fight for that.) All told, the journey from San Francisco International to Dad's bedside took twenty-six hours flat.

Dad was still alive when I got there. I leaned in to listen for his breath, which I could barely make out under the roar of the IV drip, the heart monitor, and the elevator in the hallway. Every few seconds, it clanked like a hammer hitting a nail. This was not the place where I'd hoped Dad would die, but it was the place where I could easily see it happening.

"Papi, I'm here." I leaned in and kissed his forehead. It was greasy, scaly. He needed a scrub. At least he wasn't burning up.

"Doll? My doll?" he said. He was awake.

"Looking good, papi! You enjoying your vacation?!"

He was a train wreck—thinner, much thinner. When I put on the lights and lifted the sheets, it looked like someone had taken a machete to his thigh. It was covered in blood from his hip down to his knee. Only, the blood wasn't on the outside. It was on the inside—a terrible case of bedsores. The mattress was too firm, and he couldn't roll over on his own.

"Papi, what kind of music you want?" I asked him. I held one of his hands in both of mine, careful not to touch the needle taped to his vein. His fingers were swollen. "Mukesh? Should I put on some Mukesh for us?" He was one of five Hindi singers I could name.

Dad didn't respond. I made the playlist on Spotify and sat on the sofa by his bed. It was long enough to spread out and take a nap.

The next three days were devoid of emotion. That has become for me the sign of a real crisis. When I'm teeming with rage or wallowing in sadness, I know it's because I have the luxury of feeling. When there's a real crisis, there's no time to feel.

The doctor made his rounds at 5 A.M. He was a squat, friendly man. "You should call your brother and sister to come," he told me.

"OK. When should they arrive?"

"My dear, how will I know the exact time? Ask Him." The doctor pointed to the sky.

I glanced up, where I saw chipped paint and a mold spore. "Right, Doctor," I said. "My dad hasn't died before, so I'm just asking dumb questions."

Relatives shuffled in and out with conflicting looks: "I'm sorry for your loss" and "he'll get better soon." I didn't always know who I was related to. I accidentally kissed a couple of nurses. They wore saris; I thought they were my aunties.

Indian hospitals are the opposite of American ones in a key way: in India, they assume every patient has a family member there to help. The role of family is embedded in the design. The long sofa in Dad's room was there for dutiful relatives to sleep over. In the many U.S. hospital rooms we'd visited for him, there would be one armchair at most.

Mom and I had to go to the "pharmacy"—a line that snaked through the atrium, where we and others elbowed each other to get meds. One lady walked by, a clear plastic bag with red liquid bulging from the fold of her sari. "Blood," Mom whispered. "Here we have to bring the blood for the transfusions."

By the end of the second day, Dad's prognosis had changed profoundly. "My dear, he's more and more alive," the doctor said, metal-wire specks resting on the bridge of his nose. "If this continues, take him home tomorrow."

I glanced at Dad, who was just lying there, his eyes half-open. "Papi, did you do all this just to see if I'd come for you?" He shook his head as if I were being ridiculous. Then I asked him a serious question. "Do you want us to stay here or go back? It's your choice."

I didn't want to force him this time. I didn't want to have it my way. I didn't want to shut him up. I wanted to listen for once, to hear him make a decision for himself.

"Go back," he said, no trace of doubt in his frail voice. "Take me home. I want to go home."

Dad could not sit upright for two minutes, let alone the sixteen-hour flight from Mumbai to Newark. The bedsores were too severe. I had to buy two business-class tickets—one for him, the other for me (to monitor him). Mom would fly later. If the plane had to make an emergency landing in Europe, it would be too hard for me to manage both of them.

Each ticket cost seven thousand dollars—money I did not yet have and could not charge. My credit line wasn't that big. Mom suggested I call one of Dad's brothers, who'd become a millionaire in the Middle East.

"Aarti *beti*, how is Papa?" My uncle picked up the phone when I rang. "You must stay there as long as he needs. Take care of him. That is your duty. Forget everything else. Job, this, that. Your duty is your father."

I was a bit disoriented by the command. I'd spoken with this uncle only a few times in my life. Perhaps he was not aware that I'd been financially independent since I was seventeen, paying all my bills and then some of my parents'. Still, I didn't pick a fight.

"Uncle, the doctor says I should take my dad home." I explained the prognosis. "He says it's fine and we should go home now. I showed the charts to another doctor here, who agreed."

"Oh, very good, *beti*. Very good." *Beti* means "daughter."

"Uncle, I've been spending my money on the hospital bills and medications here. We have to buy everything out-of-pocket." I proceeded with my ask. "Can you help us get the plane tickets? We need business class—two seats—so I can sit with Dad."

His response was priceless. "I've given your family so much. So much. I cannot tell you how much. I'm in a meeting, very important business. Call me back in ten minutes." He hung up before I could say another word.

I didn't call back. Maybe he deserved another chance to help his dying or living brother. But I didn't feel like groveling.

Mom's little sister and her husband—the same ones who got us green cards and nursed Mom when the car hit her—swooped in and picked up the bill. They happened to be passing through India, and, when they heard their brother-in-law was in trouble, they found their way to the hospital and walked into Dad's room.

Somewhere in the flurry of activity, another unexpected visitor came. It was Akshay. "Dadu, where are you going? You just got here."

Standing before me, I was seeing with my own eyes the child my parents described on the phone. I pulled him into me like Mom would—

234

without restraint. It was the only moment in that entire trip—and it was quick—when my emotions tried to jump out. I had to put a stop to it. *Not now, Aarti,* I told myself, sternly. *Now is not the time.*

Dad's eyes shot open. "Akshay, my boy," he whispered, and tried to stretch out his arm, which he couldn't lift on his own.

"I'm sorry I didn't come earlier," Akshay apologized. "I've been studying for exams."

"That's OK," Mom said. "We missed you! Why don't you stay with us here and study?"

"NO." I jumped in before he could respond for himself. "This is a distracting place. He can't study here." Even if he'd wanted to, I didn't want him to make the choices I made. I wanted him to know his family, but not at the expense of his future.

Akshay left and then reappeared when it was time to go. He asked a nurse to step aside, and he lifted his granddad from the bed to the wheelchair and then again from the wheelchair to the taxi.

"We've seen each other after so long," he told Dad. "We have to spend more time together."

Dad looked at him and pointed to the sky. God willing.

Our family with the elevator house in Mumbai insisted we make a stop before the airport, for a prayer. Tears streamed down the face of Dad's kid sister as she lit the wick, preparing the tray we'd hold together at the family altar, for the *aarti*. Her husband, standing beside her, was also weeping. He had fond memories of Dad when they were younger. So did a few others they'd hastily gathered from across Mumbai—complete strangers to me, long-lost friends to Dad.

"*Namu-bhai,* please come back to us," my auntie told him. "We'll be waiting for you." He was barely conscious.

"We need to get going," I pleaded. "It'll take a while to get him to the gate."

"This would be too hard for me," a cousin said, looking worried at what I had to pull off. "You're a very strong girl."

"Oh! That's all the girls in America."

A lot could go wrong, fairly easily: while Dad had a catheter, he could still soil himself. Badly. I would not be able to clean up the mess without attracting a lot of attention. His phantom pain could take over, and he could start screaming and convulsing, sending fellow passengers into mile-high hysterics. Or Dad could die.

I increased the chances of that by playing with his medicine. He had to take twenty-four pills total—blood thinners, sugar, vitamins, Valium. Dad protested when I tried to force-feed them. It hurt to swallow. His throat was inflamed. Just before takeoff, I hastily googled the names on the bottles and selected a few that seemed the most relevant to diabetes and pain management.

Business-class seats are like space-travel capsules. There are buttons to recline the back, the legs, the feet. You can adjust into a horseback-riding pose or a flat, spacious bed. I pressed Dad's buttons, in a good way, until the pressure was off his bedsores.

"You're doing great, Dad." I felt his forehead, which was not hot. "Just rest and we'll be home soon."

Flight attendants walked up and down the aisles serving complimentary wine and cheese. They had Johnnie Walker too. I wished Dad was well and we could share a much-needed drink. I set the TV to the channel that showed the trip in progress. The small plane icon moved over the world—from Indian and Pakistani airspace to the Middle East and North Africa, finally beginning to cross the Atlantic, which was the longest stretch of the journey. Dad and I were retracing his steps, compressing into one night a lifetime of movement.

My eyes darted back and forth between the screen and his neck. I looked for that millimeter of rise and fall that told me he was still breathing. I held his hand—his long fingers, which I used to call Marlboros, now swollen. Still, they were elegant, strong. I loved putting my face in his hands.

Once we were halfway across the Atlantic, when I felt certain we were too close to America to turn back, I got up to tell the crew we'd need a doctor to meet us at the gate.

"Do you want us to see if there's a doctor on board?" one of them asked me.

"No. My dad's resting fine right now. I don't want to wake him. We'll just need help as soon as we land."

"All right, honey. Let us know if anything changes."

There were two hours left. Dad woke up just once. "Where is Mumah?" he asked me.

"She's in India. She's coming soon," I said. And I had to add, "She wanted to go for elephant rides first."

This whole trip, I had the nagging feeling I was supposed to tell Dad about the chance meeting with the judge who sentenced him. "We made a mistake," I almost said to him in the hospital and then on this flight. But with him so close to death, the fact no longer felt relevant. It was of earth, not of heaven, more for the living than the dying.

The lights, which were off in the cabin, came back on with an announcement. "Ladies and gentlemen, we are beginning our initial descent." I waited for as long as I could to put Dad's seat back up. He didn't wince or shriek.

"Your grandfather did very well on such a long flight," a man sitting across the aisle leaned in to say. "Very well done, sir."

"He's my father." I made the familiar correction.

When the wheels hit the ground—the moment I'd usually grab my phone, excited to see whatever I'd missed while offline—I sat immobilized, taking deep breaths, fighting back tears. You can live life in many places; you can only die in one. Dad chose here.

"Everyone, please stay seated," a crew member announced. "We have a sick passenger on board this flight."

Two medical workers boarded the plane and lifted Dad from his seat. I followed them, holding his meds, the catheter, and my backpack. They checked his blood sugar in the vestibule. "It's twenty," one said. "Amazing this guy is still alive." They gave him an injection.

A customs agent eyeballed our passports and escorted us through an emergency exit so that we wouldn't have to wait in the immigration line. For once, it felt, we got a break from the government.

Dad was at his hospital within twenty minutes of landing at Newark Liberty International. Deepak and Ang were already there waiting for us when we arrived.

Over the next few weeks, Dad miraculously made another swift recovery. He was moved from the hospital to a rehab center, where he'd rebuild muscle mass. Mom was back, too. All of us together again, I told my family about our flight from Mumbai. Dad didn't know I played Russian roulette with his medicine. "You're the one who taught me to gamble!" I reminded him.

He smiled, and then, in the tone a parent takes when truly confounded by their child, Dad added one detail to my story: "You were so patient, my doll. I never knew you could be patient. Never have I seen you that way before."

Ang snickered. Finally, a backhanded compliment to make her laugh.

My cousin—the one who went to college because Dad advocated for her—came with her two eight-year-olds. The twins were in a Bollywood dance class. They'd come from rehearsal for an upcoming recital.

"Show Grandpa what you learned," their mom told them. They called Dad "Grandpa" because his younger brother—their actual grandpa—had passed before their birth. She took out her iPhone to play the song. The twins lined up, hands on hips, waiting for the first drumbeat to begin their steps. Dad watched while slurping hot and sour soup with extra tofu. He looked happy. I kissed his forehead and slipped out of the room to catch my flight to California.

A few days later, I was jogging one of my favorite trails in the hills, which had sweeping panoramic views of the bridges, reservoirs, and islands that were becoming as familiar as the Manhattan skyline. A good friend decided to join me. We scaled the gentle slopes, each going at our own pace.

When I came to a lane of eucalyptus trees—the mintiness in the air was refreshing—I suddenly felt nauseated. My mouth began to water. I needed to stop running or even standing. I curled into a ball and rested my cheek against the earth. It smelled ashen, like it does in the first seconds of rain. Only, the sun was shining.

My friend came back for me. "I don't know what's wrong," I told him. "This has never happened before." He helped me up, and we walked back to the car.

A couple hours later, Mom called. "He, he died," she sobbed and stuttered. "Pah-, pah-, Papa died. He died."

"What? When?" I asked her.

It happened at the same moment I'd laid on the ground.

EPILOGUE
Dear Dad

YOU TOLD ME AND I heard you. It wasn't a mistake. Thank you.

For your funeral, the past came to join us. The priests recited the Guru Granth Sahib. Mom's little sister explained they'd take turns to read the whole book from beginning to end without stopping. "That's what we do when someone in our culture dies." It hit me: you're the first person from "our culture" I've ever lost.

I stayed with Mom that week. We hugged each other to sleep every night. Neither of us wanted to be alone—and we get along best when we're sleeping.

She woke up each morning before dawn to chant for you. Tears flooded her face. They came so hard there was no point wiping them away. How much she loved you. I watched her in the dark, pretending to be asleep. For all you both fought, for all you hurt each other, what she wouldn't do for you. In those moments I felt you'd died a lucky man.

Uncle Ratan couldn't come because he wasn't allowed into the United States—not even for a prayer. Still, he prayed from afar.

I imagined what my life would have been had our family stayed in Morocco or somewhere else in the Arab world or Indian subcontinent. Mom told me about the sleeping pills she swallowed in Casablanca to not wake up again. I thought I knew the heaviest weights inside you. I didn't. And so it goes: even the ones you love most in life are forever strangers.

Our relationship gave me a working definition of love: where passion meets duty. Though sometimes I worry I take it too far. I know there should be no regrets, but there's one I have. I wish I had known how to be there for you differently—not so focused on outcomes, more able to stop and listen to how you were doing, really doing. I was driving so hard toward goals, I was too afraid to slow down.

Every once in a while, in my new fancy life, a person says: your father would have been so proud. And, like clockwork, my throat contracts. Deep breath—hold it, hold it. Is that how you felt at the mention of your father, whose funeral you could not attend? I know he would have been proud of you, Dad.

What is the word for the memories one has that are not lived personally but inherited from one's ancestors? Pieces of your life are caught inside me. I can see the blood flowing in the streets of Karachi; the waves breaking in the moonlight of Beirut; the ice sheets on Broadway; and the bed where you slept at Rikers Island. The distance you'd traveled didn't carry over in the eyes of the law. But I saw it. It carried over in my eyes.

I told the guru at your funeral that I wanted to take your ashes to California, to spread them in the Pacific. "No, *beti*." He thought I didn't know the rules. "A *chokri* cannot touch the ashes. It must be the son, not the daughter." That's one rule I was well aware of. But we'd come so far, I thought we could go a little farther. I got ahead of myself.

Deepak carried your ashes to India. His son, your grandson, joined him. They took you together to the Ganges.

You have two more grandchildren. Deepak had another boy, Izak (named after the scientist who discovered the laws of motion). He is strong and fast like his mom and has melancholic eyes like his dad. Angelly had a girl, Khaleesi (named after a fierce TV character). She is Ang's spitting image and makes us all laugh. We'll tell them stories of you.

We each saved enough to become homeowners. My house is the West Coast outpost for the Shahani family. Your picture is on my altar. And—God works in strange ways—Akshay got his U.S. passport and showed up one day. He lives with me, goes to college, and makes chai tea lattes at Peet's Coffee. He's hardworking, like us.

One day I spoke with the woman in charge of deportations in the United States. She'd retired from that job and agreed to take my call. When I told her about your case—the arrest, the "aggravated felony," our win in the end (it happened right under her nose, while she was chief)—she said to me, "How your dad worked his way out of that is somewhat miraculous." It didn't sound like she meant the good type of miracle. No matter. I know for myself: it was the great type.

I recently imagined us all on a game show, the host (maybe the same one from *The Price Is Right*) asking us each what it took to make this country our home. You would say patience; Mom, sharing; Deepak, Sylvester Stallone movies; Angelly, humor; and I, rage. Or rage is the first word that comes to mind. Maybe it's actually hope.

Your nephew, my cousin in Dubai, has a green card. His American wife and I sponsored him. How wild it is that he will be a citizen of this country in just a few years, when the land of his birth wouldn't grant him citizenship. I feel our country is special in this way. I hope to bring many more people over.

America is going through upheaval again, not unlike what we saw after 9/11. There's no point getting into politics with the departed. But there is a person I need to tell you about. Her family reminded me of us.

This young woman came here as a child. Her parents brought her. When she was little, her dad—a janitor—put her in his trash bin and snuck her into the office building he cleaned. They rented a small room in an apartment with many men. He didn't want to leave her home alone.

She went on to graduate from the best schools. But, unlike me, she didn't have a way to get her papers. No one in her family did. She's now at risk of being deported, because of political changes.

I had to interview her. When I asked my final question—"Do you have any message for America?"—she blurted out through her tears, "It's not my fault. I didn't choose to come here. I didn't do anything wrong. My parents broke the law—not me."

I thought of you. Of your choices and why you made them. As fast as I talk, somehow the words didn't come in time, but I meant to tell her: *your parents did it because they love you, and love is above the law.*

I miss you every day.

ACKNOWLEDGMENTS

This book is my first child. It takes a village.

My agent, Jim Levine: you knew those were more than journal entries. And when I thought I needed two months to clean up a draft, you said, "You're closer than you think. Get it done in a week." You're like the dog whisperer for authors.

My editor, Deb Futter: you held my hand through the most important creative project of my life, protected me from some of my worst instincts, and reminded me to stop and explain how things actually felt. Thank you for reading so many iterations with patience, humor, and confidence in our vision. You're so right. The truth always resonates.

Team Celadon: may every writer experience just once the care you've shown me, these pages, and the cover art. Christine Mykityshyn, you make it matter. Randi Kramer, you make it happen. Thank you, fierce ladies.

NPR is where I learned to hold a microphone instead of a bullhorn, to ask questions and welcome the unexpected, even crave it. I could not have written this story without that training. Pallavi Gogoi and Uri Berliner, in particular, thank you for hearing me and making it possible to step away from the business desk at such a frenetic moment.

I needed deep solitude to write this story—a still place where the sediment could settle and the water clear. Spirit Rock and Esalen in California, the Insight Meditation Society and Barre Center for Buddhist Studies in Massachusetts: thank you for giving me quiet (and the chance to shovel manure in exchange for food and shelter). Will Kabat-Zinn, only in America does a desi from Queens return to Buddhism through a white guy in Berkeley. Thank you for teaching me how to see my fears less and what's there more; and then putting your own eagle eyes on this text.

Esther Sanchez, McKaylah Austin, and Mariana Suarez: your invaluable research propelled this book forward. (And thanks to your professor Eric Tang for bringing us together.)

DJ, M'Liss, and Dennis DiDonna: you run the best writer's colony in town. Thanks for adopting me in and making sure I was OK in there (Dennis, I didn't turn into a mushroom).

My beloved friends: Avideh Moussavian, nurturer, trainer, culture critic, and comedian, you're my rock. Brilliant Rajan Lukose, we just keep going deeper and deeper together. Sarahi Uribe, *mi hermanita*, we're showing others who've lived this story that everything is gonna be all right. Geetha Vallabhaneni, didi, mountain cat, old soul, you bring us to so many places I can't find on my own. Gautam Mukunda, that day we landed at the same table, it was the hand of God, and I'm so grateful. Bazi Robert Banda, *Americanah* gave me the courage you knew I needed. Deepa Vora, you radiate light and made the hardest part—getting started—inordinately more fun (MYLY). Tarun Agarwal, I wish my dad had gotten to meet you. Rai Cockfield, I love the prescient promise you made us make. Kwame Owusu-Kesse, your daughter is blessed with a feminist father (whether or not we use the word). Luis Elizondo Thompson, homie, let's always remind each other to cherish where we came from. Ginny Too, we'll find a long trail to hike and unpack these heavy lifts of ours. Benita Jain, each major step of the way—from Dad's case, to my California move, to this book—you've been a guardian angel. Thanks to each of you for reading drafts at various phases, providing invaluable feedback and encouragement.

Uncle Kumar and Auntie Rita, you made Dad smile like no one else. Uncle Sham, when I see your face I remember his (and the lottery). *Tias Duru y Jasoti, cuando venga a Barcelona, les leeré extractos de este libro y aprenderé mejor sus historias para el próximo.* Auntie Ione, you shielded us with so much grace and kindness; also, I miss your pancakes. Thanks to each of you for getting us here.

Acknowledgments

Uncle Ratan, yes, we clashed. But it was always clear: you loved your brother and family deeply. May your soul rest in peace.

Auntie Nimi and Uncle Bhagwan: we would not have survived in this country without you. You've always been a silent pillar in our lives, and a dazzling example of love, sacrifice, and family.

Angelly: no one's feedback mattered more to me than yours. I know it wasn't easy to revisit many of these memories. Thank you for going there with me, and pushing me to be sharper, hit harder where it mattered.

Deepak: when we were little, you used to complain about how I never listened to you. But when you told me to write this book, I listened. I hope you find here a bit of justice, a sense of closure you've long deserved.

Mom: you're one of the strongest human beings I've ever met. Thank you for holding my hand through every step of this process, clearing your schedule for hours on end to talk about moments you'd rather forget, finding long lost photographs and numbers, and always getting what's in my heart.

Dad: you taught me integrity. "You should always be able to look a man in the eye." That's the standard I held when writing about the men and women who appear in these pages.

This memoir draws from my memories, interviews with about 100 sources, legal records, historical archives, and scholarship on colonialism, race, criminal justice, and migration. A few names and personal details have been altered or omitted to protect privacy. Any mistakes are mine alone.

CELADON
BOOKS
——
NEW YORK

Founded in 2017, Celadon Books, a division of
Macmillan Publishers, publishes a highly curated list
of twenty to twenty-five new titles a year. The list of
both fiction and nonfiction is eclectic and focuses
on publishing commercial and literary books and
discovering and nurturing talent.